W9-BVT-853

America's
TEST KITCHEN

FROM OUR

Grandmothers'

KITCHENS

A TREASURY OF LOST RECIPES
TOO GOOD TO FORGET

FROM THE EDITORS OF *COOK'S COUNTRY* MAGAZINE

COLOR PHOTOGRAPHY Keller + Keller
FOOD STYLING Mary Jane Sawyer and Catrine Kelty
BLACK AND WHITE PHOTOGRAPHY Daniel J. van Ackere

Copyright © 2011 by the Editors of *Cook's Country* Magazine

All rights reserved. No part of this book may be reproduced
or transmitted in any manner whatsoever without written
permission from the publisher, except in the case of brief
quotations embodied in critical articles or reviews.

America's Test Kitchen
17 Station Street
Brookline, MA 02445

Library of Congress Cataloging-in-Publication Data

From our grandmothers' kitchens : a treasury of lost recipes too
good to forget / from the editors of Cook's Country magazine.
  p. cm.
 Includes bibliographical references and index.
 ISBN-13: 978-1-933615-80-6
 ISBN-10: 1-933615-80-X
 1. Cooking, American. 2. Grandmothers. 3. Cookbooks. I.
America's Test Kitchen (Firm) II. Cook's Country. III. Title:
Treasury of lost recipes too good to forget.
 TX715.C78535 2011
 641.5973--dc22
                    2011013764

Manufactured in Thailand
10 9 8 7 6 5 4 3 2 1

Distributed by America's Test Kitchen,
17 Station Street, Brookline, MA 02445

Editorial Director: Jack Bishop
Executive Editor: Elizabeth Carduff
Executive Food Editor: Julia Collin Davison
Senior Editor: Louise Emerick
Associate Editor: Chris O'Connor, Dan Zuccarello
Test Cook: Jennifer Lalime
Assistant Test Cook: Kate Williams
Editorial Assistant: Alyssa King
Design Director: Amy Klee
Art Director: Greg Galvan
Associate Art Director: Matthew Warnick
Photography: Keller + Keller
Staff Photographer: Daniel J. van Ackere
Food Styling: Mary Jane Sawyer, Catrine Kelty
Illustration: © Greg Stevenson/www.i2iart.com
Production Director: Guy Rochford
Senior Production Manager: Jessica Lindheimer Quirk
Senior Project Manager: Alice Carpenter
Production and Traffic Coordinator: Kate Hux
Workflow and Imaging Manager: Andrew Mannone
Production and Imaging Specialists: Judy Blomquist,
Heather Dube, Lauren Pettapiece
Copy Editor: Jeff Schier
Proofreader: Christine Corcoran Cox
Indexer: Elizabeth Parson

Pictured on front cover: Grated Bread and Chocolate Cake
(page 133)
Pictured opposite title page: Biggum's Fried Pies (page 186)
Pictured on back cover: Tomato Soup Cake (page 116),
Italian Love Nests (page 41), Date and Nut Bread (page 100)

Contents

WELCOME TO AMERICA'S TEST KITCHEN **vi**

INTRODUCTION BY CHRISTOPHER KIMBALL **vii**

CHAPTER 1: Church Socials and Potlucks **1**

CHAPTER 2: Sunday Suppers and Special Occasion Dinners **23**

CHAPTER 3: Comfort Food Classics **57**

CHAPTER 4: Breads with a Story to Tell **81**

CHAPTER 5: Cakes Plain and Simple **111**

CHAPTER 6: A Legacy of Cookies **139**

CHAPTER 7: Pies Worth Coming Home For **161**

CHAPTER 8: Putting Food By **189**

CONVERSIONS & EQUIVALENCIES **204**

INDEX **206**

Welcome to America's Test Kitchen

THIS BOOK HAS BEEN TESTED, WRITTEN, AND EDITED BY THE FOLKS at America's Test Kitchen, a very real 2,500-square-foot kitchen located just outside of Boston. It is the home of *Cook's Country* magazine and *Cook's Illustrated* magazine and is the Monday-through-Friday destination for more than three dozen test cooks, editors, food scientists, tasters, and cookware specialists. Our mission is to test recipes over and over again until we understand how and why they work and until we arrive at the "best" version.

We start the process of testing a recipe with a complete lack of conviction, which means that we accept no claim, no theory, no technique, and no recipe at face value. We simply assemble as many variations as possible, test a half dozen of the most promising, and taste the results blind. We then construct our own hybrid recipe and continue to test it, varying ingredients, techniques, and cooking times until we reach a consensus. The result, we hope, is the best version of a particular recipe, but we realize that only you can be the final judge of our success (or failure). As we like to say in the test kitchen, "We make the mistakes, so you don't have to."

All of this would not be possible without a belief that good cooking, much like good music, is indeed based on a foundation of objective technique. Some people like spicy foods and others don't, but there is a right way to sauté, there is a best way to cook a pot roast, and there are measurable scientific principles involved in producing perfectly beaten, stable egg whites. This is our ultimate goal: to investigate the fundamental principles of cooking so that you become a better cook. It is as simple as that.

You can watch us work (in our actual test kitchen) by tuning in to *Cook's Country from America's Test Kitchen* (www.cookscountrytv.com) or *America's Test Kitchen* (www.americastestkitchen.com) on public television, or by subscribing to *Cook's Country* magazine (www.cookscountry.com) or *Cook's Illustrated* magazine (www.cooksillustrated.com), which are each published every other month. We welcome you into our kitchen, where you can stand by our side as we test our way to the "best" recipes in America.

Introduction

IT IS A VERY GOOD THING THAT THIS BOOK DID NOT INCLUDE RECIPES from my grandmother. As far as I can remember, she rarely cooked and her diet was appallingly monotonous: well-done roast beef, potatoes, and vanilla ice cream with chocolate sauce for dessert. My mother did cook but was an early proponent of organic ingredients and low-heat cooking, which unfortunately resulted in "unadulterated" dishes (no seasonings, herbs, or spices) and an utter lack of flavor development. The good news is that I spent a good part of my childhood on a subsistence farm in the mountains of Vermont, enjoying the prodigious skills and output of Marie Briggs, the town baker. Her Molasses Cookies, Baking Powder Biscuits, and Anadama Bread are constant reminders of what one can do with the simplest of ingredients and the most elementary of kitchens.

Fortunately, this book, *From Our Grandmothers' Kitchens*, takes a sweeping view of the culinary heritage of our grandmothers through a nationwide call for recipes. The winner, Grated Bread and Chocolate Cake, won first prize and $25,000, and the four runners-up (Mom's Gone with the Wind Heavenly Pie, Genuine Danish Kleiner, Chapel Squares, and Italian Love Nests) received $1,000 each. This unearthed a wealth of culinary history, story-telling, and recipes from dozens of countries ranging from the African-based Gullah Gratin (a gratin of sausage, greens, potatoes, and shrimp) of the coastal Carolina and Georgia Low Country to recipes based on the various cuisines of Europe, China, and the Americas, and many points in between.

The joy of this sort of cooking is that it has practical roots, not just in a particular family but, more broadly, in a way of living and cooking. That reminds me of the story of the youngster from New York City who spent most of the summer with a host family in Vermont back in the 1930s. When he returned home, he was asked about his experience.

"You know, they have a nice bathroom upstairs, but they don't use it except when they are feeling poorly and, for the toilet, they go out back. We all took a bath in the brook and when we got ready to eat, we all washed up at the kitchen sink. Gee, we didn't mind at all."

When asked what they talked about at dinner, the boy thought a bit and then replied, "When they eat they don't talk, they just eat!"

That was my experience in Vermont as well back in the 1950s and it is a nice reminder that food wasn't for sport or amusement, it was to feed hungry people. That notion of practicality married to a bit of creative recipe development is what makes this collection so special. There is not one frivolous recipe in the bunch.

For many families, Sunday supper was a light meal, the big sit-down dinner having occurred at noon. So, Suzanne Banfield remembers the perfect simple supper recipe, Sunday Supper Strata, made from sandwich bread, apples, cheese, bacon, milk, and eggs; and it was make-ahead as well. Carol Swain Lewis, from Poplar Bluff, MO, sent along a family recipe for Minute Muffins that are a snap to make: a dump-and-stir mixture of buttermilk, mayonnaise, flour, salt, and baking powder.

Many recipes reflect American adaptations of old-country recipes, including Rum Tum Tiddy, the New World version of Welsh rarebit, and Sergeant Meatloaf, which is filled with prosciutto-wrapped hard-boiled eggs. Lovie May's Rice Muffins are the essence of practicality since they use leftover cooked rice, and Grated Bread and Chocolate Cake was a miracle of texture, flavor, and New World frugality. I will never look at stale, leftover bread the same way again.

Grandma Alpha's Barbecue Ribs was born in a tavern in rural Ohio. Grandma lived in a shotgun apartment upstairs and made these ribs for the farmers eating dinner below. There is no shortage of breads and cakes from the European repertoire, including stollen and coffee bread. But our grandmothers were often more inventive than that and we showcase Grandma Pearl's Upside-Down Tomato Pan Bread, Bubbles (drop doughnuts), Pennsylvania Dutch Shoofly Cake, Scripture Cake, and Butternut-Pecan Cake. For cookies there are Scrumptious Orange Bites, Estelle's Black Walnut Chocolate Pixies, Peppernuts, and Blarney Stones plus a mix of churchy recipes, Cathedral Windows (marshmallows, nuts, and chocolate), Chapel Squares, and The Bishop's Bars. Pies are often spectacular, as with Mom's Gone with the Wind Heavenly Pie (Clark Gable purchased a lemon-flavored Heavenly Pie from Sandy Farler's mother in the 1950s in Encino, CA), Roly-Boley (blackberry tarts served with crème anglaise), Ina's Butter Tarts, and a delicious Brown Sugar Pie.

I am not convinced that the world needs more 30-minute recipes, especially when they are made up like sausages from a factory. Good recipes, like interesting people, come from somewhere; they have an accent, a personality, and a special way of pleasing the palate that tells the story of their beginnings and even how they changed as they grew up and evolved. At the same time, I know that old cookbooks are very much a hit or miss proposition, and the benefit of a strong test kitchen to vouch for these recipes, modernizing and streamlining them, if you will, is worth its weight in culinary gold. None of the recipes in this volume have to be interpreted for today's home cook—we have done that work for you.

So let our grandmothers (well, not mine) tell their stories through this book, through their recipes and their cooking. *From Our Grandmothers' Kitchens* is much like being adopted and instantly connected to a past that others are eager to share, as you stand at their elbow watching them cook up history. Starting today, please consider this collection your own, dishes that you too will hand down to future generations.

And just like that city kid who spent the summer in Vermont, you may find that there is considerably more eating around the dinner table and a whole lot less conversation!

Christopher Kimball
Founder and Editor, *Cook's Country* and *Cook's Illustrated*
Host, *Cook's Country from America's Test Kitchen* and *America's Test Kitchen*

SPRING POTATO CASSEROLE

Church Socials and Potlucks

Ox Roast of Beef 2

Slumgullion 3

Edison Street Italian Baptist Church Spaghetti and Meatballs 4

Sausage Soup 6

Tamale Loaf 8

Squash Casserole with Cheese 9

Lynne's Zucchini Parmesan 11

Eggplant Parmigiana 12

Mom's Eggplant Deluxe 13

Gnocchi alla Romana 14

Spring Potato Casserole 16

Gullah Gratin 17

New Orleans Shrimp, French Quarter–Style 19

Potato-Mac Salad 20

Sweet and Sour German Potato Salad 21

Ox Roast of Beef

LINDA CORSO | SAN FRANCISCO, CALIFORNIA

"Growing up in the '50s in Erie, Pennsylvania, everyone ate ox roast sandwiches," Linda tells us. "The firemen had ox roast picnics, as did churches and schools. When I moved to California, the closest thing I could get was a French Dip. Good, but not the same." More common in the Midwest and mid-Atlantic states, ox roasts, a tradition brought here from England, are typically held at town festivals, at political or military victory celebrations, or as fundraisers for local organizations. An entire ox was roasted in a closed pit, though today more manageable rounds of beef are typically cooked over open pits on spits. And some cooks (including Linda) roast or braise the meat in ovens. The meat might be pulled or shredded, sliced or shaved, but no matter what, it is usually served on hamburger buns. "I was thrilled when I got my grandmother's cookbook and found this recipe. Couple this with Calico Beans and I'm in heaven."

SERVES 16 TO 18

- 2 tablespoons vegetable oil
- 1 small onion, chopped coarse
- 1 carrot, peeled and chopped coarse
- 1 celery rib, chopped coarse
- 2 garlic cloves, minced
  Salt and pepper
- 2 cups beef broth
- 2 cups water
- ½ (1-ounce) packet onion soup mix
- 1 (5-pound) boneless beef eye-round roast, halved crosswise
  Hamburger buns, for serving

1. Adjust oven rack to lower-middle position and heat oven to 200 degrees. Heat oil in large Dutch oven over medium heat until shimmering. Add onion, carrot, and celery and cook, stirring occasionally, until softened and well browned, 8 to 10 minutes. Stir in garlic and ¼ teaspoon pepper and cook until fragrant, about 30 seconds. Stir in broth, water, and onion soup mix, scraping up any browned bits.

2. Season beef with salt and pepper and nestle into braising liquid. Bring to simmer, cover, and transfer to oven. Cook until centers of roasts register 125 degrees (for medium-rare) on instant-read thermometer, 35 to 45 minutes.

3. Remove pot from oven and transfer roasts to large bowl. Let braising liquid settle for 5 minutes, then remove fat from surface using large spoon. Return liquid to medium heat and simmer until reduced to 3 cups, 15 to 20 minutes. Let sauce cool to room temperature, then pour over meat. Cover and refrigerate for at least 12 hours or up to 1 day.

4. Adjust oven rack to middle position and heat oven to 350 degrees. Transfer roasts to carving board and slice thin. Transfer sauce to saucepan, bring to simmer over medium heat, and season with salt and pepper to taste. Shingle sliced beef in 13 by 9-inch baking dish and pour warmed sauce over top. Bake until meat is heated through, about 10 minutes. Serve sliced beef on buns, passing sauce separately.

Notes from the Test Kitchen
This crowd-friendly recipe is a fun change from the usual barbecue or burgers. We cut Linda's recipe, which would serve forty, back to serve a smaller group of 16 to 18. We browned the vegetables for more flavor and cooked the meat to medium-rare in step 2 since it would cook further in step 4.

Slumgullion

CAROL LOVEJOY | YARMOUTH PORT, MASSACHUSETTS

We weren't sure what to expect given the name, but after baking up this cheesy spaghetti and ground beef casserole with its bread-crumb topping, we were sold. "I grew up loving my Aunt Kit's slumgullion," Carol tells us. "To my knowledge no one outside of our immediate family had ever heard of it." However, she recently learned it has actually been around for years. Slumgullion first appeared in mid 19th century mining camps, referring to a watery stew. Later it was applied to military mess hall and hobo camp stews. In the domestic setting, however, it came to refer to a thrifty (and far more tasty) dish of ground meat, onions, tomatoes, and cheese served over potatoes, biscuits, spaghetti, or crackers. Carol simplifies it further by making it a casserole.

SERVES 6 TO 8

- 1 tablespoon olive oil, plus extra as needed
- 1 onion, chopped fine
- 1 green bell pepper, stemmed, seeded, and cut into ½-inch pieces
- 1 pound 85 percent lean ground beef
- 3 garlic cloves, minced
- 1 tablespoon minced fresh oregano or 1 teaspoon dried
- 2 tablespoons all-purpose flour
- 1 (28-ounce) can diced tomatoes
- 1 cup low-sodium chicken broth
  Salt
- ¼ teaspoon pepper
- 1 pound spaghetti
- 1 pound extra-sharp cheddar cheese, shredded (4 cups)
- 1 ounce Parmesan cheese, grated (½ cup)
- ½ cup dry plain bread crumbs
- 2 tablespoons unsalted butter, melted

1. Adjust oven rack to middle position and heat oven to 350 degrees. Grease 13 by 9-inch baking dish.

2. Heat oil in large saucepan over medium heat until shimmering. Add onion and bell pepper and cook until softened, about 5 minutes. Stir in ground beef and cook, breaking up any large pieces with wooden spoon, until no longer pink, about 3 minutes.

3. Stir in garlic and oregano and cook until fragrant, about 30 seconds. Stir in flour and cook for 1 minute. Stir in tomatoes, broth, 1 teaspoon salt, and pepper, scraping up any browned bits. Bring to simmer and cook until mixture is thickened but still saucy, about 5 minutes. Remove from heat and cover to keep warm.

4. Meanwhile, bring 4 quarts water to boil in large Dutch oven. Add pasta and 1 tablespoon salt and cook, stirring often, until al dente; drain pasta. (If drained pasta sits for longer than 5 minutes, toss with 1 tablespoon olive oil.)

5. Spread ½ cup sauce into prepared baking dish. Spread half of cooked pasta into baking dish, then spoon 2¼ cups sauce over top and sprinkle with 2 cups cheddar and ¼ cup Parmesan. Repeat layering with remaining pasta, sauce, cheddar, and Parmesan. Combine bread crumbs and melted butter and sprinkle over top. Bake until filling is bubbling and topping begins to brown, 30 to 40 minutes. Let casserole cool for 10 minutes before serving.

Notes from the Test Kitchen
We made the sauce saucier and gave it more binding power by adding broth and flour. Tossing the crumbs with melted butter created a crisper crust. Oregano and garlic lent a flavor boost.

Edison Street Italian Baptist Church Spaghetti and Meatballs

KATHERINE HAYNES | VAN NUYS, CALIFORNIA

"My Italian family immigrated to the United States around the mid 1890s from the Abruzzo region of Italy to Buffalo, New York. They had left the Catholic church in Italy and started the First Italian Baptist Church in America, now the Edison Street Baptist Church. One of the yearly big fund-raisers for the Men's Club of the church was the annual Spaghetti and Meatball Supper. My own memory is of a thick, wonderful tomato sauce and baseball-size meatballs with tons of flavor and smooth texture. I probably only got to eat at one or two dinners at the church when I was really little, but I do remember leftovers, which were brought home and stored in the freezer. It was still so good even months later. When I first asked for the recipe for the meatballs, my grandfather sent me a recipe to make 100 meatballs. I am now a chef and have a use for a recipe for 100 meatballs, but at the time I had no idea what to do with it. I love the rich history of this unique church supper and think it should be preserved and shared with others." This is a pared down version of Katherine's grandfather's original congregation-size recipe.

MAKES 12 CUPS SAUCE PLUS 20 MEATBALLS, ENOUGH FOR 2 POUNDS OF PASTA

SAUCE

- 2 tablespoons olive oil
- 1 onion, chopped fine
- 4 garlic cloves, minced
- ¼ teaspoon red pepper flakes
- ½ cup dry red wine
- 12 cups water, plus extra as needed
- 6 (6-ounce) cans tomato paste
- 8 ounces beef ribs (optional; see note on page 5)
- 4 ounces thinly sliced pepperoni, quartered
- 1 pound Italian sausage, sliced 1 inch thick

MEATBALLS

- 2 pounds 85 percent lean ground beef
- 8 ounces ground pork
- 2 onions, chopped fine
- 2 cups dry plain bread crumbs
- 1 ounce Pecorino Romano cheese, grated (½ cup)
- ½ cup whole milk
- 6 garlic cloves, minced
- 2 tablespoons dried parsley
- 2 large eggs
  Salt and pepper
- ⅓ cup coarsely chopped fresh basil
  Sugar

1. **FOR THE SAUCE:** Heat oil in 12-quart stockpot over medium heat until shimmering. Add onion and cook until softened, about 5 minutes. Stir in garlic and red pepper flakes and cook until fragrant, about 30 seconds. Stir in wine and cook until almost completely evaporated, about 1 minute.

2. Stir in water, tomato paste, beef ribs (if using), and pepperoni and bring to gentle simmer. Cover partially (leaving about 1 inch of pot open), reduce heat to medium-low, and simmer gently, stirring occasionally, until thickened slightly, about 2 hours. Stir in sausage and continue to cook, partially covered, until sausage is cooked through and sauce is deeply flavored, about 1 hour longer.

3. Transfer ribs (if using) to carving board, let cool slightly, then shred meat into bite-size pieces, discarding fat and bones. Stir shredded meat into sauce and adjust consistency with additional hot water as needed. (Sauce can be refrigerated in airtight container for up to 3 days, or frozen for up to 1 month. If frozen, let sauce thaw completely before returning to simmer in pot.)

4. **FOR THE MEATBALLS:** Meanwhile, adjust oven rack to upper-middle position and heat oven to 475 degrees. Grease rimmed baking sheet.

5. Mix ground beef, ground pork, onions, bread crumbs, Pecorino Romano, milk, garlic, parsley, eggs, 2 teaspoons salt, and 2 teaspoons pepper together in bowl using hands. Pinch off and roll mixture into 2½-inch meatballs (about 20 meatballs total) and arrange on prepared baking sheet. Bake until well browned, about 20 minutes. (Baked meatballs can be refrigerated in airtight container for up to 3 days, or frozen for up to 1 month. If frozen, do not thaw before using.)

6. Nestle meatballs into sauce and cook until heated through, 10 to 20 minutes. (Avoid excess stirring to prevent meatballs from breaking apart.) Gently stir in basil and season with salt, pepper, and sugar to taste before serving.

Notes from the Test Kitchen

Spaghetti suppers have long been a traditional fund-raiser at churches across the country, and we loved the unique history behind Katherine's recipe, not to mention the oversized, ultra-tender meatballs. She provided a recipe to serve 100 as well as a scaled-down version; we went with the more practical latter recipe, though we liked the meatballs so much we made a few more of those. She noted to add bread crumbs or cheese to thicken the sauce but tasters found it wasn't necessary; we actually added more water to loosen it up. We skipped browning the sausage first to ensure it wouldn't dry out, and we added the beef and pepperoni at the start of simmering for deeper flavor (Katherine simmered just the water and tomato paste). Eight ounces of beef ribs is a small amount, and since a butcher might not cut such a modest quantity, we made it optional.

Sausage Soup

JUDITH PEASE | MORRISVILLE, VERMONT

With its combination of Italian sausage, macaroni, cannellini beans, and topping of grated Parmesan, this soup is quintessential Italian-style comfort food. (Although, Judith notes, "This recipe originally came from my grandmother-in-law, who was 'not Italian, but Genoese.'") Adds Judith, "I usually make three times the recipe to serve the workers at our annual church fair in Stowe, Vermont. I make it the night before the fair and set it outside (covered) on the porch to cool. On a fair day, it is heated slowly on the large range in the church's kitchen." What better choice could there be for feeding a crowd on a chilly day?

SERVES 8 TO 10

- 1 tablespoon olive oil
- 1 pound Italian sausage, casings removed
- 2 onions, chopped fine
- 4 celery ribs, chopped fine
- 2 (14.5-ounce) cans diced tomatoes with basil, oregano, and garlic, drained and juice reserved
- 4 cups low-sodium chicken broth
- 3½ cups water
- 4 ounces elbow macaroni (1 cup)
- 2 (15-ounce) cans cannellini beans, drained and rinsed
- ¼ cup minced fresh parsley
  Salt and pepper
  Grated Parmesan cheese, for serving

1. Heat oil in large Dutch oven over medium-high heat until just smoking. Cook sausage, breaking up large pieces with wooden spoon, until it is well browned, about 5 minutes; transfer to bowl. Pour off all but 2 tablespoons fat left in pot, add onions, celery, and tomatoes and cook over medium heat until softened and lightly browned, 7 to 10 minutes.

2. Stir in browned sausage, reserved tomato juice, broth, and water and bring to boil. Add pasta and cook, stirring often, until al dente. Stir in beans and cook until heated through, about 5 minutes. Stir in parsley, season with salt and pepper to taste, and serve with Parmesan.

Notes from the Test Kitchen

The smell of Judith's soup simmering in our test kitchen one cold afternoon brought tasters running. A simple recipe with great flavor, it's easy to make in a big batch for a potluck. Judith's recipe didn't need many changes. Rather than cook the aromatics and sausage together and then add the liquid, we sautéed the two components separately so that we could avoid overcooking the meat while cooking the aromatics long enough to ensure they were tender. To cut back on prep time, Judith called for seasoned diced tomatoes; you can also use plain diced tomatoes and add 3 minced garlic cloves and 1 teaspoon dried basil or oregano along with the aromatics in step 1.

Tamale Loaf

ANNE MAHONEY-KRUSE | LA JOLLA, CALIFORNIA

"Southwest comfort food at its finest, tamale loaf was very popular in Tucson during the 1940s," relates Anne. "My grandmother Grove moved from Pennsylvania to Tucson right after the Spanish flu epidemic in 1918, and this is her version of this classic casserole." Given its name, you'd expect her recipe to be made in a loaf pan, but it is actually baked in a casserole, much like tamale pie, though Anne's recipe certainly has its own unique spin that puts it somewhere between an authentic tamale and the 1950s-style tamale pie casseroles we're most familiar with (made with ground meat, cornmeal, and a cheesy topping). Here, the fluffy cornmeal base is mixed with shredded meat, diced tomatoes, corn, onions, black and green olives, and plenty of herbs and spices. "My mother would always make this recipe with leftover holiday turkey and serve it with a simple salad on New Year's Day. We still enjoy this timeless recipe every holiday season."

SERVES 6 TO 8

- 1 (28-ounce) can diced tomatoes
- 2 (6-ounce) cans pitted ripe black olives, drained and ½ cup juice reserved
- 1 (8-ounce) can corn, drained
- 1 (7-ounce) jar pimento-stuffed green olives, drained
- 2 cups shredded cooked chicken, turkey, or pork
- 1 cup vegetable oil
- 1 onion, chopped fine
- 2 tablespoons unsalted butter
- 4 teaspoons chili powder
- 1 teaspoon dried oregano
- 1 garlic clove, minced
- 1 teaspoon salt
- 1 cup whole milk
- 3 large eggs
- 2 cups cornmeal

1. Adjust oven rack to middle position and heat oven to 350 degrees. Grease 13 by 9-inch baking dish.

2. Bring tomatoes, black olives and reserved juice, corn, green olives, chicken, oil, onion, butter, chili powder, oregano, garlic, and salt to simmer in large Dutch oven and cook until flavors meld, about 30 minutes.

3. Whisk milk and eggs together in medium bowl, then whisk in cornmeal until incorporated and smooth. Slowly pour cornmeal mixture into pot, stirring constantly. Transfer tamale mixture to prepared baking dish and bake until dry to touch and lightly browned, about 45 minutes. Let casserole cool for 10 minutes before serving.

Notes from the Test Kitchen

Just when we felt we'd tried every type of tamale pie–style casserole out there, we happily came across Anne's recipe. The olives were an ingredient that made her Tamale Loaf stand out, and our tasters agreed they were a fun addition to the mix. We didn't change a thing about her recipe.

Squash Casserole with Cheese

NAN CORBY | LONG BEACH, CALIFORNIA

Combining fresh summer squash browned briefly on the stovetop with a rich custard, cheddar cheese, and a crunchy fresh bread-crumb topping makes this a casserole sure to be polished off at your next social gathering. "This recipe was developed by my mother-in-law, Irene Kyser Rhodes, of Jackson, Mississippi (1905–1992)," notes Nan. "My husband remembers having it as early as 1941 and he later modified it, and I also modified it subsequently, including changing the order of preparation of the ingredients so that it took only one pan to make, not two or three. My mother-in-law's grandchildren now serve it to their children. We serve this recipe with home-grown sliced tomatoes drizzled with extra-virgin California olive oil and home-grown blanched green beans in a mustard vinaigrette."

SERVES 6

- 2 slices hearty white sandwich bread, torn into quarters
- 2 tablespoons olive oil
  Salt
- 1 onion, chopped fine
- 1½ pounds summer squash, cut into ¾-inch pieces
- ½ cup low-sodium chicken broth or vegetable broth
- ¼ teaspoon white pepper
- ¼ cup whole milk
- 1 large egg
- 3 ounces extra-sharp cheddar cheese, shredded (¾ cup)

1. Adjust oven rack to middle position and heat oven to 350 degrees. Pulse bread, 1 tablespoon oil, and ¼ teaspoon salt in food processor to coarse crumbs, about 10 pulses.

2. Heat remaining 1 tablespoon oil in large skillet over medium heat until shimmering. Add onion and cook until softened, about 5 minutes. Stir in squash, broth, ½ teaspoon salt, and pepper, cover, and cook until squash is softened, about 10 minutes. Uncover, increase heat to medium-high, and continue to cook until squash is dry and beginning to brown, 5 to 7 minutes longer. Transfer mixture to bowl.

3. Whisk milk and egg together in large bowl. Gently stir in squash mixture and cheddar. Transfer mixture to 8-inch square baking dish. Sprinkle with bread-crumb mixture and bake until center of casserole is set and topping is lightly browned, 20 to 25 minutes. Let casserole cool for 10 minutes before serving.

Notes from the Test Kitchen

We loved the simplicity of this summery casserole. We added a couple tablespoons more milk to Nan's custard to make it creamier, and rather than pour it into the skillet with the squash, where it would start cooking, we added the squash to the bowl of custard mixture. Her original recipe called for mashing some of the squash and leaving some chunks after it had browned, but we found it broke down on its own. Nan toasted the bread crumbs in the skillet, but because we found they had a tendency to overbrown we simply added a little oil as we pulsed them in the food processor and sprinkled them over the casserole before baking.

Lynne's Zucchini Parmesan

LYNNE WILLIAMS | SAN JOSE, CALIFORNIA

"As a child, I watched my Italian grandmother cook in her tiny apartment kitchen. She never used a cookbook and there always seemed to be at least five things cooking at once. It was the best food you could ever eat!" One of Lynne's favorites, Eggplant Parmesan, inspired her to come up with this creative variation. "I winged the recipe, added my own touch to things, and it is still one of my family's favorites."

SERVES 8 TO 10

SAUCE
- 1 (28-ounce) can whole tomatoes
- 3 tablespoons olive oil
- 1 onion, chopped fine
- 3 garlic cloves, minced
- 2 teaspoons minced fresh rosemary
- 1 teaspoon minced fresh thyme

LAYERS
- 2 cups all-purpose flour
- ½ teaspoon salt
- ¼ teaspoon pepper
- 4 large eggs
- 2 cups dry Italian bread crumbs
- 4 ounces Parmesan cheese, grated (2 cups)
- ½ teaspoon garlic powder
- 2½ pounds zucchini, sliced lengthwise ¼ inch thick
- 1½ cups vegetable oil
- 4 ounces mozzarella cheese, shredded (1 cup)

1. FOR THE SAUCE: Process tomatoes in food processor until smooth, about 30 seconds. Heat oil in large saucepan over medium heat until shimmering. Add onion and cook until softened and lightly browned, 5 to 7 minutes. Stir in garlic, rosemary, and thyme and cook until fragrant, about 30 seconds. Stir in processed tomatoes, bring to simmer, and cook until thickened, about 10 minutes. Remove from heat and cover to keep warm.

2. FOR THE LAYERS: Adjust oven rack to lower-middle position and heat oven to 400 degrees.

Combine flour, salt, and pepper in large zipper-lock bag. Beat eggs in shallow dish. Combine bread crumbs, ½ cup Parmesan, and garlic powder in second shallow dish.

3. Working in batches, place several zucchini slices in bag with flour, shake bag to coat, then remove from bag and shake off excess flour. Using tongs, coat floured zucchini with beaten eggs, allowing excess to drip off. Coat all sides of zucchini with bread crumbs, pressing on crumbs to help adhere. Lay breaded zucchini slices on wire rack set over rimmed baking sheet.

4. Heat oil in large skillet over medium-high heat until shimmering. Working in batches, carefully add breaded zucchini to skillet and cook until well browned on both sides, 2 to 3 minutes per side. Transfer cooked zucchini to wire rack.

5. Spread ½ cup sauce into 13 by 9-inch baking dish. Shingle half of zucchini in baking dish, then spoon ½ cup more sauce over zucchini and sprinkle with ½ cup mozzarella. Shingle remaining zucchini over top, and cover with remaining sauce, remaining mozzarella, and remaining Parmesan. Bake until filling is bubbling and cheese is melted and beginning to brown, 20 to 25 minutes. Let casserole cool for 10 minutes before serving.

Notes from the Test Kitchen
Lynne didn't specify how many layers to make; we found two fit tidily in the dish. For balance we used one can of tomatoes rather than the two her recipe called for. We also cut back on the oil in the sauce to let the vegetables' flavors shine through.

Eggplant Parmigiana

JOANNE BELLANTONI | PORT CHESTER, NEW YORK

With its hard-boiled eggs, Joanne's authentic Italian recipe is a fun change from the standard version. "My great-grandmother, who emigrated from Italy, fed her family very well with very little, and my grandmother fed her family the same way. Every Italian family makes Eggplant Parmigiana, and some make it with hard-boiled eggs."

SERVES 6 TO 8

SAUCE
- 2 tablespoons olive oil
- 4 garlic cloves, minced
- ¼ teaspoon red pepper flakes
- 1 (28-ounce) can crushed tomatoes
- 1 (14.5-ounce) can diced tomatoes
- Salt and pepper

LAYERS
- 3 large eggs
- 2 cups dry Italian bread crumbs
- 2 medium eggplants, sliced crosswise ¼ inch thick
- ¾ cup olive oil, plus extra as needed
- 4 hard-boiled eggs, peeled and sliced thin
- 8 ounces mozzarella cheese, shredded (2 cups)
- ½ cup coarsely chopped fresh basil
- Vegetable oil spray

1. FOR THE SAUCE: Cook oil, garlic, and red pepper flakes in large saucepan over low heat, stirring often, until garlic is sticky and just golden, about 10 minutes. Add tomatoes, bring to simmer, and cook, stirring occasionally, until sauce measures 4 cups, about 15 minutes. Remove from heat, season with salt and pepper to taste, and cover to keep warm.

2. FOR THE LAYERS: Adjust oven rack to middle position and heat oven to 350 degrees. Beat eggs in shallow dish. Spread bread crumbs into second shallow dish. Using tongs, coat eggplant slices with beaten eggs, allowing excess to drip off. Coat all sides of eggplant with bread crumbs, pressing on crumbs to help adhere. Lay breaded eggplant slices on wire rack set over rimmed baking sheet.

3. Working in batches, heat 2 tablespoons oil in large nonstick skillet over medium-high heat until shimmering. Add breaded eggplant in single layer and cook until well browned on both sides, 2 to 3 minutes per side. Transfer cooked eggplant to wire rack. Wipe crumbs out of skillet with paper towels, and repeat with more oil and remaining eggplant.

4. Spread ½ cup sauce into 13 by 9-inch baking dish. Shingle one-third of eggplant slices in baking dish, then top with half of sliced hard-boiled eggs, ⅔ cup mozzarella, and ¼ cup basil. Spoon 1 cup more sauce over top. Repeat layering once more with half of remaining eggplant, remaining hard-boiled eggs, ⅔ cup mozzarella, and remaining basil.

5. For final layer, shingle remaining eggplant in baking dish and top with 1½ cups sauce and remaining mozzarella. Cover dish tightly with aluminum foil that has been sprayed with vegetable oil spray (or use nonstick foil) and bake for 30 minutes.

6. Uncover and continue to bake until filling is bubbling and cheese is melted and beginning to brown, 10 to 20 minutes longer. Let casserole cool for 10 minutes. Serve with remaining sauce.

Notes from the Test Kitchen
We used our sauce recipe (plus extra for serving) since Joanne only called for "tomato sauce." Doubling the bread crumbs lent texture, and a third beaten egg made a better eggplant coating.

Mom's Eggplant Deluxe

ROBERTA BRITT | WHITE SETTLEMENT, TEXAS

"Back in the 1950s there was a place in Tampa, Florida, called The Cricket Tea Room. Mother took us there to eat often, as the food was outstanding. I hated eggplant as a child, but would eat this. My mother asked for the recipe, and they were nice enough to share it. I've never tasted any eggplant casserole quite as good since." As any home cook is likely to do, Roberta's mother took the restaurant's recipe and made a few adjustments of her own. As Roberta said, this is not your typical eggplant casserole that involves tomatoes or tomato sauce. Instead, with its mix of eggplant baked in a custard of eggs, half-and-half, and cheese, it falls more in the camp of stratas, frittatas, and soufflés. "It is really an outstanding side dish and I've found even the little kids will eat this. My mother is gone now, but I still bake this for my family and they love it too."

SERVES 4 TO 6

- 2 tablespoons unsalted butter, plus extra for baking dish
- 1 medium eggplant, cut into 1-inch pieces
- 1 onion, chopped fine
- 1 garlic clove, minced
- 1 cup half-and-half
- 3 large eggs
- 12 Ritz crackers, pulsed in food processor to coarse crumbs
- 1 teaspoon salt
- ¼ teaspoon pepper
- ⅛ teaspoon hot sauce
- 2 ounces Swiss cheese, shredded (½ cup)
- 2 tablespoons chopped fresh basil

1. Adjust oven rack to middle position and heat oven to 350 degrees. Grease 9-inch square baking dish with butter.

2. Melt 1 tablespoon butter in large skillet over medium-high heat. Brown eggplant lightly on all sides, 5 to 7 minutes; transfer to large bowl. Melt remaining 1 tablespoon butter in skillet over medium heat. Add onion and cook until softened and lightly browned, 5 to 7 minutes. Stir in garlic and cook until fragrant, about 30 seconds; transfer to bowl with eggplant.

3. Whisk half-and-half, eggs, Ritz crackers, salt, pepper, and hot sauce together in large bowl, then gently stir in eggplant mixture and Swiss cheese. Transfer mixture to prepared baking dish and bake until center of casserole is set and top is lightly browned, about 30 minutes. Let casserole cool for 10 minutes, then sprinkle with basil and serve.

Notes from the Test Kitchen

This one-of-a-kind recipe will add nice variety to any potluck's spread. Instead of steaming or boiling the eggplant as Roberta's recipe directed, we opted to brown it to deepen its flavor and also to rid the vegetable of some of its water. We added onion for balance and bite, and basil for a little garnish that nicely complemented the eggplant and lent color. Roberta's recipe called for any cheese but noted that her mother typically used Swiss, so we followed her lead. Parmesan would probably also work well.

Gnocchi alla Romana

LILY JULOW | GAINESVILLE, FLORIDA

When most of us think of gnocchi, we think of the classic little dumplings made from potatoes. That's why Lily's recipe, made by shaping cooked grits into squares, shingling them in a gratin dish, and sprinkling them with cheese and baking, is such a revelation. "I brought the idea for this memorable dish back from a trip to Rome forty years ago, in the 1970s. Without a specific recipe to go on, I experimented until I came up with this close approximation. I always thought that gnocchi was the potato dumpling kind, but this was made of a grain similar to our grits." The making of gnocchi in Italy goes back at least to the mid 1850s, and gnocchi was made not just from potatoes but from a variety of ingredients, including ricotta, bread, winter squash, and corn semolina (cornmeal), clearly what Lily had tried in Rome. Says Lily of her version: "It worked out so well, it's passed along as a family treasured recipe." This cheesy, starchy side dish would be perfect served with ham.

SERVES 8 TO 10

- 4 cups whole milk
- 2 tablespoons unsalted butter, plus extra for baking dish
- 1 cup old-fashioned white grits
- 1 teaspoon salt
- ¼ teaspoon white pepper
- 2 ounces Gruyère cheese, shredded (½ cup)
- 1 ounce Parmesan cheese, grated (½ cup)

1. Line 13 by 9-inch baking dish with foil lengthwise and widthwise, letting excess foil hang over edges. Grease foil.

2. Bring milk and butter to simmer in large saucepan over medium-high heat, stirring occasionally to melt butter. Slowly pour grits into milk mixture, stirring constantly. Reduce heat to low and cook, stirring occasionally, until mixture has thickened and all liquid has been absorbed, about 5 minutes. Stir in salt and pepper.

2. Transfer grits to large bowl and beat with electric mixer on medium-high speed until light and creamy, about 5 minutes. Pour grits mixture into prepared baking dish and spread into even layer. Cover and refrigerate until well chilled and set, at least 4 hours or up to 1 day.

3. Adjust oven rack to middle position and heat oven to 400 degrees. Remove cooled grits from baking dish using foil sling and cut into 18 rectangles. Grease baking dish with butter.

4. Shingle grits rectangles into prepared baking dish, then sprinkle with Gruyère and Parmesan. Bake until grits are heated through and cheese is melted and beginning to brown, about 30 minutes. Let cool for 5 minutes before serving.

Notes from the Test Kitchen

We jumped at the chance to add this upscale comfort food to our repertoire. With all the rich cheese, we found we could substantially decrease the butter in the original (almost 1 cup). Since Lily didn't specify a size for the rectangles, we settled on 3 by 2½ inches because they were easy to arrange and serve. We decreased the white pepper from ⅓ teaspoon (an odd amount) to ¼ teaspoon. Make sure to use regular grits, not quick-cooking or instant.

Spring Potato Casserole

ALICE KNISLEY MATTHIAS | STATEN ISLAND, NEW YORK

"As someone who loves to garden and cook, nothing makes me happier than to see the first bits of herbs come up. My children now accompany me on the walks around the spring garden, and I love that they get as much of a thrill as I do to see the garden return each growing season. This recipe is one that I have tinkered with through the years, and it has become a tradition for our Easter family meal. When it emerges from the oven I send my son out to his herb garden to get some chives to scatter over this dish of potatoes, cream, caramelized onions, and shredded Gruyère cheese. The taste of this potato casserole, with the onion flavor of fresh chives, has come to mean spring to me as much as the flowers blooming and the Easter egg hunt my children have in the yard before we sit down to dinner."

SERVES 8 TO 10

- 3 tablespoons unsalted butter
- 1 tablespoon olive oil
- 2 Vidalia onions, halved and sliced thin
- 2 sprigs fresh thyme
- 1 teaspoon honey
  Salt and pepper
- 2 tablespoons all-purpose flour
- 1 cup heavy cream
- 1 cup low-sodium chicken broth
- 3 tablespoons minced fresh chives
- 3 pounds russet potatoes, peeled and sliced ⅛ inch thick
- 6 ounces Gruyère cheese, shredded (1½ cups)

1. Adjust oven rack to middle position and heat oven to 350 degrees. Grease 13 by 9-inch baking dish.

2. Heat 1 tablespoon butter and oil in large skillet over medium heat until butter is melted. Add onions, thyme sprigs, honey, and ¼ teaspoon salt and cook until onions are softened and lightly browned, 5 to 7 minutes; discard thyme sprigs.

3. Melt remaining 2 tablespoons butter in large saucepan over medium heat. Add flour and cook for 1 minute. Slowly whisk in cream and broth, bring to simmer, and cook until thickened, about 2 minutes. Stir in 2 tablespoons chives, ¾ teaspoon salt, and ¼ teaspoon pepper.

4. Spread ½ cup sauce into prepared baking dish. Shingle half of potato slices in baking dish, then sprinkle with ¾ cup Gruyère and half of onions. Shingle remaining potatoes over top and sprinkle with remaining Gruyère and remaining onions. Pour remaining sauce over top and press with spatula to compact. Cover dish tightly with foil that has been sprayed with vegetable oil spray (or use nonstick foil) and bake for 1 hour.

5. Uncover and continue to bake until fork can be inserted into center of casserole with little to no resistance, about 1 hour longer. Let casserole cool for 10 minutes, then sprinkle with remaining 1 tablespoon chives, and serve.

Notes from the Test Kitchen

This rich casserole had our tasters going back for seconds. We covered the dish for the first half of baking and increased the overall cooking time to ensure the potatoes were done, and we cut back on the cheese and added broth for a less greasy result. Slicing the potatoes ⅛ inch thick is crucial; use a mandoline, a V-slicer, or a food processor fitted with a ⅛-inch slicing blade.

Gullah Gratin

ROBIN KESSLER | SARASOTA, FLORIDA

For those unfamiliar with Gullah culture and cuisine, this one-dish meal of potatoes, shrimp, sausage, and collard greens is a great introduction. The Gullah, African descendants who live in fishing and farming communities in Georgia and on the Sea Islands of South Carolina, have a cuisine that combines African and Low Country (coastal South Carolina and Georgia) traditions. From the late 1700s through the mid 1800s, some of the Gullah settled in Florida, and given Robin's recipe title, their influence clearly endured. "I suspect the origins of this family favorite are in my grandmother's ability to stretch a few ingredients into a satisfying meal," says Robin, a trait also notable in Gullah cooking. "This is our favorite recipe and still our most requested potluck dish."

SERVES 8

- 2 tablespoons olive oil
- 1 pound collard greens, stemmed and leaves cut into 1-inch pieces
- 12 ounces andouille sausage, cut into ½-inch pieces
- ½ cup beer
- ¼ teaspoon red pepper flakes
- 2 tablespoons unsalted butter
- 3 celery ribs, chopped fine
- 1 large onion, chopped fine
- 3 tablespoons Old Bay seasoning
- 3 tablespoons all-purpose flour
- 1½ cups low-sodium chicken broth
- 1½ cups heavy cream
- 2 teaspoons Worcestershire sauce
- 2 pounds russet potatoes, sliced ⅛ inch thick
- 12 ounces medium shrimp (40 to 50 per pound), peeled and deveined
- 1½ cups frozen corn

1. Adjust oven rack to middle position and heat oven to 350 degrees. Grease 13 by 9-inch baking dish.

2. Heat oil in large Dutch oven over medium heat until shimmering. Add collard greens, sausage, beer, and red pepper flakes and cook until collard greens begin to soften, 10 to 15 minutes. Transfer mixture, with liquid, to prepared baking dish.

3. Melt butter in pot over medium heat. Add celery and onion and cook until softened, 5 to 7 minutes. Stir in Old Bay and cook until fragrant, about 30 seconds. Stir in flour and cook for 1 minute. Slowly whisk in broth, cream, and Worcestershire, scraping up any browned bits. Bring to simmer and cook until thickened, about 2 minutes.

4. Stir in potatoes and bring to simmer. Cover, reduce heat to low, and cook, stirring occasionally, until potatoes are almost tender, 15 to 20 minutes. Stir in shrimp and corn.

5. Spoon potato mixture over collard greens mixture and press into even layer. Bake until fork can be inserted into center of casserole with little to no resistance, 50 to 60 minutes. Let casserole cool for 10 minutes before serving.

Notes from the Test Kitchen

We scaled Robin's recipe so it could fit in a single casserole, and we parcooked the potatoes to ensure they were done by the end. Switching from milk and half-and-half to broth and cream gave us a sauce less likely to break. Any mild beer will work here. Slicing the potatoes ⅛ inch thick is crucial; use a mandoline, a V-slicer, or a food processor fitted with a ⅛-inch slicing blade.

New Orleans Shrimp, French Quarter–Style

HELEN CONWELL | PORTLAND, OREGON

"While I was born (88 years ago) and raised in Mobile, I consider New Orleans to be my spiritual home. I had part of my medical residency there at the late lamented Charity Hospital (a casualty of Hurricane Katrina), practiced there, met and married my husband there, flew or took a ship from New Orleans after each home leave while we lived in South America, and during 30 years of retirement in coastal Alabama often spent short holidays there, sometimes even driving over just for lunch. (My husband David always said you couldn't get a bad meal in New Orleans.) So this recipe, a variation of a New Orleans classic, conjures up wonderful memories for me. While it is derived from a dish served for many decades in a famous restaurant, I call it just 'New Orleans Shrimp,' since every cook there has put his or her own spin on it." We weren't sure what restaurant Helen was referring to, but her recipe for marinating shrimp in a spicy mixture of mustard, cider vinegar, horseradish, and of course Tabasco sauce, and serving it over iceberg lettuce, has a kick and elegance all at once that certainly says New Orleans.

SERVES 8 TO 10

½	cup fresh parsley leaves
½	cup olive oil
½	cup cider vinegar
⅓	cup whole grain mustard
¼	cup prepared horseradish
2	scallions, chopped fine
1	celery rib, chopped fine
2	tablespoons ketchup
2	teaspoons paprika
1	garlic clove, minced
1	teaspoon salt
¼	teaspoon pepper
¼	teaspoon Tabasco sauce
3	pounds cooked and peeled large shrimp
1	head iceberg lettuce, cored and sliced ¼ inch thick

1. Process parsley, oil, vinegar, mustard, horseradish, scallions, celery, ketchup, paprika, garlic, salt, pepper, and Tabasco in food processor until mostly smooth, about 30 seconds; transfer to large bowl. Stir in shrimp, cover, and refrigerate for at least 8 hours or up to 1 day.

2. Spread lettuce onto large platter or individual plates. Using slotted spoon, remove shrimp from marinade and lay over lettuce. Spoon additional marinade over shrimp and lettuce to taste. Serve.

Notes from the Test Kitchen

Helen didn't specify a size of shrimp in her recipe; we opted for smaller shrimp to make this dish a little easier to eat. The marinade was a little oily so we cut back there and upped the mustard, Tabasco, and horseradish. Helen's recipe called for Creole mustard; we substituted the more readily available equivalent of whole grain mustard.

Potato-Mac Salad

KATHY TSARK | AIEA, HAWAII

Mixing potato and macaroni salads and then adding crabmeat may seem odd at first, but as Kathy tells us, "This recipe is a salad that is commonly served in Hawaii. Some version of it will be found in almost every 'plate lunch' sold at takeout and/or eat-in restaurants. This version was taught to me by my mother, Margaret Hodge, who learned to make it while working in a Japanese take-out restaurant in Honolulu in the 1930s." The plate lunch, a perfect example of the merging of cuisines in Hawaii, has been around since the 1920s and traditionally consists of sticky rice, a large portion of meat (typically prepared Asian-style), macaroni or potato salad, and perhaps kimchi or lettuce, all eaten with chopsticks. It seems likely that at some point both types of salad ended up on a plate and were mixed together. The addition of crabmeat to Kathy's recipe gives it another welcome spin. "My mother always made this salad for family gatherings. She was one of ten children born on the Rice Sugar Plantation on Kauai. Eventually they all moved to Oahu and we would have huge family dinners at my grandparents' home in Makiki. It was always the favorite salad of everyone in our family, and I made sure my mother taught me how to make it."

SERVES 8 TO 10

8	ounces bucatini, broken into 3-inch pieces
	Salt and pepper
1½	pounds red potatoes, cut into ½-inch pieces
¼	cup rice vinegar
2	tablespoons sugar
1½	cups mayonnaise
2	celery ribs, chopped fine
2	carrots, peeled and shredded
1	small onion, chopped fine
6	hard-boiled eggs, peeled and chopped medium
8	ounces crabmeat, picked over for shells

1. Bring 4 quarts water to boil in large Dutch oven. Add pasta and 1 tablespoon salt and cook, stirring often, until al dente. Drain pasta and transfer to large bowl.

2. Meanwhile, cover potatoes with water in large saucepan. Bring to boil, add 2 teaspoons salt, reduce to simmer, and cook until tender, about 10 minutes. Drain potatoes thoroughly and transfer to bowl with pasta.

3. Combine vinegar and sugar in bowl, then pour over pasta mixture and gently toss to combine. Cover and refrigerate until cooled, about 2 hours.

4. Add mayonnaise, celery, carrots, and onion to cooled pasta mixture and gently toss to combine. Cover and refrigerate until well chilled, about 30 minutes. (Salad can be refrigerated in airtight container for up to 2 days.) Before serving, gently fold in eggs and crabmeat, and season with salt and pepper to taste.

Notes from the Test Kitchen

This picnic-perfect recipe didn't require more than a single test to confirm it was a winner. We simply settled on a specific amount of mayonnaise (her recipe called for 1 to 2 cups). Kathy noted that imitation crab also works well. If you can't find bucatini you can substitute spaghetti.

Sweet and Sour German Potato Salad

SUSAN SMITH | TUCSON, ARIZONA

"German potato salad is an occasional menu side dish at Friday night fish fries throughout Wisconsin," Susan tells us, which is no surprise given Wisconsin's large population of German descendants. The local tradition surrounding Friday night fish fries grew out of the Catholic population's Lenten custom of eating fish on Fridays, combined with the readily available fish from the nearby Great Lakes. "My mother learned the basics of this recipe at a church picnic back in the 1950s from an old German immigrant in northeast Wisconsin. She added her own touches, and over the years has probably made thousands of pounds of this salad, as it's been requested for nearly every family and church function for the past 60 years. I made 20 pounds of it with her last month, so had an opportunity to learn what goes into it, how much, and her method so that I could write it down to share for the first time."

SERVES 6 TO 8

3 pounds medium red potatoes
6 slices bacon, chopped medium
1 onion, chopped fine
1 teaspoon celery seeds
1 teaspoon mustard seeds
½ teaspoon dry mustard
1 tablespoon all-purpose flour
½ cup cider vinegar
½ cup white vinegar
¼ cup granulated sugar
¼ cup packed light brown sugar
 Salt and pepper

1. Cover potatoes with water in large Dutch oven. Bring to boil, reduce to simmer, and cook until tender, 35 to 45 minutes. Drain potatoes thoroughly, let cool slightly, then slice ¼ inch thick.

2. Meanwhile, cook bacon in large skillet over medium heat until crisp, 5 to 7 minutes; transfer to paper towel–lined plate. Pour off all but 3 tablespoons bacon fat left in skillet.

3. Add onion to fat in skillet and cook over medium heat until beginning to soften, about 3 minutes. Add celery seeds, mustard seeds, and dry mustard and cook until fragrant, about 30 seconds. Stir in flour and cook for 1 minute. Slowly whisk in cider vinegar and white vinegar, scraping up any browned bits. Stir in granulated sugar, brown sugar, 1 teaspoon salt, and ¼ teaspoon pepper, bring to simmer, and cook until thickened, about 2 minutes.

4. Gently fold in cooked potatoes and crisp bacon until well combined. Season with salt and pepper to taste and serve warm or at room temperature.

Notes from the Test Kitchen

This version of potato salad stood out to our tasters, with its big sweet and sour flavor that would most definitely make a good match to mild-tasting fried fish. Her recipe called for ¾ cup white sugar, which struck us as too far in the sweet direction, so we cut it back some. Susan suggests making this salad one day in advance for the best flavor.

MAINE LOBSTER QUICHE

Sunday Suppers and Special Occasion Dinners

Grandma Lillian's Oxtail Stew 24

Nannie's Delicious Beef and Dumplings 25

Bubbe's Passover Brisket 26

Grandma's Sweet and Sour Rabbit 28

Grandma Alpha's Barbecue Ribs 30

Mt. Vernon Short Ribs 33

Ribs and Rigatonies 34

Beef Kapama 35

Beef Rollettes with Spaghetti 38

Italian Love Nests 41

Apple Cabbage Rolls 42

Tootie's Tourtière Pie 44

Grandma's Polish Pierogi 45

My Grandmother's Chicken Biryani 47

Chinese Five-Spice Chicken and Mushrooms 50

Coronation Chicken 52

Maine Lobster Quiche 53

Sunday Supper Strata 55

Grandma Lillian's Oxtail Stew

MICHAEL ANDREWS | KNOXVILLE, TENNESSEE

Oxtail stew is an English classic that is hearty and healing yet worthy of a special occasion. Few people make it these days, likely because oxtails seem obscure, but they can be found at most butcher shops and grocery stores (in the freezer section). Michael has been a longtime fan of this stew that is deeply flavored and rich in body. "This is my favorite recipe from my grandmother. I made sure I was somewhere close so that when she called my name for dinner, I wouldn't have far to run." Her recipe is clever because she tosses the oxtails in Worcestershire, then roasts them with vegetables before they go in the soup. This deepens the flavors and color of her stew. Oxtails require a slow braise, making this stew ideal for preparing on a Sunday afternoon.

SERVES 4 TO 6

- 3 pounds oxtails
- 2 tablespoons Worcestershire sauce
- Salt and pepper
- 1½ pounds russet potatoes, peeled and cut into 1-inch pieces
- 1 pound carrots, peeled and cut into 1-inch pieces
- 2 tablespoons vegetable oil
- 3 tablespoons unsalted butter
- 1 onion, chopped fine
- 1 celery rib, chopped fine
- 5 garlic cloves, minced
- 1 tablespoon minced fresh oregano or 1 teaspoon dried
- ¼ cup all-purpose flour
- 8 cups beef broth
- 3 tablespoons chopped fresh basil

1. Adjust oven racks to upper-middle and lower-middle positions and heat oven to 350 degrees. Pat oxtails dry with paper towels, toss with Worcestershire, and season with pepper. Lay oxtails on rimmed baking sheet. Toss potatoes and carrots with oil, ½ teaspoon salt, and ¼ teaspoon pepper in large bowl and spread over second rimmed baking sheet. Roast oxtails and vegetables until oxtails are well browned and vegetables are tender, 45 to 60 minutes, switching and rotating baking sheets halfway through cooking.

2. Melt butter in large Dutch oven over medium heat. Add onion and celery and cook until softened and well browned, 8 to 10 minutes. Stir in garlic and oregano and cook until fragrant, about 30 seconds. Stir in flour and cook for 1 minute. Slowly whisk in broth, scraping up any browned bits, and bring to simmer.

3. Nestle browned oxtails, along with any accumulated juice, into pot. Bring to simmer, cover, and transfer to oven to lower-middle rack. Cook until oxtails are tender, about 2½ hours. Stir in roasted potatoes and carrots and continue to cook in oven until heated through, about 10 minutes longer.

4. Remove pot from oven. Let stew settle for 5 minutes, then remove fat from surface using large spoon. Stir in basil, season with salt and pepper to taste, and serve.

Notes from the Test Kitchen
We opted to precook the aromatic vegetables in the Dutch oven so we could build a more flavorful soup base, and moving the stew from stovetop to oven allowed for more even cooking. Oxtail pieces can vary widely in diameter; try to buy thicker pieces, which will have more meat.

Nannie's Delicious Beef and Dumplings

MARY MEIER | MIAMI, FLORIDA

"My grandmother, Anna Marie Schneider, lived to be 103 years old and cooked countless meals for generations of loved ones," writes Mary. "I treasure her old spiral notebook containing recipes, with clippings from newspapers all the way back to 1916. Her most beloved recipe is for dumplings cooked in a simple dish of braised beef and onions. We loved them when my mother made them, but she always said they weren't as good as her mother's. When I make them, I always feel they aren't as perfect as I remember. Funny thing is, everyone loves them, no matter who makes them." With its hearty dumplings, rich stew, and tender meat, you are sure to love it too.

SERVES 4 TO 6

STEW

- 1 (2-pound) boneless beef chuck-eye roast, trimmed and cut into 1½-inch pieces
  Salt and pepper
- 2 tablespoons vegetable oil
- 2 onions, chopped fine
- 2 garlic cloves, minced
- 1 tablespoon minced fresh thyme or 1 teaspoon dried
- ¼ cup all-purpose flour
- 3 cups low-sodium chicken broth
- 2 cups water
- 2 bay leaves

DUMPLINGS

- 2 cups all-purpose flour
- 1¼ teaspoons baking powder
  Pinch salt
- 1 tablespoon unsalted butter, softened
- 1 cup whole milk

1. FOR THE STEW: Adjust oven rack to lower-middle position and heat oven to 300 degrees. Pat beef dry with paper towels and season with salt and pepper. Heat 1 tablespoon oil in large Dutch oven over medium-high heat until just smoking. Brown beef well on all sides, 8 to 10 minutes; transfer to bowl.

2. Heat remaining 1 tablespoon oil in pot over medium heat until shimmering. Add onions and cook until softened and lightly browned, 5 to 7 minutes. Stir in garlic and thyme and cook until fragrant, about 30 seconds. Stir in flour and cook for 1 minute. Slowly whisk in broth and water, scraping up any browned bits, and bring to simmer.

3. Stir in browned meat, along with any accumulated juice, and bay leaves. Bring to simmer, cover, and transfer to oven. Cook until meat is tender, about 2 hours. Remove pot from oven, discard bay leaves, and season with salt and pepper to taste.

4. FOR THE DUMPLINGS: Whisk flour, baking powder, and salt together in large bowl. Add butter and cut into flour mixture using fork (or two butter knives) until evenly distributed. Stir milk into flour mixture until just incorporated (dough will be very thick).

5. Return stew to simmer. Using two spoons, drop ¼-cup-size dumplings into stew about 1 inch apart (you should have about 6 dumplings). Cover, reduce heat to gentle simmer, and cook until dumplings have doubled in size, about 10 minutes. Serve.

Notes from the Test Kitchen

We made only a few changes to Nannie's recipe. We cooked the stew in the oven for more even heat, and we substituted chicken broth for some water. Thyme and bay leaf lent flavor.

Bubbe's Passover Brisket

REGGIE GRINER | SAN FRANCISCO, CALIFORNIA

"The Passover Brisket is a recipe by my mother, 'Bubbe,' as she was known to everyone after she had grandchildren. She grew up in a shtetl in Poland. The brisket was placed in the baker's oven on Friday night and stayed there until the Sabbath on Saturday night." Bubbe braises her brisket with potatoes, carrots, prunes, and apricots, which creates a meal that is wonderfully savory and sweet at once. "It came to be served for every Passover in the United States," adds Reggie, "and I have made it for the last 30 years to much acclaim from all who join my family for Passover."

SERVES 8 TO 10

- 1 (4- to 5-pound) brisket, preferably flat-cut, trimmed
  Salt and pepper
- 2 tablespoons vegetable oil
- 1½ pounds carrots, peeled and sliced 2 inches thick
- 2 onions, chopped coarse
- 12 ounces sweet potatoes, peeled and cut into 2-inch pieces
- 6 cups low-sodium chicken broth, plus extra as needed
- 2 cups prunes
- 1 cup dried apricots
- 2 bay leaves

1. Adjust oven rack to lower-middle position and heat oven to 350 degrees. Pat brisket dry with paper towels and season with salt and pepper. Heat 1 tablespoon oil in large Dutch oven over medium-high heat until just smoking. Brown brisket on both sides, 12 to 14 minutes; transfer to large plate.

2. Heat remaining 1 tablespoon oil in pot over medium heat until shimmering. Add carrots, onions, and sweet potatoes and cook until softened, 5 to 7 minutes. Stir in broth, prunes, apricots, and bay leaves and bring to simmer.

3. Nestle browned brisket, along with any accumulated juice, into pot. (If necessary, add more broth to cover all but top of meat.) Bring to simmer, cover, and transfer to oven. Cook until brisket is tender and fork can be inserted into meat with little to no resistance, 3 to 4 hours, turning brisket every hour.

4. Remove pot from oven and transfer brisket to large plate. Let braising liquid settle for 5 minutes, then remove fat from surface using large spoon. Discard bay leaves. Return brisket to pot and let cool to room temperature. Cover and refrigerate for at least 12 hours or up to 1 day.

5. Adjust oven rack to middle position and heat oven to 350 degrees. Transfer brisket to carving board and slice against grain into ½-inch-thick slices. Bring sauce to simmer in pot over medium heat and season with salt and pepper to taste. Shingle sliced brisket in 13 by 9-inch baking dish and pour warmed sauce over top. Bake until meat is heated through, 10 to 20 minutes. Serve.

Notes from the Test Kitchen

We loved the combination of sweet and savory flavors here. Refrigerating the brisket overnight deepens the flavors and allows the meat to become more tender, but you can make and serve it on the same day. In step 4, transfer the brisket to a carving board rather than letting it cool. Let the brisket rest 15 minutes, then slice against the grain and serve with the sauce.

Grandma's Sweet and Sour Rabbit

NIKKI LORE | ROCHESTER, NEW YORK

Affordably priced yet worthy of a special occasion, rabbit tends to be an overlooked, underrated centerpiece these days—which makes Nikki's dish a perfect addition to this collection of forgotten special occasion recipes. "My grandmother came from Sicily in 1912 with her father and mother, leaving two older sisters and one brother behind," Nikki tells us. "It had been arranged for her to meet a gentleman who would soon become her husband. They were married within the year, but unfortunately he died, along with so many others, of the Spanish influenza in 1918. She married my grandfather two years later. He was an avid hunter, and his sons followed him down every country road imaginable, bringing home deer, pheasant, rabbit, even woodchuck and squirrel, and Grandma cooked it all with love for her family. Grandma prided herself on being able to cook any wild game. Her Sweet and Sour Rabbit is the one we all loved best because of its unique blend of flavors. Her legacy was love of family and cooking."

SERVES 4

- 1 (3-pound) whole rabbit
  Salt and pepper
- 3 tablespoons olive oil
- 2 celery ribs, cut into ½-inch pieces
- 1 onion, chopped fine
- 1 large carrot, peeled and cut into ½-inch pieces
- 4 garlic cloves, minced
- 1 tablespoon all-purpose flour
- 1 cup dry red wine
- 1 (14.5-ounce) can diced tomatoes
- ½ cup pitted Italian green olives, chopped
- ⅓ cup red wine vinegar
- ⅓ cup raisins
- 4 teaspoons sugar
- 2 bay leaves

1. Following photos on page 29, cut rabbit into 7 pieces. Pat rabbit dry with paper towels and season with salt and pepper. Heat 1 tablespoon oil in large Dutch oven over medium-high heat until just smoking. Brown half of rabbit well on both sides, 6 to 8 minutes; transfer to medium bowl. Repeat with 1 tablespoon more oil and remaining rabbit; transfer to bowl.

2. Heat remaining 1 tablespoon oil in pot over medium heat. Add celery, onion, and carrot and cook until softened and lightly

browned, 8 to 10 minutes. Stir in garlic and cook until fragrant, about 30 seconds. Stir in flour and cook for 1 minute. Slowly whisk in wine, scraping up any browned bits. Stir in tomatoes, olives, vinegar, raisins, sugar, and bay leaves and bring to simmer.

3. Nestle browned forequarters, hindquarters, and neck into pot (reserve loin pieces for later). Bring to simmer, cover, and reduce heat to medium-low. Simmer gently until rabbit is almost tender, 45 to 55 minutes.

4. Nestle browned loin pieces into pot, cover, and continue to simmer gently until rabbit is tender, about 10 minutes longer. Discard bay leaves, season with salt and pepper to taste, and serve.

Notes from the Test Kitchen

With vinegar, sugar, red wine, raisins, and vegetables, Nikki's recipe is packed with flavor. We did bring the sweet and sour into better balance, as it was fairly tart, by reducing the amount of vinegar from ½ cup to ⅓ cup and increasing the sugar from 2 to 4 teaspoons. A little flour added to the sauce gave it body. To ensure the tenderloin pieces didn't overcook, we added them toward the end of cooking. Rabbits are available in several sizes. If necessary, you can substitute two (1½-pound) rabbits (the cooking time will remain the same). Nikki suggested green or black olives; we preferred the former. Make sure to buy green olives that are not pimento-stuffed.

CUTTING UP A WHOLE RABBIT

1. Using a chef's knife, cut the hindquarters from the loin, then cut the hindquarters into 2 pieces by slicing through the spine.

2. Trim and discard the thin flap that hangs between the rib cage and loin.

3. Remove the loin from the forequarters by cutting through the spine at the point where the rib cage is attached, then cut the loin in half crosswise.

4. Separate the two forequarters from the neck by cutting through the rib cage on either side of the neck.

Grandma Alpha's Barbecue Ribs

JOYCE CONWAY | WESTERVILLE, OHIO

"My first memory of enjoying these mouthwatering ribs is still vivid in my mind. Grandma owned a tavern in a small rural Ohio town and lived above it, in a shotgun-style apartment. I loved visiting her on weekends when the farmers came to town to drop off grain at the feed store next door. Grandma's place was quite the social center. The farmers gathered to play cards on small wooden tables with chalkboards on each corner, while they drank their libations and chewed their Mail Pouch tobacco. But the main attraction was the Blue Plate Special: Grandma Alpha's Barbecue Ribs. They were served on oval platters with a big side dish of homemade coleslaw and biscuits. She would prebake the ribs and marinate them in her (then secret) sauce overnight. The next day, she finished them in her broiler. Her timeless recipe is faithfully and regularly re-created, the lone concession to 21st century convenience being a gas-fired grill." The key to the flavor of Grandma Alpha's ribs is her balance between a spice rub, which includes paprika, cayenne, and garlic, and a tangy-sweet, ketchup-heavy sauce. This recipe achieves unbelievably tender meat by first braising the ribs in beer for several hours, then finishing them on the grill. "Grandma Alpha, who passed in 1966, would be proud that her 'social centerpiece' is still the rage of family and friends."

SERVES 4 TO 6

SPICE RUB AND RIBS
- 1 tablespoon pepper
- 2 teaspoons salt
- 1½ teaspoons smoked paprika
- ¾ teaspoon garlic powder
- ½ teaspoon cayenne pepper
- 6 pounds baby back ribs or St. Louis–style spareribs, membrane removed and cut into 4- to 5-rib sections
- 1 cup beer

SAUCE
- 2 cups ketchup
- 1 cup packed brown sugar
- ½ cup cider vinegar
- ½ cup soy sauce
- ¼ cup yellow mustard
- 6 garlic cloves, minced
- Salt and pepper

(Continued on page 32)

1. FOR THE SPICE RUB AND RIBS: Adjust oven rack to middle position and heat oven to 375 degrees. Combine pepper, salt, paprika, garlic powder, and cayenne in bowl. Pat ribs dry with paper towels and rub evenly with spice mixture. Arrange ribs in roasting pan, overlapping as needed. Pour beer over ribs, cover tightly with foil, and transfer to oven. Roast until meat is tender and beginning to pull away from bones, about 2½ hours.

2. FOR THE SAUCE: Combine all ingredients in bowl and season with salt and pepper to taste. Refrigerate sauce until needed.

3. Brush ribs thoroughly with 1 cup sauce, transfer to rimmed baking sheet, and let cool to room temperature. Cover and refrigerate for at least 6 hours or up to 1 day. (Let ribs sit at room temperature for 1 hour before grilling.)

4A. FOR A CHARCOAL GRILL: Open bottom grill vents completely. Light large chimney starter half full with charcoal briquettes (50 briquettes; 3 quarts). When coals are hot, pour them evenly over grill. Set cooking grate in place, cover, and heat grill until hot, about 5 minutes.

4B. FOR A GAS GRILL: Turn all burners to high, cover, and heat grill until hot, about 15 minutes. Turn all burners to medium. (Adjust burners as needed to maintain medium fire.)

5. Clean and oil cooking grate. Place ribs on grill, overlapping as needed. Cook ribs, flipping and brushing with more sauce every few minutes, until hot and well glazed, about 20 minutes.

6. Transfer ribs to carving board, tent loosely with foil, and let rest for 30 minutes. While ribs rest, heat remaining sauce in microwave. Serve ribs with warmed sauce.

Notes from the Test Kitchen

There certainly weren't any leftovers in the test kitchen when we made these fall-off-the-bone tender ribs. We made only a few tweaks to the recipe. Joyce's original recipe yielded enough to feed a dozen people. We decided to scale down to make enough to feed a family or small group, knowing it could be doubled if necessary. Because granulated garlic is hard to find, we switched to using garlic powder, and since Joyce didn't specify what type of mustard to use, we assumed classic yellow. Either baby back or St. Louis spareribs will work here; baby back ribs weigh 1½ pounds per rack, while St. Louis–style spareribs weigh about 3 pounds per rack.

REMOVING THE MEMBRANE FROM RIBS

1. At one end of the rack, loosen the edge of the membrane with the tip of a paring knife.

2. Grab the membrane with a paper towel and pull slowly—it should come off in one piece. The membrane is very thin, so removing it should not expose the rib bones.

Mt. Vernon Short Ribs

PATRICIA BEDOR | SEATTLE, WASHINGTON

As far as we can tell, Mt. Vernon Short Ribs was created in honor of—not by—our famous forefather. The first instance we found of a similarly titled dish appeared in a 1965 Maryland newspaper, which noted that George Washington had a Pennsylvania Dutch cook and was fond of beer, making short ribs braised in beer a perfect dish for Presidents' Day. (Similarly, Patricia suspects her mother found the recipe in a Detroit newspaper.) Notes Patricia: "This recipe comes from my mother, and I have doctored it up quite a bit from her take on it." The beans and garlic were Patricia's touches, both of which are nice additions. She likes to serve this recipe over rice.

SERVES 6

- 6 pounds bone-in English-style short ribs, trimmed
  Salt and pepper
- 2 tablespoons olive oil
- 1 onion, halved and sliced ½ inch thick
- 3 garlic cloves, minced
- 2 tablespoons all-purpose flour
- ¾ cup beer
- 2 cups low-sodium chicken broth
- 1 (8-ounce) can tomato sauce
- 2 tablespoons brown sugar
- 1 tablespoon white vinegar
- 1 teaspoon dry mustard
- 1 teaspoon (1 cube) beef bouillon
- 1 pound carrots, peeled and cut into 1-inch pieces
- 1 (15-ounce) can pinto beans, drained and rinsed

1. Adjust oven rack to lower-middle position and heat oven to 300 degrees. Pat short ribs dry with paper towels and season with salt and pepper. Heat 1 tablespoon oil in large Dutch oven over medium-high heat until just smoking. Brown half of ribs well on all sides, 7 to 10 minutes; transfer to large plate. Repeat with remaining 1 tablespoon oil and remaining short ribs; transfer to plate.

2. Pour off all but 1 tablespoon of fat left in pot. Add onion and ¼ teaspoon salt and cook over medium heat until softened and lightly browned, 5 to 7 minutes. Stir in garlic and cook until fragrant, about 30 seconds. Stir in flour and cook for 1 minute. Slowly whisk in beer, scraping up any browned bits. Stir in broth, tomato sauce, sugar, vinegar, mustard, and bouillon and bring to simmer.

3. Nestle browned short ribs, bone side up, into pot along with any accumulated juice. Bring to simmer, cover, and transfer to oven. Cook until meat is almost tender, about 2½ hours. Stir in carrots and beans, cover, and continue to cook in oven until meat is tender, about 45 minutes longer.

4. Transfer short ribs to platter and tent loosely with foil. Let braising liquid settle for 5 minutes, then remove fat from surface using large spoon. Season with salt and pepper to taste. Spoon 1 cup sauce over short ribs and serve with remaining sauce.

Notes from the Test Kitchen
We gobbled up these ultra-tender ribs and flavorful sauce. Adding a little flour slightly thickened the sauce so it would cling better, and we swapped her water for broth for more flavor.

Ribs and Rigatonies

CYNTHIA WALLACE | TUCSON, ARIZONA

"This recipe came from my father-in-law's mother, Josephine Wallace, who lived in Rock Springs, Wyoming. The story is that she got it from an Italian friend who reportedly was at one time somehow associated with a 'house of ill repute.' Maybe the cook?'" No matter the recipe's background, with its tender pork ribs and concentrated, deeply flavored tomato sauce with just a hint of heat, Cynthia is right that it is a dish that is both simple and delicious. "I love to serve it for company and always get rave reviews. Since the work is done ahead of time, you can relax and visit when company arrives—the sauce is ready and simmering on the stove just waiting for pasta."

SERVES 4

- 2 pounds baby back ribs, racks halved lengthwise, then cut into individual ribs (see note)
  Salt and pepper
- 2 tablespoons olive oil
- 8 tablespoons (1 stick) unsalted butter
- 2 celery ribs, chopped medium
- 1 onion, chopped medium
- 1 green bell pepper, stemmed, seeded, and cut into ½-inch pieces
- 4 garlic cloves, minced
- 2 cups water
- 1 (15-ounce) can tomato sauce
- 1 (6-ounce) can tomato paste
- 3 dried Thai, tepín, or de árbol chiles
- ¼ teaspoon baking soda
- 1 pound rigatoni
  Grated Parmesan cheese, for serving

1. Pat ribs dry with paper towels and season with salt and pepper. Heat oil in large Dutch oven over medium-high heat until just smoking. Brown ribs on all sides, 6 to 8 minutes; transfer to bowl.

2. Melt butter in pot over medium heat. Add celery, onion, and bell pepper and cook until softened and lightly browned, 8 to 10 minutes. Stir in garlic and cook until fragrant, about 30 seconds. Stir in water, scraping up any browned bits. Stir in tomato sauce, tomato paste, Thai chiles, baking soda, ½ teaspoon salt, and ¼ teaspoon pepper and bring to simmer.

3. Stir in browned ribs, along with any accumulated juice, and bring to simmer. Cover partially (leaving about 1 inch of pot open), reduce heat to medium-low, and simmer gently until meat is tender and sauce is deeply flavored, about 3 hours.

4. Bring 4 quarts water to boil in large pot. Add pasta and 1 tablespoon salt and cook, stirring often, until al dente. Reserve ½ cup of cooking water, then drain pasta and return to pot.

5. Let sauce settle for 5 minutes, then remove fat from surface using large spoon. Add sauce and ribs to pasta and toss to combine, adjusting sauce consistency with reserved cooking water as desired. Season with salt and pepper to taste and serve with Parmesan.

Notes from the Test Kitchen

This Italian-American take on classic Italian ragu is great for company or a hearty supper. Cynthia called for tepín chiles; we found both Thai and de árbol chiles were good, easier-to-find substitutes. Adding some pasta cooking water to the sauce, rather than tap water, lent starch to thicken the sauce. While Cynthia's father-in-law broke down the ribs using a meat cleaver, we found it easiest (and safest) to ask our butcher to do it.

Beef Kapama

PENELOPE MANDIS | CHICAGO, ILLINOIS

"My grandmother was one of the earliest Greek immigrants to Chicago. She was a great cook. My grandfather owned a small grocery and, especially during the Depression, there was always a crowd around Yia-Yia's (Greek for 'grandma's') table, particularly after Sunday services. Of all her recipes," notes Penelope, "my favorite is Beef Kapama." Kapama, a dish of Turkish origin that is hugely popular in Greece, refers to any kind of meat cooked in a slightly sweetened and warmly spiced tomato sauce with onions. It has been a popular pre-Lenten supper at numerous Greek Orthodox churches. It can be served over various starches, such as potatoes, rice, or buttered noodles, and it is often served with, if not topped by, string beans. Though Penelope's grandmother's recipe omits the green beans, it gets an incredible boost in flavor because she tosses the noodles in browned butter, as well as a traditional Greek hard, sharp cheese called Myzithra (both of which are techniques we found in a few other recipes), before topping them with the meat and sauce. Though chicken and lamb are the most common versions of kapama, Penelope notes the following about her grandmother's recipe made with beef: "In her poor village, chicken kapama was rare, lamb kapama even more so. But when she arrived here, Yia-Yia discovered beef and the recipe for Beef Kapama was born!"

SERVES 6

- 2 onions, 1 onion peeled and 1 onion chopped fine
- 6 whole cloves
- 1 (3½- to 4-pound) boneless beef chuck-eye roast, trimmed and cut into 1½-inch pieces
- 1 tablespoon fresh lemon juice
- ¼ teaspoon ground cinnamon
- ⅛ teaspoon ground allspice
  Salt and pepper

- 3 tablespoons olive oil
- 2 cups water
- 1 (28-ounce) can tomato puree
- 1 (6-ounce) can tomato paste
- 1 pound mostaccioli or penne
- 8 tablespoons (1 stick) unsalted butter
- 2 ounces Greek Myzithra cheese, ricotta salata, or Pecorino Romano, grated (1 cup)
- 3 tablespoons minced fresh parsley
- 2 shallots, minced

(Continued on page 37)

1. Adjust oven rack to lower-middle position and heat oven to 325 degrees. Stud peeled onion with cloves; set aside. Toss beef with lemon juice, cinnamon, and allspice and let sit for 15 minutes.

2. Pat beef dry with paper towels and season with salt and pepper. Heat 1 tablespoon oil in large Dutch oven over medium-high heat until just smoking. Brown half of beef well on all sides, 7 to 10 minutes; transfer to medium bowl. Repeat with 1 tablespoon more oil and remaining beef; transfer to bowl.

3. Heat remaining 1 tablespoon oil in pot over medium heat until shimmering. Add chopped onion and cook until softened, about 5 minutes. Stir in water, scraping up any browned bits. Stir in tomato puree, tomato paste, and clove-studded onion and bring to simmer.

4. Stir in browned beef, along with any accumulated juice, and bring to simmer. Cover, transfer to oven, and cook until meat is tender, 2 to 2½ hours.

5. Remove pot from oven and discard clove-studded onion. Season stew with salt and pepper to taste.

6. Meanwhile, bring 4 quarts water to boil in large pot. Add pasta and 1 tablespoon salt and cook, stirring often, until al dente. Drain pasta and return to pot.

7. Melt butter in small skillet over medium heat and cook, swirling pan constantly, until butter is light brown and has faint nutty aroma, 3 to 5 minutes. Pour browned butter over noodles, add Myzithra cheese, and toss to combine. Serve stew over noodles, sprinkling each portion with parsley and shallots.

Notes from the Test Kitchen

We had never had kapama before Penelope's recipe, and it turned us into huge fans. The spiced, slightly sweet sauce melded with the brown butter noodles to create a fantastic combination. Her recipe called for beef and noted a preference for sirloin, but we opted for chuck-eye roast, the test kitchen's favorite stew meat, and we upped the amount of meat so the recipe could serve six (having a bigger yield seemed logical since the recipe takes some time to prepare). We also moved the pot from the stovetop to the oven for more even cooking. Cutting back from two cans of tomato paste to one helped pull the tomato flavor into balance. Myzithra cheese is hard to find, but we found ricotta salata was the next best thing, though Pecorino Romano will also work. Penelope's recipe called for mostaccioli, noodles that resemble a smooth penne. We couldn't find these but we did like it with penne, as well as wide egg noodles.

Beef Rollettes with Spaghetti

SALLY REILLY | FORT WORTH, TEXAS

"My mother made this dish for my family as we were growing up during the '60s and '70s," Sally tells us. "She found the recipe shortly after she was married, in a magazine advertisement for Hunt's tomato paste. It featured an Italian mother proudly displaying a platter of the meat rolls with pasta." Going back to that original advertisement (we found a copy in a 1962 issue of *McCall's*), we saw that the picture is just as Sally notes, putting an American spin on old-world cooking with its sense of celebration and family coming together over hearty, satisfying recipes. Sally followed that original recipe by rolling steaks, which were pounded thin, around a mixture of bread crumbs, Parmesan cheese, onion, and herbs, and then simmering them in a tomato sauce. But it seems like she also added a few touches of her own. For one, she added the bacon to the filling (she says Thuringer, a type of summer sausage, works well too, but it can be hard to find). She also opted for top round over the cube steak specified by Hunt's. And though the folks at Hunt's might disapprove, she swapped some of the tomato paste for V8. Her changes give these beef rollettes a huge boost in flavor, making them a meal that will definitely bring the family to the table.

SERVES 4

1 slice hearty white sandwich bread, torn into quarters
2 ounces Parmesan cheese, grated (1 cup)
¼ cup finely chopped onion
1 (1½-pound) top-round steak, about ¾ inch thick, trimmed
  Salt and pepper
4 slices bacon, halved crosswise
2 (6-ounce) cans tomato paste
1½ cups V8 vegetable juice
1½ cups water
2 garlic cloves, minced
2 teaspoons minced fresh oregano or ½ teaspoon dried
½ teaspoon dried basil
2 tablespoons vegetable oil
1 pound spaghetti
1 tablespoon minced fresh parsley

1. Pulse bread in food processor to fine crumbs, about 10 pulses. Combine bread crumbs, Parmesan, and onion in bowl.

2. Following photos, cut steak into 8 equal pieces, then pound each to ⅛-inch thickness. Pat steaks dry with paper towels and season with salt and pepper. Working with one piece of steak at a time, lay 1 bacon piece down center. Gently pack 3 tablespoons bread crumb mixture on top of meat. Roll and tie steak with butcher's twine into tight rollette.

3. Combine tomato paste, vegetable juice, water, garlic, oregano, basil, ¼ teaspoon salt, and ¼ teaspoon pepper in bowl. Heat oil in large nonstick skillet over medium-high heat until just smoking. Brown rollettes on all sides, 6 to 8 minutes. Pour tomato paste mixture over rollettes and bring to gentle simmer. Cover, reduce heat to medium-low, and simmer gently until meat is tender, about 1½ hours.

4. Transfer rollettes to carving board, remove twine, and cover to keep warm. Let sauce settle for 5 minutes, then remove fat from surface using large spoon. Season with salt and pepper to taste.

5. Meanwhile, bring 4 quarts water to boil in large Dutch oven. Add pasta and 1 tablespoon salt and cook, stirring often, until al dente. Reserve ½ cup of cooking water, then drain pasta and return to pot.

6. Add 3 cups sauce to pasta and toss to combine, adjusting sauce consistency with reserved cooking water as desired. Divide pasta among four individual bowls, then top each bowl with two rollettes. Sprinkle with parsley and serve with remaining sauce.

Notes from the Test Kitchen

We loved the smoky flavor the bacon lent to Sally's mother's recipe, but it also added a fair amount of rendered fat, so we defatted the sauce before serving. We also cut back on the salt since the bacon lent plenty on its own, and we switched out a few convenience products for their fresher counterparts: fresh Parmesan we grated ourselves for the less-flavorful pregrated cheese, and fresh parsley in lieu of dried. We also scaled up the sauce because the original yielded a scant 2 cups, not enough to sauce the pasta to our liking.

MAKING ROLLETTES

1. Slice the steak crosswise into 8 equal pieces.

2. Working with one piece of steak at a time, layer it between two sheets of plastic wrap and gently pound it to a ⅛-inch thickness.

3. Working with one piece of steak at a time, lay one piece of bacon down the center, then gently pack 3 tablespoons of the bread-crumb mixture over the bacon and piece of steak.

4. Roll the meat around the filling into a tight rollette, then tie the rollette with butcher's twine to secure.

Italian Love Nests

TRACY ZAMPAGLIONE | ORLANDO, FLORIDA

"When I married into an Italian-American family, I was immediately fascinated by the food and family traditions that make the Italian ways so endearing. My husband would fondly describe specialties his grandmother made for Sunday dinners. Since both his grandmother and mother passed away prior to our marriage, I was challenged with re-creating these dishes based solely on description. I succeeded with Sunday red sauce and chicken cacciatore. Next, I was on a mission to replicate 'Italian Love Nests,' which my husband's grandmother created for him as a child. Essentially, these are individual nests of pasta in a Parmesan sauce, topped with chopped prosciutto and finely grated Parmesan, and baked to perfection. The finishing touch was a large green olive, which represented an eye since my husband's grandmother always told him that he was 'the apple of her eye.' They've become a favorite of my own children." These spirals of cheesy, prosciutto-flecked pasta prepared in a muffin tin are as tasty as they are fun. Tracy notes they are good with roast chicken or veal chops; we also think they would make a great lunch or light dinner served with a green vegetable.

SERVES 6 TO 8

8	ounces angel hair pasta
1	cup heavy cream
2½	ounces Parmesan cheese, grated (1¼ cups)
6	thin slices prosciutto, chopped fine
¼	cup dry white wine
2	large eggs
2	teaspoons minced fresh sage
1	teaspoon white pepper
½	teaspoon salt
½	teaspoon ground nutmeg
⅛	teaspoon hot sauce
12	pimento-stuffed green olives

1. Adjust oven rack to middle position and heat oven to 350 degrees. Lightly grease 12-cup muffin tin. Bring 4 quarts water to boil in large Dutch oven. Add pasta and 1 tablespoon salt and cook, stirring often, until al dente. Drain pasta and return to pot.

2. Whisk cream, ¾ cup Parmesan, prosciutto, wine, eggs, sage, pepper, salt, nutmeg, and hot sauce together, then pour over pasta and toss to combine.

3. Using tongs, portion pasta mixture into prepared muffin tins, twisting pasta in cups to form uniform nests. Pour any remaining sauce evenly over pasta, sprinkle with remaining ½ cup Parmesan, and press one olive into each nest.

4. Bake until centers are set and tops are golden brown, 20 to 25 minutes, rotating pan halfway through baking. Let nests cool in pan for 5 minutes, then run small knife around edges, unmold, and serve warm.

Notes from the Test Kitchen

Not only are these nests cute as can be, but they also have wonderful flavor from the combination of Parmesan, prosciutto, sage, and nutmeg. We swapped out Tracy's fresh pasta for easier-to-find dried, and we used fresh sage instead of ground. Tracy lined the muffin tin cups with Parmesan, but we found this made the nests too greasy so we sprayed the muffin cups with vegetable oil spray.

Apple Cabbage Rolls

LAINA LAMB | MARION, OHIO

Cabbage rolls stuffed with ground meat and simmered in a tomato sauce are a classic retro comfort food, but Laina puts a few twists on the typical recipe to make her version stand out from the crowd. She adds pearl barley to the ground meat filling, which creates an appealingly rustic texture and earthy flavor, and she layers the rolls in the pot with thin slices of apple and then pours the sauce over the top. As the rolls, sauce, and apples cook together, the apples dissolve into the sauce, lending a balancing sweetness to the dish. For her, it's a special occasion favorite. "This is an old Hungarian recipe from my paternal side," Laina tells us. "I added the apples to reduce the bitterness of the cabbage so that my kids would eat it too. I got the idea from an old Polish recipe. We enjoy this recipe every New Year's Day, and various other times throughout the year."

SERVES 8

Salt and pepper

2 large heads green cabbage, cored

1 pound 85 percent lean ground beef

1 pound ground pork

3 cups sour cream

1 cup pearl barley

1 onion, chopped fine

¼ cup paprika

4 cloves garlic, minced

2 Granny Smith apples, peeled, cored, and sliced thin

4 cups canned tomato sauce

2 cups low-sodium chicken broth

1. Bring 4 quarts water and 1 tablespoon salt to boil in large Dutch oven. Add 1 head cabbage and cook until outer leaves begin to wilt, 3 to 5 minutes. Following photos on page 43, use tongs to remove outer 15 leaves from cabbage, one at a time, as they wilt. Transfer wilted leaves to colander and let cool. Remove remaining cabbage heart from water, and repeat with second head cabbage. Discard water and dry pot.

2. Pat wilted cabbage leaves dry with paper towels, and trim away any tough ribs. Using hands, mix ground beef, ground pork, 2 cups sour cream, barley, onion, 2 tablespoons paprika, garlic, and ½ teaspoon salt together in bowl. Working with 18 to 20 largest cabbage

leaves, pack and roll ⅓ cup meat mixture into each leaf following photos.

3. Cover bottom of Dutch oven with 5 more wilted cabbage leaves. Top with one-third apples. Arrange half of cabbage rolls in pot, seam side down, fitting them snugly to prevent unrolling. Repeat layering process with half of remaining apples, followed by remaining cabbage rolls, then remaining apples. Combine tomato sauce and chicken broth, and pour evenly into pot. Top with remaining 5 wilted cabbage leaves to cover.

4. Bring to simmer over medium-high heat. Cover, reduce heat to medium-low, and simmer gently until cabbage is tender and filling is cooked through, about 2 hours.

5. Using slotted spoon, transfer cabbage rolls to serving platter, discarding loose cabbage leaves. Stir remaining 2 tablespoons paprika into

sauce. Combine 1 cup sauce with remaining 1 cup sour cream (to temper), then stir mixture into pot. Season sauce with salt and pepper to taste. Spoon 1 cup sauce over cabbage rolls and serve with remaining sauce.

Notes from the Test Kitchen

We were all fans of the modern touches Laina gave to this old-fashioned dish. To prevent the sour cream from curdling, we tempered it before stirring it all into the pot, and we cut the amount of sour cream back from 4 cups because the sauce seemed a little too heavy and dairy-rich. Because the sauce was slightly bitter, we also swapped out the cabbage cooking water for chicken broth. Two apples rather than four seemed sufficient and helped keep the flavors in balance. Note that the recipe requires about 30 cabbage leaves, which is about 2 heads of cabbage.

STUFFING CABBAGE LEAVES

1. Cut out the cabbage core with a paring knife and discard, then place the head of cabbage in a large pot of boiling water.

2. Using tongs, gently transfer the outer leaves of cabbage to a colander as they blanch and wilt. When the cabbage leaves are cool enough to handle, pat them dry and remove any tough ribs from the base.

3. With the core end of the cabbage leaf facing you, arrange ⅓ cup of the filling just above the area where the thick rib has been removed.

4. Fold the sides of the cabbage leaf over the filling, then roll the bottom edge of the leaf up over the filling into a tight and tidy roll.

Tootie's Tourtière Pie

SUE LOUISELLE | MAPLE GROVE, MINNESOTA

This old-fashioned meat and potato pie, seasoned with spices such as clove, allspice, and turmeric, has been a Christmastime tradition in Quebec since at least the 18th century. Early French settlers made savory pies with *tourtes* (passenger pigeons), and although this bird became extinct by the early 20th century, tourtière continued on as a holiday tradition, instead made with ground pork. Says Sue, "My father-in-law's mother used to make tourtière pie for breakfast on Thanksgiving and Christmas mornings." Sue suggests serving this pie with a fried egg. In Canada, it is often served with ketchup.

SERVES 6 TO 8

1	recipe Double-Crust Pie Dough (page 167)
12	ounces ground pork
8	ounces 90 percent lean ground beef
2	tablespoons vegetable oil
1	pound russet potatoes, shredded
1	onion, chopped fine
2	garlic cloves, minced
1½	teaspoons minced fresh thyme or
	¾ teaspoon dried
¼	teaspoon ground allspice
¼	teaspoon dried sage
¼	teaspoon ground turmeric
	Salt and pepper
1½	cups low-sodium chicken broth

1. Following photos on page 167, roll one disk of dough into 12-inch circle on lightly floured counter, then fit into 9-inch pie plate, letting excess dough hang over edge; cover with plastic wrap and refrigerate 30 minutes. Roll second disk of dough into 12-inch circle on lightly floured counter, then transfer to parchment-lined baking sheet; cover with plastic wrap and refrigerate for 30 minutes.

2. Cook ground pork and ground beef in large nonstick skillet over medium-high heat, breaking up any large pieces with wooden spoon, until no longer pink, about 5 minutes; transfer to bowl.

3. Heat oil in skillet over medium heat until shimmering. Add potatoes and onion and cook until softened, 5 to 7 minutes. Stir in garlic, thyme, allspice, sage, turmeric, ¼ teaspoon salt, and ¼ teaspoon pepper and cook until fragrant, about 30 seconds. Stir in broth and bring to simmer. Reduce heat to medium-low and simmer gently until potatoes are just tender, about 10 minutes.

4. Mash potatoes with back of wooden spoon until mostly smooth, then stir in meat mixture, along with any accumulated juice. Continue to cook until mixture is heated through, about 5 minutes. Remove from heat and season with salt and pepper to taste.

5. Adjust oven rack to middle position and heat oven to 450 degrees. Spread filling into dough-lined pie plate and smooth surface. Loosely roll second dough circle around rolling pin and gently unroll over pie. Trim, fold, and crimp edges. Cut 3 oval-shaped vent holes, each about 1 inch long, in center of top.

6. Bake for 10 minutes, then reduce oven temperature to 350 degrees and continue baking until filling is hot and crust is golden brown, 30 to 40 minutes longer. Let cool 15 minutes before serving.

Notes from the Test Kitchen

Some tasters felt the filling needed a binder, so we mirrored other tourtière recipes and mashed some of the shredded potatoes. To boost flavor, we switched from water to broth and upped the garlic.

Grandma's Polish Pierogi

LOIS SZYDLOWSKI | TAMPA, FLORIDA

Today, frozen pierogi are easy enough to find in the supermarket and they're certainly quick to prepare (just boil), but these versions are also gummy and lacking much flavor. A good from-scratch recipe for these classic Eastern European dumplings, like this one from Lois, is a revelation in flavor and texture, making them well worth the effort. She submitted several fillings, but the version here—with cabbage, bacon, and dried porcini mushrooms—has a deep, rich flavor that is unique and irresistible. "When I was a little girl," Lois writes, "my grandma would make pierogi with my mother and her two sisters. Then, for about ten years, my mom, my two sisters, my two nieces, and I would make Polish pierogi in my mom's kitchen every year the week before Christmas. We would make about 500 of them in cheese, sauerkraut, and potato. My mom would make the fillings, I would make the dough and roll it out, and my two nieces would cut and fill, while my two sisters would crimp and fork. They were our main entrée on Christmas Eve every year. Everyone loved them. Now only my mom, one sister, and her married daughter make them every Christmas, but not in the quantities of 500!"

MAKES 18 TO 20

DOUGH

- 2 cups all-purpose flour
- ¾ teaspoon salt
- 2 large egg yolks
- 2 tablespoons unsalted butter, melted
- 8–10 tablespoons whole milk, warmed

FILLING

- 4 slices bacon, chopped medium
- 1 onion, chopped fine
- ¾ ounce dried porcini mushrooms, rinsed and minced
- ¼ teaspoon salt
- ¼ small head green cabbage, cored and sliced thin (2 cups)
- ½ teaspoon pepper
- 2 tablespoons unsalted butter
  Sour cream, for serving
  Melted butter, for serving

1. FOR THE DOUGH: Pulse flour and salt together in food processor until combined, about 4 pulses. With machine running, slowly add egg yolks, followed by melted butter, and process until mixture resembles wet sand, about 30 seconds. Add ½ cup milk and continue to process until large clumps of dough form and no powdery bits remain, about 5 seconds. If dough doesn't clump, add remaining milk, 1 tablespoon at a time, and pulse until dough clumps form (you may not use all of milk).

2. Transfer dough to lightly floured counter and knead by hand until dough firms slightly and becomes smooth, about 1 minute.

(Continued on page 46)

Divide dough into 2 even pieces, and flatten into 6-inch round disks. Wrap each dough tightly in plastic wrap and let rest at room temperature for at least 15 minutes or up to 2 hours.

3. FOR THE FILLING: Cook bacon in large skillet over medium heat until crisp, 5 to 7 minutes. Transfer bacon to paper towel–lined plate. Add onion, mushrooms, and salt to fat left in skillet and cook over medium heat until softened and lightly browned, 5 to 7 minutes. Stir in cabbage and cook until wilted, 5 to 7 minutes. Remove from heat and stir in crisp bacon and pepper; let cool.

4. Dust rimmed baking sheet liberally with flour. Roll one disk dough into 15-inch circle, about $\frac{1}{16}$ inch thick, on lightly floured counter. Using 4-inch round cookie cutter, cut out as many rounds as possible (about 6 rounds). Carefully gather up dough scraps, wrap in plastic wrap, and set aside.

5. TO ASSEMBLE: Following photos, place 1 tablespoon filling in center of each dough round. Moisten edges with water using your finger or a pastry brush, fold dough in half over filling, and crimp edges with fork to seal. Transfer pierogi to prepared baking sheet and cover with damp cloth. Repeat with remaining dough disk.

6. Gently knead all dough scraps together into ball, cover, and let rest for 5 minutes. Roll out, cut, and assemble additional pierogi, discarding any remaining dough scraps. (At this point pierogi can be refrigerated for up to 4 hours or frozen for up to 1 month. If frozen, do not thaw before boiling.)

7. Bring 4 quarts water to boil in large Dutch oven. Add half of pierogi and 1 tablespoon salt and cook, stirring often, until edges are al dente, about 10 minutes. Transfer pierogi to colander using slotted spoon. Return water to boil and cook remaining pierogi.

8. Melt 1 tablespoon butter in large skillet over medium heat. Add half of pierogi and brown on both sides, about 2 minutes. Transfer to platter and cover to keep warm. Repeat with remaining 1 tablespoon butter and remaining pierogi. Serve with sour cream and melted butter.

Notes from the Test Kitchen

Lois sent us several dough and filling recipes, but this flavorful combination was our favorite, hands down. The original recipe was fairly loose on directions, so we filled in the gaps for preparing the dough and sautéing the filling with our own test kitchen pierogi method. Lois's recipe noted to roll the dough $\frac{1}{8}$ to $\frac{1}{16}$ inch thick, and we found that the thinnest end of that range, about the thickness of a quarter, was the way to go; any thicker and the pierogi were gummy. We also increased the cooking time to make sure the dumplings cooked through. Don't be tempted to reroll scraps; we tried this and the resulting pierogi were very tough.

MAKING PIEROGI

1. After placing filling in the center of each dough round, moisten the edges with water and fold the dough over the filling to make a half-moon shape.

2. Using a fork, crimp the edges to seal the pierogi before transferring them to the prepared baking sheet.

My Grandmother's Chicken Biryani

SHEEMA AAMER | FONTANA, CALIFORNIA

America, a melting pot of cultures since its beginning, is home to countless ethnic cuisines, and Sheema's biryani recipe is the perfect example of the traditional Indian food that her family continues to prepare here in the States. "My family is originally from India but my ancestors migrated to Pakistan back in 1947. I belong to a traditional family. We are proud of our heritage, cherish our culture and traditional values, and love our typical, ancestral cuisine. Since the days of the Mughal emperors, a lot of stress had been laid on delicacies in culinary arts in India. The cuisine of that era was rich in flavor (and calories) but the number of dishes could be counted on the fingertips. Although the recipe choices were fewer, the quality and flavor of the food made the painstaking preparation of the dishes well worth the effort. My mother taught me to prepare Chicken Biryani when I was in my late teens, saying that 'this is the food that adorned the tables of the Shahs.'" And indeed, this biryani, with its combination of aromatic rice, tender chicken thighs, sweet tomatoes, and infusion of warm spices, is a blend of flavors and textures that is fit for a king. "She learned the recipe from my grandmother, who in turn learned it from her mother and aunts. Biryani is traditionally prepared on every special occasion and for special guests. It makes people feel welcomed and cherished; it shows them how much time and effort was put into preparing this delicacy only for them."

SERVES 8

STEW

- 3 medium tomatoes, cored and chopped coarse
- ¼ cup olive oil
- 3 onions, halved and sliced ¼ inch thick
- 4½ teaspoons ground coriander
- 4 garlic cloves, minced
- 1 tablespoon grated fresh ginger
  Salt and pepper
- 1½ teaspoons chili powder
- 1 teaspoon ground cardamom
- ½ teaspoon cumin seeds
- ¼ teaspoon ground turmeric
  Pinch ground mace
  Pinch ground cloves
- 2 pounds boneless, skinless chicken thighs, trimmed and cut into 1½-inch pieces
- 2 large russet potatoes, peeled and cut into 1-inch pieces
- ½ cup plain whole-milk yogurt

(Continued on page 49)

RICE

2 cinnamon sticks

Salt

4 green cardamom pods (optional)

2 black cardamom pods (optional)

2 bay leaves

2½ cups basmati rice, rinsed

TOPPINGS

¼ teaspoon saffron threads, crumbled

2 tablespoons hot water

2 tablespoons rose water

1 drop orange food coloring (optional)

2 tablespoons unsalted butter, cut into
    ¼-inch pieces

1 tomato, cored and sliced thin

¼ cup minced fresh cilantro

1. FOR THE STEW: Process tomatoes in food processor until smooth, about 15 seconds.

2. Heat oil in large saucepan over medium heat until shimmering. Add onions and cook until softened and well browned, 8 to 10 minutes. Stir in coriander, garlic, ginger, 1½ teaspoons salt, chili powder, cardamom, cumin seeds, turmeric, mace, and cloves, and cook until fragrant, about 30 seconds. Stir in chicken and potatoes, coat well with spices, and cook until beginning to brown, about 5 minutes.

3. Combine pureed tomatoes and yogurt, then stir into pot. Bring to gentle simmer and cook until chicken and potatoes are tender and sauce is thickened, 30 to 40 minutes. Season with salt and pepper to taste.

4. FOR THE RICE: Meanwhile, bring 3 quarts water, cinnamon sticks, 1 tablespoon salt, cardamom pods (if using), and bay leaves to boil in large Dutch oven. Add rice and cook, stirring often, until just tender, 7 to 15 minutes. Drain and rinse rice, discarding cinnamon sticks, bay leaves, and cardamom pods.

5. FOR THE TOPPINGS: Combine saffron and hot water in small bowl and let steep for 5 minutes. Stir in rose water and food coloring (if using).

6. To assemble, spread half of rice into bottom of Dutch oven. Ladle stew into pot, then top with remaining rice. Pour the saffron mixture over top in swirl design. Dot with butter, shingle tomato slices over top, and sprinkle with cilantro. Cover and cook over medium-low heat until bubbling on sides and casserole is heated through, about 15 minutes. Serve.

Notes from the Test Kitchen

Biryani is simple in appearance but boasts wonderfully complex flavors. Sheema's recipe was fairly rice-dominant, so we tweaked the chicken-to-rice ratio to make this a heartier meal. Her original recipe cooked the chicken and potatoes with whole spices, which we had trouble fishing out before serving, so we switched to ground spices instead. And in lieu of cooking the chicken and potatoes in stages, we cooked them together. She called for parboiling the rice for an unspecified amount of time; we achieved perfect grains in the final dish by boiling it until just tender.

Chinese Five-Spice Chicken and Mushrooms

ALBERTA FUJIHARA | GRANTS PASS, OREGON

Five-spice powder, a mixture of various warm spices, can be found in countless Asian recipes, and Alberta matches it here with wild mushrooms and plenty of soy sauce to take braised chicken to new, flavorful heights. "This succulent, hearty dish is one of those comfort foods that I was fortunate to grow up with," she says. "My Chinese father and mostly Hawaiian mother used to make this for Sunday supper, and I remember my father relishing the task of carving the bird. I loved watching him do the carving, and he loved teaching me how to cut up a chicken. Now I make this for a special dinner and it always brings rave reviews." Alberta suggests serving her recipe with steamed rice and stir-fried or steamed vegetables. Sliced scallions add a nice hint of color.

SERVES 4

- 1 (4½- to 5-pound) whole chicken
- 1 (2-inch) piece fresh ginger, peeled and sliced ½ inch thick
- 2 teaspoons five-spice powder
- 2 tablespoons peanut or vegetable oil
- 2 cups low-sodium chicken broth
- ¼ cup soy sauce, plus extra as needed
- 2 tablespoons bourbon or whiskey
- 2 tablespoons oyster sauce
- 2 teaspoons sugar, plus extra as needed
- 1 pound mixture of shiitake, white, portobello, chanterelle, and/or oyster mushrooms, trimmed and sliced thin
- 2 tablespoons cornstarch
- 2 tablespoons water

1. Adjust oven rack to lowest position and heat oven to 250 degrees. Pat chicken dry with paper towels. Tuck wings behind back and tie legs together with butcher's twine. Rub chicken skin with 2 slices ginger, then place inside cavity. Rub five-spice powder evenly over chicken.

2. Heat oil in large Dutch oven over medium-high heat until just smoking. Add chicken, breast side down, and scatter remaining 2 slices ginger around chicken. Cook until chicken breast is lightly browned, about 5 minutes.

Flip chicken breast side up and continue to cook until back of chicken is well browned, 6 to 8 minutes. Transfer chicken to large plate.

3. Stir broth, soy sauce, bourbon, oyster sauce, and sugar into pot, scraping up any browned bits. Place chicken, breast side up, into pot. Scatter mushrooms around chicken. Cover, transfer to oven, and cook until thickest part of breast registers 160 to 165 degrees and/or thickest part of thigh registers 175 degrees on instant-read thermometer, 1 hour and 20 minutes to 1 hour and 50 minutes.

4. Remove pot from oven. Transfer chicken to carving board, tent loosely with foil, and let rest for 20 minutes. Let braising liquid settle for 5 minutes, then remove fat from surface using large spoon. Discard ginger slices.

5. Whisk cornstarch and water together in bowl. Bring braising liquid to simmer, whisk in cornstarch mixture, and continue to simmer until thickened, about 4 minutes. Season sauce with additional soy sauce and sugar to taste. Carve chicken and serve with sauce.

Notes from the Test Kitchen

This elegantly simple recipe is perfect for all occasions. We made few changes, moving the pot from the stovetop to the oven for more even cooking, and cutting a little soy sauce to reduce saltiness.

Coronation Chicken

GLADYS MCCONNELL | MANHASSET, NEW YORK

"This recipe was created in 1953 by the Cordon Bleu school in London to celebrate the coronation of Queen Elizabeth," notes Gladys. "The tart-sweet flavor of the apricots is tempered by the addition of the red wine sparked by a touch of curry powder. The cream softens the flavor to make a most delicious sauce." From Gladys's description, it certainly sounds exotic, but what is Coronation Chicken exactly? It is actually an upscale twist on none other than the humble chicken salad. When you swap out some of the mayonnaise in the standard version for heavy cream and stir pureed apricots, curry powder, red wine, and just a touch of tomato paste into the rich sauce base, it indeed becomes a whole new dish, one worthy of its royal pedigree. "I have been making it for over 50 years and it always gets rave reviews." While you might not be hosting a royal banquet anytime soon, you'll find Coronation Chicken perfectly suited to a brunch, luncheon, or summertime dinner where you want to offer a dish with a little zing. Gladys suggests serving it with thinly sliced cucumbers.

SERVES 8

- 1 tablespoon unsalted butter
- 1 small onion, chopped fine
- 1 teaspoon curry powder
- ½ cup dry red wine
- 2 tablespoons fresh lemon juice, plus extra as needed
- 1 teaspoon tomato paste
- 1 bay leaf
- 1 (15-ounce) can apricot halves in light syrup, drained
- ½ cup heavy cream
- ½ cup mayonnaise
- 2 pounds cooked chicken, cut into ½-inch pieces
  Salt and pepper

1. Melt butter in medium skillet over medium heat. Add onion and cook until beginning to soften, about 3 minutes. Stir in curry powder and cook until fragrant, about 30 seconds. Stir in wine, lemon juice, tomato paste, and bay leaf, bring to simmer, and cook until thick and syrupy, about 5 minutes. Strain liquid into large bowl and let cool to room temperature.

2. Process apricots in food processor until smooth, about 30 seconds. In large bowl, whip cream with electric mixer on medium-low speed until frothy, about 1 minute. Increase speed to high and continue to whip cream to stiff peaks, 1 to 3 minutes.

3. Stir apricot puree and mayonnaise into cooled syrup. Gently fold in whipped cream, then fold in chicken. Season with salt, pepper, and additional lemon juice to taste. Serve.

Notes from the Test Kitchen
The secret to this recipe is the apricots, which lend a sweet-tart flavor that works well with curry. The original recipe called for 1 teaspoon tomato puree, but we didn't want to buy a whole can of puree for 1 teaspoon, so we swapped it out for 1 teaspoon tomato paste. This is meant to be a rich dish, but it seemed overly sauced to us, so we reduced the cream from ⅔ cup to ½ cup and cut the mayonnaise in half—it is still plenty rich.

Maine Lobster Quiche

JOANNE LEONI | CANANDAIGUA, NEW YORK

This elegant, rich quiche, made with chunks of delicate lobster, is a surefire special occasion winner. "One of my old friends from high school would go to the family house in Maine every summer back in the '50s and '60s," Joanne writes. "Of course, the family would have lobster several times during their stay. My friend Hope would get the job of picking over the leftover lobster shells for hunks of meat to make this quiche the next day. She got pretty good at this duty over the years. This quiche is worth the trouble." One taste and you are sure to agree. This recipe is particularly well suited to a festive midday event like a Mother's Day brunch.

SERVES 6 TO 8

- 1 tablespoon unsalted butter
- 1 celery rib, chopped fine
- 1 shallot, minced
- 1 garlic clove, minced
- ½ teaspoon curry powder
- 12 ounces cooked lobster meat, chopped medium
- ¼ cup minced fresh parsley
- 1 recipe Single-Crust Pie Dough, fitted into a 9-inch deep-dish pie plate and chilled (page 166)
- 2 cups heavy cream
- 4 large eggs
- 2 tablespoons dry sherry
- ½ teaspoon salt
- ¼ teaspoon ground nutmeg
- ¼ teaspoon white pepper

1. Melt butter in medium skillet over medium heat. Add celery and shallot and cook until softened, about 5 minutes. Stir in garlic and curry powder and cook until fragrant, about 30 seconds. Transfer celery mixture to medium bowl and stir in lobster and parsley. Cover and refrigerate until needed.

2. Adjust oven rack to middle position and heat oven to 375 degrees. Line chilled crust with double layer of foil, covering edges to prevent burning, and fill with pie weights.

Bake until pie dough looks dry and is light in color, 25 to 30 minutes. Transfer pie plate to wire rack and remove weights and foil. Reduce oven temperature to 350 degrees. (The crust must still be warm when the filling is added.)

3. Spread lobster mixture evenly into warm pie shell. Whisk cream, eggs, sherry, salt, nutmeg, and pepper together, then transfer to 4-cup liquid measuring cup.

4. Set pie shell on rimmed baking sheet and place in oven. Carefully pour custard mixture into shell and bake until top is lightly browned and knife inserted about 1 inch from edge comes out clean, 40 to 50 minutes. Let quiche cool for at least 1 hour or up to 3 hours. Serve slightly warm or at room temperature.

Notes from the Test Kitchen

This winning quiche is supremely rich and decadent. We tweaked Joanne's method for more consistent results, parbaking the crust longer and cooking the quiche at a consistent 350 degrees, rather than starting high and reducing the temperature partway through. Because stirring the celery into the filling just before baking resulted in still-crunchy celery, we precooked it, along with the garlic, shallot, and curry on the stovetop. Make sure to use a deep-dish pie plate here. You can either buy cooked lobster meat or cook two 1¼- to 1½-pound lobsters and shell the meat.

Sunday Supper Strata

SUZANNE BANFIELD | BASKING RIDGE, NEW JERSEY

While some families might have reserved Sunday evening for their main meal, in many families the big meal of the day was at noon. This meant that supper, in the evening, was something light and easy to make. Such was the case with Suzanne's family. "We always had our main meal at midday on Sunday, usually something like roast beef, roast chicken, or lasagna with lots of sides. So Sunday supper was a simpler meal, more like soup and sandwiches, scrambled eggs, an omelet, or a make-ahead casserole like this baked strata. My mother would put it together first thing in the morning, and it rested in the refrigerator all day until we were ready to bake it that evening. Sometimes mom added leftover vegetables, meat, or chicken, but the dish always included cheese and bacon. Of all the variations, this version with apple was my all-time favorite." Most stratas are made by cutting bread into cubes and combining them with various add-ins, then soaking the mixture in a custard before baking. Suzanne simply layers the add-ins between whole slices of bread in the baking dish (essentially, she makes sandwiches) and then pours the custard over the top. It's a snap to make, and the combination of sweet apples, smoky bacon, and cheddar cheese is hard to beat.

SERVES 6 TO 8

12 slices bacon, chopped medium
12 slices hearty white sandwich bread, crusts removed
2   McIntosh or Golden Delicious apples, peeled, cored, and sliced thin
8   ounces sharp cheddar cheese, shredded (2 cups)
3   cups whole milk
6   large eggs
1   teaspoon spicy brown mustard
½   teaspoon salt
¼   teaspoon pepper
2   tablespoons unsalted butter, melted
1   ounce Parmesan cheese, grated (½ cup)

1. Cook bacon in large skillet over medium heat until very crisp, about 10 minutes; transfer to paper towel–lined plate.

2. Grease 13 by 9-inch baking dish. Arrange six slices bread in single layer in prepared baking dish, cutting bread as needed to fit. Spread half of apples over bread, sprinkle evenly with crisp bacon and cheddar, then top with remaining apple. Arrange remaining bread slices in single layer over top, cutting bread as needed to fit.

3. Whisk milk, eggs, mustard, salt, and pepper together, then pour over bread. Press gently on bread to submerge. Cover with plastic wrap and refrigerate for at least 8 hours or up to 1 day.

4. Adjust oven rack to middle position and heat oven to 350 degrees. Unwrap strata, drizzle melted butter over top, and sprinkle with Parmesan. Bake until strata is puffed and golden brown, 50 to 60 minutes. Serve hot.

Notes from the Test Kitchen

We were sold on this autumnal-themed strata. Suzanne didn't specify what variety of apple to use so we picked our favorites. We switched from sliced cheddar to shredded for better distribution, and since whole slices of bacon were tricky to eat, we chopped it first.

CHILAQUILES

Comfort Food Classics

Sergeant Meatloaf **58**

Taglerina **61**

Polpette alla Nonna **62**

Grandma Lucy's Creamed Tomatoes over Biscuits **63**

Rum Tum Tiddy **65**

Big Wheel **67**

Potato and Escarole Soup **68**

Swedish Pea Soup **70**

Potato Crust Quiche **71**

Lulie's Pork Chop Casserole **72**

Spaetzle and Sauerkraut **73**

Easy Amazing Noodle Pudding **75**

Chilaquiles **76**

Hurry Curry **77**

Greek Shrimp with Feta and Peppers **78**

Sergeant Meatloaf

JOHN MARTONE | AIKEN, SOUTH CAROLINA

"Our Italian mother made this recipe often in the '50s, and when my brother was drafted into the army as a cook in 1953, he made this recipe for the army men and their officers. My brother's colonel was so impressed by the meatloaf that he promoted my brother to sergeant on the spot, hence the recipe name, Sergeant Meatloaf! Unfortunately for my brother, he got back from a weekend pass a little late and he was back to a private!" What makes this recipe stand out enough to have earned John's brother a promotion? One look and you'll notice it's no basic meatloaf recipe. Several hard-boiled eggs, wrapped in prosciutto, are nestled into the loaf before it's cooked. Traditional Italian meatloaf recipes vary in their method and ingredients, but many include a line of hard-boiled eggs. They were added not just because they lent a decorative touch but also because, when times were tough, the hard-boiled eggs helped to extend the meat. Wrapping a little prosciutto around the eggs was a simple way to add a punch of flavor and another visual accent. John's cooking technique is also unique. While familiar versions are cooked through in the oven, this version is cooked through on the stovetop—with surprisingly tender, evenly cooked results. Mashed potatoes would be a perfect match for his recipe.

SERVES 6 TO 8

- 6 slices hearty white sandwich bread, crusts removed, torn into quarters
- ½ cup whole milk
- 2 pounds meatloaf mix
- 1 small onion, chopped fine
- 2 large eggs
- ¼ cup olive oil
- 1 tablespoon grated Parmesan cheese
- 1 garlic clove, minced
  Salt and pepper
- 3 hard-boiled eggs, peeled
- 3 thin slices prosciutto or deli ham
- 2 (8-ounce) cans tomato sauce
- 4 ounces white mushrooms, sliced thin
- ½ cup frozen peas

1. Mash bread and milk into paste in large bowl using fork. Using hands, mix in meatloaf mix, onion, eggs, 2 tablespoons oil, Parmesan, garlic, 1½ teaspoons salt, and ½ teaspoon pepper.

2. Following photos on page 60, transfer two-thirds of meat mixture to rimmed baking sheet and pat into 9 by 5-inch loaf using wet hands. Wrap each hard-boiled egg with 1 slice prosciutto, then nestle them lengthwise down center of meatloaf. Top with remaining meat mixture, pressing on seams and sides to form compact loaf. Cover and refrigerate until set, about 30 minutes.

3. Heat remaining 2 tablespoons oil in large Dutch oven over medium-high heat until just smoking. Using two spatulas, carefully transfer

(Continued on page 60)

meatloaf to pot and cook, undisturbed, until bottom is well browned, about 5 minutes.

4. Add tomato sauce and mushrooms around meatloaf and bring to simmer. Cover, reduce heat to medium-low, and simmer gently until center of meatloaf registers 160 degrees on instant-read thermometer, 45 to 60 minutes.

5. Position oven rack 6 inches from broiler element and heat broiler. Set wire rack over foil-lined rimmed baking sheet. Using two spatulas, carefully transfer meatloaf to prepared baking sheet. Brush ½ cup sauce over meatloaf and broil until lightly caramelized, about 10 minutes.

6. Meanwhile, add peas to remaining sauce and bring to brief simmer over medium heat.

Off heat, season with salt and pepper to taste and cover to keep warm. Let broiled meatloaf rest for 15 minutes, then serve with sauce.

Notes from the Test Kitchen

A panade helps make this meatloaf tender, but we swapped out the water in John's panade for milk for more tenderness and flavor. John's recipe called for searing all sides of the meatloaf, but we found this hard to do given the fragility of the uncooked loaf, so we browned only one side and used the broiler to finish the job. We swapped canned peas for frozen and canned mushrooms for fresh. If meatloaf mix isn't available, substitute 1 pound 85 percent lean ground beef and 1 pound ground pork.

MAKING SERGEANT MEATLOAF

1. Using wet hands, pat two-thirds of the meat mixture into a 9 by 5-inch loaf on a rimmed baking sheet.

2. Nestle the prosciutto-wrapped eggs lengthwise down the center of the meatloaf, then top with the remaining meat mixture, pressing on the seams and sides to form a compact loaf. Cover and refrigerate the loaf until it is set.

3. Using two spatulas to support the bottom of the meatloaf, carefully transfer the chilled meatloaf to a large Dutch oven. After adding the sauce and mushrooms, cover and simmer until the meatloaf is cooked through, 45 to 60 minutes.

4. Using the spatulas, transfer the meatloaf to a wire rack set over a foil-lined baking sheet. Brush the meatloaf with ½ cup sauce and broil until lightly caramelized.

Taglerina

MARY JO WEISS | VALLEY CITY, OHIO

"When my six brothers and sisters and I were growing up, one of our favorite meals that our dad would prepare was Taglerina. Our dad loved to cook, and I have many fond memories of him in the kitchen wearing his white butcher's apron. Taglerina particularly stands out because nothing compares to its mouthwatering aroma as it cooks. He got the recipe from the *Presbyterian Cook Book*, which was published in 1928 by the First Presbyterian Church of Huntington, Indiana (his hometown)." Mary Jo notes her father is of German descent, but this sauce, a bright tomato sauce with chunks of steak, mushrooms, and loads of chopped onions, comes across as thoroughly Italian. While we're not positive of the origin of the recipe's name, given the process of cutting up the meat and chopping the onions, we have a hunch it comes from the Italian verb *tagliare,* which means "to cut or chop." Mary Jo adds, "To this day whenever the brothers and sisters get together for our week at the beach, Taglerina has to be one of the meals. It is a joint effort, with everyone wanting to help either by chopping ingredients or stirring the pot." Serve this sauce over spaghetti.

MAKES 9 CUPS, ENOUGH FOR 2 POUNDS OF PASTA

1 (1½-pound) top-round steak, trimmed and cut into ½-inch pieces
  Salt and pepper
2 tablespoons unsalted butter
6 onions, chopped fine
1 (28-ounce) can whole tomatoes
2 cups water, plus extra as needed
8 ounces white mushrooms, trimmed and sliced thin
1 (8-ounce) can tomato sauce
1 (6-ounce) can tomato paste

1. Pat beef dry with paper towels and season with salt and pepper. Melt 1 tablespoon butter in large Dutch oven over medium-high heat. Brown half of beef well on all sides, 7 to 10 minutes; transfer to medium bowl. Repeat with remaining 1 tablespoon butter and remaining beef; transfer to bowl.

2. Stir onions, tomatoes, water, mushrooms, tomato sauce, tomato paste, and 1 teaspoon salt into pot, scraping up any browned bits, and bring to simmer. Stir in browned beef, along with any accumulated juice, and bring to simmer.

3. Cover partially (leaving about 1 inch of pot open), reduce heat to medium-low, and simmer gently until meat is tender and sauce is thickened slightly, 2 to 2½ hours. Adjust sauce consistency with additional water as needed. Season with salt and pepper to taste and serve.

Notes from the Test Kitchen

All the onions in Mary Jo's recipe make it stand out from the crowd. She called for browning the meat in 1 stick of butter; we found 2 tablespoons were sufficient. We simmered the meat in the sauce longer than she had suggested to ensure tender meat. Because of the longer cooking time, we added 2 cups of water and partially covered the pot to minimize reduction.

Polpette alla Nonna

JULIE BARON | NEW YORK, NEW YORK

"My nonna originally hailed from Perugia. At barely 4 feet 10 inches tall, my nonna was a sight in the kitchen. Many of my happiest childhood times were at her apron strings," writes Julie, "stirring and measuring at first, chopping and frying as I grew older. When she came to America, Nonna brought with her many wonderful recipes from the old country, and one of my favorites was her famous meatballs." Julie's grandmother's meatballs are not dressed in the tomato sauce you'd likely expect. Rather, they resemble old Italian preparations for meatballs cooked in broth. Her recipe is also thrifty, as bread crumbs and cheese play double duty, used both as binders for the meatballs and as thickeners for the sauce. "Polpette alla Nonna (Nonna's meatballs) are simply prepared with very common ingredients," notes Julie, "but they form a rich sauce that warms the bones on cold winter nights quite unlike anything else."

SERVES 4 TO 6

- 1 pound 85 percent lean ground beef
- 8 ounces ground pork
- 3½ ounces Parmesan cheese, grated (1¾ cups)
- 1¼ cups dry plain bread crumbs
- 1 large egg
- 1 shallot, minced
- 2 tablespoons whole milk
- 2 tablespoons minced fresh parsley
- 3 garlic cloves, minced
  Salt and pepper
- 3 tablespoons olive oil
- 1 onion, chopped fine
- 1 cup low-sodium chicken broth
- 1 cup water

1. Using hands, mix ground beef, ground pork, ¾ cup Parmesan, ½ cup bread crumbs, egg, shallot, milk, parsley, garlic, 1 teaspoon salt, and 1 teaspoon pepper together in bowl. Pinch off and roll mixture into 1½-inch meatballs (about 30 meatballs total).

2. Spread ½ cup more bread crumbs into shallow dish. Coat meatballs with bread crumbs, shaking off excess, and transfer to large plate.

3. Heat 1 tablespoon oil in large nonstick skillet over medium-high heat until just smoking. Brown half of meatballs well on all sides, 6 to 8 minutes; transfer to large paper towel–lined plate. Repeat with 1 tablespoon more oil and remaining meatballs; transfer to plate.

4. Heat remaining 1 tablespoon oil in skillet over medium heat until shimmering. Add onion and cook until softened, about 5 minutes. Stir in broth and water, then slowly whisk in remaining 1 cup Parmesan and remaining ¼ cup bread crumbs until smooth and bring to simmer.

5. Nestle meatballs into skillet and bring to simmer. Cover, reduce heat to medium-low, and simmer gently until meatballs are cooked through and sauce is deeply flavored, 10 to 15 minutes. Season with salt and pepper to taste and serve.

Notes from the Test Kitchen

This recipe offers a great change from the usual meatballs in tomato sauce. We cut back on the 2 cups bread crumbs to create a saucier consistency, and we swapped out some broth for water for better balance. We also added milk to the meatballs to keep them tender. Julie drizzled the meatballs with more olive oil at the end, but we felt this dish was plenty rich as is.

Grandma Lucy's Creamed Tomatoes over Biscuits

JIM ERVIN | COLUMBUS, OHIO

Southern-style comfort food doesn't get much better than biscuits and gravy, and Jim's recipe gives this old favorite a sweet, fresh-tasting flavor boost by incorporating tomatoes into the gravy. "This recipe is from Dad's side of the family, for how many generations, I'm not sure. Our family roots are in West Virginia, though my mother, the daughter of a tobacco family, was raised in Maryland. I remember she always insisted this recipe should be called Creamed Tomatoes, not Tomato Gravy! It's a good recipe for a cold winter morning or a hearty dinner after a long day of work." Despite Jim's mother's insistence, this recipe clearly aligns with recipes called Southern Tomato Gravy, which tend to be country-style and chunkier. (In fact, there is a strikingly similar recipe titled "Tomato Gravy" by the iconic southern cook Edna Lewis.) In comparison, to make creamed tomatoes, one would traditionally fry sliced tomatoes, prepare a gravy, then pour the prepared gravy over the tomatoes and serve. But no matter the name, Jim's recipe is a sure bet for satisfying your hunger. Jim's recipe calls for serving his creamed tomatoes over biscuits with bacon, sausage, or any cut of pork such as chops on the side, but we actually prefer to mix sausage right in.

SERVES 6

BISCUITS

3¾	cups all-purpose flour
2	tablespoons sugar
4	teaspoons baking powder
1½	teaspoons salt
1	teaspoon baking soda
12	tablespoons (1½ sticks) unsalted butter, cut into ½-inch pieces and chilled
4	tablespoons vegetable shortening, cut into ½-inch pieces and chilled
1¼	cups buttermilk

CREAMED TOMATOES

12	ounces bulk sausage meat
3	tablespoons all-purpose flour
2	cups whole milk
1	(14.5-ounce) can diced tomatoes
	Salt and pepper
	Sugar

1. **FOR THE BISCUITS:** Adjust oven rack to middle position and heat oven to 450 degrees. Line rimmed baking sheet with parchment paper. Pulse flour, sugar, baking powder, salt, and baking soda together in food processor to

(Continued on page 64)

combine, about 3 pulses. Scatter butter and shortening evenly over top and pulse until mixture resembles coarse cornmeal, about 15 more pulses.

2. Transfer mixture to large bowl and stir in buttermilk with rubber spatula until dough begins to form. Transfer dough and any floury bits to well-floured counter. Lightly flour your hands and dough, and knead dough gently until uniform, about 30 seconds. Shape dough into 10-inch round, about 1 inch thick.

3. Using floured 2½-inch cookie cutter, stamp out 12 biscuits, gently patting dough scraps back into uniform, 1-inch-thick piece as needed. Arrange biscuits, upside down, on prepared baking sheet, spaced about 1½ inches apart.

4. Bake biscuits for 5 minutes. Rotate pan, reduce oven temperature to 400 degrees, and continue to bake until golden brown, 12 to 15 minutes longer. Transfer to wire rack and let cool slightly.

5. FOR THE CREAMED TOMATOES: While biscuits bake, cook sausage in large skillet over medium-high heat, breaking up any large pieces with wooden spoon, until no longer pink, about 5 minutes; transfer to bowl. Pour off all but 1 tablespoon fat left in skillet. (Substitute vegetable oil if you don't have enough rendered fat.)

6. Stir flour into fat left in skillet and cook over medium heat for 1 minute. Slowly whisk in milk, scraping up any browned bits. Bring to simmer and cook until thickened slightly, about 1 minute. Stir in tomatoes and mash with potato masher until mostly smooth. Stir in cooked sausage and cook until heated through, 3 to 5 minutes. Season with salt, pepper, and sugar to taste.

7. To serve, place two split biscuits on individual plates, and spoon creamed tomatoes over top.

Notes from the Test Kitchen
This satisfying recipe is great for any meal of the day, not just breakfast. The sausage didn't render much fat, so we added extra oil to the pan. Because of the sweetness of the tomatoes, we found we could cut Jim's 3 tablespoons of sugar (as well as the salt and pepper) back to just enough for seasoning at the end. We reduced the amount of flour just slightly, as well as the cooking time, for a smoother, less thickened sauce. We had trouble with the gravy breaking in the original recipe so we used a foolproof roux. Because Jim didn't provide a biscuit recipe, we included our own here.

Rum Tum Tiddy

LAURIE DAGOSTINO | ROCHESTER, NEW YORK

"This story follows my father's smile all the way back to 1936, when he took his annual summer camp trip to Middleton, Massachusetts. He sat down one night in the hot musty cabin for his nightly meal. It was then that my father encountered Rum Tum Tiddy. He asked the cook how to make the delectable treat, and memorizing only the ingredients, he returned home. Raised by his grandmother, Dad yearned to make the dish for her and his siblings. After various experiments, he was satisfied with the product, as was his family." With such a frivolous name, Rum Tum Tiddy should pique your interest, and after one bite, this comfort food will likely draw you in like it did Laurie's father. Known variously as Rum Tum Tiddy, Rinktum Ditty, and even Rictim Chitti, among others, it is the Americanized version of the British classic Welsh rarebit. While the latter features a cheddar-brown ale sauce over toast or crackers, its stateside cousin swaps in cream and tomatoes for the beer (brown ale wasn't as readily available in American kitchens, particularly during Prohibition). Though it's unclear where the name came from, this recipe's simple yet satisfying, old-fashioned appeal is a sure thing.

SERVES 4 TO 6

3	slices bacon, chopped fine
1	small onion, chopped fine
2	tablespoons unsalted butter
1	tablespoon all-purpose flour
½	cup skim milk
2	medium tomatoes, cored and cut into ½-inch pieces
1	teaspoon Worcestershire sauce
1	teaspoon dry mustard
½	teaspoon paprika
1	pound cheddar cheese, shredded (4 cups)
2	large eggs
	Salt and pepper
8–12	slices warm toast, for serving

1. Cook bacon in large skillet over medium heat until crisp, 5 to 7 minutes; transfer to paper towel–lined plate. Pour off all but 1 tablespoon bacon fat left in skillet. Add onion and butter to fat left in skillet and cook until softened, about 5 minutes. Stir in flour and cook for 1 minute. Slowly whisk in milk, scraping up any browned bits.

2. Stir in crisp bacon, tomatoes, Worcestershire, mustard, and paprika and bring to simmer. Cover, reduce heat to medium-low, and simmer gently until tomatoes are softened, about 10 minutes. Slowly whisk in cheddar until completely melted.

3. Whisk eggs and ¼ cup of hot tomato-cheddar sauce together (to temper), then stir mixture into skillet. Continue to cook, whisking constantly, until sauce thickens, about 3 minutes longer. Remove from heat, season with salt and pepper to taste, and serve over toast (two slices toast per person).

Notes from the Test Kitchen

This recipe was a surprise winner with our tasters. We added flour to help keep the sauce from breaking, and we reduced the amount of cheese by ½ pound for a looser consistency.

Big Wheel

BARBARA "BEE" ENGELHART | BLOOMFIELD HILLS, MICHIGAN

"For generations, the Big Wheel was sold at Alban's on Woodward Avenue in Birmingham, Michigan. The round shape and title of this famous sandwich was relatable to the auto-centric culture of southeastern Michigan. Alban's is gone now, but in its day the Big Wheel was the perfect sandwich. The sandwich was too large for one, so it had to be shared. When my husband and I were dating, Alban's was our favorite casual dining destination. Later, when our lives got busier, we'd wait in line at the takeout counter to place our order. For a time, you could go into any grocery store and find round loaves of sliced pumpernickel so you could make your own at home. Today, I go to a bakery and ask them to put a pumpernickel boule, on end, through the slicing machine. We sometimes butter the exterior bread and grill our Big Wheels, swap turkey for the corned beef, and use whatever kind of mustard we like that day. Truth be told, it doesn't really matter what you put between the slices of bread. It's the shape that reminds us who we are and where we come from."

SERVES 2

- 1 (9-inch) round loaf pumpernickel or sourdough bread
- 2 tablespoons mayonnaise
- 2 teaspoons whole grain mustard
- 2 ounces thinly sliced Swiss cheese
- 1 small tomato, cored, seeded, and sliced thin
- ⅓ cup prepared coleslaw, drained
- 4 ounces thinly sliced lean corned beef

1. Adjust oven rack to middle position and heat oven to 350 degrees. Following photo, cut two round, ¾-inch-thick slices of bread from center of loaf, reserving top and bottom pieces for another use. Lay bread slices directly on oven rack and bake until lightly toasted, about 5 minutes; transfer to cutting board.

2. Combine mayonnaise and mustard and spread evenly over 1 side of each bread slice. Layer Swiss, tomato, coleslaw, and corned beef between slices of bread to make huge sandwich. Press lightly on sandwich to flatten, cut into quarters, and serve.

Notes from the Test Kitchen

We love the local history that surrounds this sandwich. We didn't need to change anything about the recipe, though Barbara said grilling or toasting was something they did only occasionally and we thought at least warming the sandwich was a must. She offered sourdough as an alternate bread choice, but given the name of the recipe and what it symbolizes, we felt the pumpernickel was a far better choice.

SLICING BREAD FOR BIG WHEEL

Stand the loaf of bread vertically on its side. Using a serrated knife, slice off the top crust. Continue to slice two ¾-inch-thick slices from the center of the bread (reserve top and bottom crusts for another use).

Potato and Escarole Soup (Menasha)

JOANNE BUCKNUM | TEMPE, ARIZONA

"Our family is from the Calabria area in southern Italy. My grandparents were very poor, and when they emigrated to America, they chose West Virginia as their home due to the work in the coal mines. My grandparents bought a farm on a pittance in Clarksburg. There, they raised seven children. They were sustained by their garden and a few hogs. They ate simply, but healthfully." This recipe is a perfect example of just that type of food. With only potatoes, greens, and seasoning, this soup is Italian peasant food that makes the most of very little. As the potatoes cook, they break down and thicken the soup, turning it into a hearty, satisfying meal. (The name, we presume, is a corruption of *minestra,* which in Italy refers to a thickened broth.) "My mother used to make this soup when I was growing up in Detroit. I dreaded this dish as a child; it looked yucky to me. Years later, my mother would come and stay with me here in Arizona. One day she decided to make the Menasha. She showed me how to make it, and after seeing how easy, tasty, and healthy it is, my opinion totally changed. It is one of my husband's and my favorite meals. On a cold winter's night, it truly warms you inside and out." Joanne suggests serving her soup with a green salad and crusty bread.

SERVES 8

- ⅓ cup extra-virgin olive oil
- 8 garlic cloves, minced
- 1 tablespoon chopped fresh basil or 1 teaspoon dried
- ½ teaspoon red pepper flakes
- 3 cups low-sodium chicken broth
- 3 cups water, plus extra as needed
- 3½ pounds russet potatoes, peeled and cut into ¾-inch pieces
- 1 pound escarole, trimmed and sliced ½ inch thick
- Salt and pepper

1. Heat oil in large Dutch oven over medium heat until shimmering. Add garlic, basil, and red pepper flakes and cook until fragrant, about 30 seconds. Stir in broth, water, and potatoes and bring to simmer. Cover, reduce heat to medium-low, and simmer gently until potatoes are almost tender, 15 to 20 minutes.

2. Stir in escarole and continue to cook until escarole and potatoes are tender, about 10 minutes longer. Mash some potatoes against side of pot with back of spoon to thicken soup. Adjust soup consistency with additional hot water as needed. Season with salt and pepper to taste and serve.

Notes from the Test Kitchen
While we loved the simplicity of this dish and admired its peasant roots, swapping in chicken broth for half of the water gave the soup a flavor boost worth the extra cost (a much more manageable one these days). Joanne sautéed the aromatics in a separate pan and added them at the end; we streamlined her method to use just one pot. And to minimize the cooking time, we mashed some of the potatoes to thicken the soup rather than wait for them to break down completely.

Swedish Pea Soup (Ärtsoppa)

LISA MALONE | SAINT PAUL, MINNESOTA

"My mother and her family lived in Sweden for a short time when she was young," writes Lisa. "Whenever she made this soup for us, my mother would reminisce about going to school in Sweden where they ate yellow pea soup, or *Ärtsoppa*, for lunch every Thursday." In Sweden, eating Ärtsoppa on Thursdays goes back to the pre-Reformation days when most Swedes were Catholic. With its meat-infused broth, hunks of pork, and plenty of yellow peas, it was a hearty soup ideal for eating the day before the Friday fast. Though Sweden is no longer predominantly Catholic, the tradition of eating yellow pea soup on Thursdays continues. Usually a little mustard is swirled in before serving, though Lisa's recipe doesn't suggest this. However, for bite she does comment, "I like this soup very peppery—it makes me think of autumn." You can find dried whole yellow peas (not split peas) in most supermarkets or order them online.

SERVES 10 TO 12

- 1 pound dried whole yellow peas, picked over
- 2 tablespoons vegetable oil
- 4 onions, chopped fine
- 4 celery ribs, chopped fine
- 2 carrots, peeled and chopped fine
- 1 tablespoon minced fresh thyme or 1 teaspoon dried
- 1 teaspoon white pepper
- 1 teaspoon ground celery seeds
- 12 cups water
- 1 bay leaf
- 1 teaspoon black peppercorns
- 1 smoked ham hock, rinsed
- 1 pound ham steak, cut into ½-inch pieces
  Salt and black pepper

1. Cover yellow peas with 4 quarts cold water in large container or pot and let sit at room temperature for at least 8 hours or up to 1 day. (Alternatively, bring 4 quarts water and peas to boil in large Dutch oven. Remove from heat, cover, and let sit for 1 hour; drain.) Drain peas, discarding soaking water.

2. Heat oil in large Dutch oven over medium heat until shimmering. Add onions, celery, and carrots and cook until softened, 5 to 7 minutes. Stir in thyme, white pepper, and celery seeds and cook until fragrant, about 30 seconds. Stir in water, bay leaf, and drained peas and bring to simmer.

3. Place peppercorns in double-layer cheesecloth pouch and tie securely with butcher's twine. Nestle ham hock and peppercorn pouch into pot and bring to simmer. Cover, reduce heat to medium-low, and simmer gently, stirring occasionally, until peas are nearly tender, about 2 hours.

4. Stir in ham steak, cover, and continue to cook, stirring occasionally, until peas are tender, 1 to 2 hours longer. Discard ham hock, peppercorn pouch, and bay leaf. Season with salt and black pepper to taste and serve.

Notes from the Test Kitchen
We all agreed the heartiness and meaty flavor of this soup make it a perfect choice for a satisfying winter meal. However, we did find it a little too chock-full of peas and meat, so we upped the water by a few cups. Given the choice between ham hock, a soup bone, or a shank, we settled on the easy-to-find and flavorful ham hock.

Potato Crust Quiche

DIANE RITCHEY | PUEBLO, COLORADO

The word "quiche" conjures images of fancy luncheons or upscale French fare, but Diane's recipe brings quiche into the comfort food realm by forgoing the fussy crust in favor of a simple layer of shredded potatoes as the base for the eggy filling. "I developed this recipe as a youngster because I loved quiche and couldn't make a decent pie crust. It is very filling and satisfying. I sometimes add ham or sausage instead of the bacon and include dill, chives, or other fresh herbs from the garden." This recipe is a perfect choice for a weekend breakfast or a quick yet filling weeknight dinner.

SERVES 6

- 3 slices bacon, chopped fine
- 1 small onion, chopped fine
- 1 pound (about 2 medium) russet potatoes, peeled and coarsely grated
- 1 teaspoon olive oil
- ¼ teaspoon salt
- ¼ teaspoon pepper
- 1 cup whole milk
- 3 large eggs
- 4 ounces cheddar cheese, shredded (1 cup)
- 2 tablespoons chopped pimentos

1. Adjust oven rack to middle position and heat oven to 350 degrees. Cook bacon in medium skillet over medium heat until very crisp, about 10 minutes; transfer to paper towel–lined plate. Pour off all but 1 teaspoon bacon fat left in skillet. Add onion to fat in skillet and cook over medium heat until softened and lightly browned, 5 to 7 minutes.

2. Meanwhile, rinse potatoes to remove excess starch and let drain. Working in batches, wrap potatoes in clean kitchen towel and squeeze out excess liquid; transfer dry potatoes to large bowl. Toss potatoes with oil, salt, and pepper and microwave until just tender, about 2 minutes.

3. Press warm potatoes into even layer over bottom of 9-inch pie plate. Whisk milk and eggs together in large bowl, then stir in crisp bacon, cooked onion, cheddar, and pimentos. Transfer mixture to 4-cup liquid measuring cup.

4. Place pie shell on rimmed baking sheet and place in oven. Carefully pour milk mixture into pie dish and bake until top is lightly browned and knife inserted 1 inch from edge comes out clean, about 30 minutes. Let quiche cool for at least 1 hour or up to 3 hours. Serve slightly warm or at room temperature.

Notes from the Test Kitchen

We loved the simplicity of this recipe. It's worth noting that, after a couple of tests, we realized the potatoes don't actually brown to form a crisp crust; rather, they form the base layer for the egg mixture, making this recipe more like a one-dish frittata over hash browns—certainly no less appealing. Diane pressed finely grated raw potatoes into the pie plate, but we found switching to coarsely grated potatoes that we first parcooked in the microwave resulted in potatoes that had better texture and were more consistently cooked through. Chopping the bacon fine ensured it didn't turn soggy. Because the original recipe cooked up slightly greasy, we cut the bacon fat from 2 tablespoons to 1 teaspoon, and scaled back the cheese from 8 ounces to 4 ounces.

Lulie's Pork Chop Casserole

KEZIA TENENBAUM | BOULDER, COLORADO

"In the early 1940s, my two uncles went off to college in Madison, Wisconsin. It was wartime, they didn't have any money, and they were always hungry. Luckily for them, they found Lulie's boardinghouse, run by Lulie (or Louise) Schumann, a German woman who ran a tight ship and loved to cook. My mother, soon following her brothers to college, found a second mother in Lulie. Of the many recipes that came down to us from Lulie, this is perhaps the most beloved by my family." It's no surprise why. With tender pork chops braised with potatoes and carrots, it is comfort food at its purest. As Kezia writes, "To this day, my children equate this yummy dish with a loving, heartfelt meal that puts the puzzle pieces of a long day back together!"

SERVES 4

- 4 (7-ounce) bone-in blade-cut pork chops, about ¾ inch thick
  Salt and pepper
- 2 tablespoons vegetable oil
- 1 onion, cut into ¼-inch rings
- 2 garlic cloves, minced
- 1 teaspoon minced fresh thyme or ¼ teaspoon dried
- 2 tablespoons all-purpose flour
- 2½ cups low-sodium chicken broth
- 3 carrots, peeled and cut into ¾-inch pieces
- 1 bay leaf
- 2 pounds Yukon Gold potatoes, peeled and cut into ¾-inch pieces

1. Adjust oven rack to lower-middle position and heat oven to 350 degrees. Following photo, cut slits in side of chops to prevent curling. Pat pork chops dry with paper towels and season with salt and pepper. Heat 1 tablespoon oil in large Dutch oven over medium-high heat until just smoking. Brown pork chops well on both sides, 6 to 8 minutes; transfer to plate.

2. Heat remaining 1 tablespoon oil in pot over medium heat until shimmering. Add onion and cook until softened, 5 to 7 minutes. Stir in garlic and thyme and cook until fragrant, about 30 seconds. Stir in flour and cook for 1 minute. Slowly whisk in broth, scraping up any browned bits. Stir in carrots and bay leaf and bring to simmer.

3. Nestle browned pork chops into pot, along with any accumulated juice, and sprinkle potatoes evenly over top. Bring to simmer, cover, and transfer to oven. Cook until pork and vegetables are tender, 60 to 75 minutes.

4. Remove pot from oven, discard bay leaf, and season with salt and pepper to taste. Serve.

Notes from the Test Kitchen
Kezia called for dredging the chops in flour; we skipped this since the extra flour made the sauce too thick. We doubled the amount of liquid for better braising and a lighter sauce and switched the water for broth.

PREPARING PORK CHOPS

To get pork chops to lie flat and cook evenly, cut two slits, about 2 inches apart, into the side of each chop.

Spaetzle and Sauerkraut

CHRISTINE PALMER | BREMERTON, WASHINGTON

The German dumplings known as *spaetzle* are one of the world's perfect starchy comfort foods. The name means "little sparrow," but Christine's oversized spaetzle are far from the traditional size. That's not a bad thing, since it allows for great contrast between the crisped exterior and doughy interior. When combined with the sauerkraut and ham, her spaetzle is hard to beat. "This recipe is traced back to the German side of my family," Christine tells us. "A more plain version originated with my great-grandma Rose. My grandma Carol modified it into its current version. Each family member liked it a different way. Some liked the dark golden brown pieces the best and others liked the more doughy pieces. Personally, I love them with extra sauerkraut!"

SERVES 6

- 3 cups all-purpose flour
- 1½ cups whole milk
- 2 large eggs
  Salt and pepper
- 6 tablespoons (¾ stick) unsalted butter
- 1 onion, chopped fine
- 1 teaspoon caraway seeds
- 4 cups sauerkraut, rinsed
- 6 ounces ham steak, cut into ½-inch pieces

1. Bring 4 quarts water to boil in large Dutch oven. In bowl, whisk flour, milk, eggs, and ½ teaspoon salt together until smooth. Let batter rest for 15 minutes.

2. Spread ⅓ cup batter into thin, even layer over small cutting board. Following photo, hold board over boiling water and, using bench scraper or chef's knife, scrape batter into water to form 2 by 1-inch shreds of spaetzle. Cook until spaetzle rise to surface, about 1 minute. Using slotted spoon, transfer spaetzle to colander; repeat with remaining batter.

3. Drain cooking water and wipe pot dry. Melt 2 tablespoons butter in pot over medium heat. Add onion and cook until softened and lightly browned, 5 to 7 minutes. Stir in caraway seeds and cook until fragrant, about 30 seconds.

Stir in sauerkraut and ham and cook until heated through, about 5 minutes.

4. Meanwhile, melt 2 tablespoons more butter in large nonstick skillet over medium-high heat. Add half of spaetzle and cook, stirring often, until golden and crisp at edges, 5 to 7 minutes; transfer to pot with sauerkraut. Repeat with remaining 2 tablespoons butter and spaetzle; transfer to pot. Season with salt and pepper to taste and serve.

Notes from the Test Kitchen

Tasters went back for thirds of Christine's recipe. Browning the spaetzle in the skillet with the sauerkraut on top was difficult, so we cooked them separately. A little onion and caraway lent complexity. We prefer sauerkraut packaged in plastic bags; two 1-pound bags are perfect here.

MAKING SPAETZLE

Spread out ⅓ cup of batter in a thin layer about 2 inches wide over a cutting board. Use a bench scraper or chef's knife to scrape 1-inch-wide pieces of batter into the boiling water. Cook until the spaetzle rise to the surface.

Easy Amazing Noodle Pudding

ELEANOR HASPEL-PORTNER | PACIFIC PALISADES, CALIFORNIA

"When my children were toddlers and quite picky eaters, a neighbor gave me this recipe. It is easy, fast, and there is almost no cleanup. Most of all, it is something between a dessert and main course dish." Eleanor's noodle pudding is essentially a noodle kugel, a standard of kosher dairy cooking that has a history going back several centuries. Kugel can be sweet or savory, but her recipe leans toward the sweet side. However, as she discovered, it can easily work for a kid-friendly entrée. While most kugel recipes call for boiling the noodles before assembling the casserole, Eleanor's version cooks the noodles right in the dish, no precooking required. "Since first making this noodle pudding/casserole, it has been a family favorite and a comfort food for my family, grandchildren, relatives, and friends."

SERVES 8 TO 10

- 4 tablespoons (½ stick) unsalted butter
- 1 (1-pound) package wide egg noodles
- 1 cup raisins
- 2 cups cottage cheese
- 6 large eggs
- 1 cup sugar
- 2 teaspoons vanilla extract
- 4 cups low-fat or skim milk

1. Adjust oven rack to middle position and heat oven to 350 degrees. Place butter in 13 by 9-inch baking dish and melt in oven, 2 to 4 minutes. Spread half of noodles into baking dish and sprinkle with ½ cup raisins. Repeat layering with remaining noodles and raisins.

2. Process cottage cheese, eggs, sugar, and vanilla in food processor until smooth, about 2 minutes, scraping down bowl as needed. Transfer cottage cheese mixture to large bowl and stir in milk. Pour over noodles and bake until center of casserole is set and top is golden and crisp, about 1 hour. Let casserole cool for 10 minutes before serving.

Notes from the Test Kitchen

The contrast between the toasted, crunchy noodles on top of the casserole and the tender, puddinglike texture below adds interest to Eleanor's recipe, and we liked that we didn't have to preboil the noodles before assembling the casserole. She topped her pudding with oats or bran, but we felt the crunchy noodles were a sufficient topping, and instead of mixing the raisins into the custard, we distributed them evenly among the noodles so some—but not all—would float to the top. Eleanor also noted that you can substitute egg whites for some of the whole eggs and cut back on the butter to make this a lighter dish. We used whole-milk cottage cheese in our testing but she noted that lower-fat options would also work.

Chilaquiles

TOM LAWSHAE | ROUND ROCK, TEXAS

A dish of Mexican origin well known in Texas and the Southwest, *chilaquiles* ("poor man's dish") was originally created to use up leftovers. A casserole of tortillas, red or green chile sauce, cheese, and anything else the cook might want to add, it offers the comforting appeal of enchiladas—without all the work. Tom's version is an old family recipe made with ground turkey, onions, and cheddar, and instead of fussing with a dried-chile sauce, he makes a simpler well-seasoned tomato sauce. "My paternal grandparents lived and worked in Mexico before my father was born," he tells us. "My grandmother learned many of the dishes she saw being prepared around her, and she opened her own catering business. This chilaquiles recipe is her adaptation of a traditional Mexican dish. We had a family tradition of going to her house for dinner on Saturday nights, and we especially looked forward to the times she served it." Garnishes like cilantro, sour cream, and avocado make this great recipe even better.

SERVES 6

- 24 (6-inch) corn tortillas, cut into ½-inch pieces
- 2 tablespoons vegetable oil
- 1 large Vidalia onion, chopped fine (1½ cups)
- 2 tablespoons chili powder
- 2 teaspoons minced fresh oregano or 1 teaspoon dried
- 1 teaspoon ground cumin
- 1 pound 93 percent lean ground turkey
- 4 cups tomato juice
   Salt and pepper
- 8 ounces cheddar cheese, shredded (2 cups)

1. Adjust oven racks to upper-middle and lower-middle positions and heat oven to 425 degrees. Spread tortilla pieces in single layer over two rimmed baking sheets. Bake tortillas, stirring occasionally, until crisp and golden brown, about 15 minutes, switching and rotating baking sheets halfway through baking. Transfer tortillas to 13 by 9-inch baking dish.

2. Adjust oven rack to middle position. Heat oil in large Dutch oven over medium heat until shimmering. Add 1 cup onion and cook until softened, about 5 minutes. Stir in chili powder, oregano, and cumin and cook until fragrant, about 30 seconds. Stir in turkey and cook, breaking up pieces with wooden spoon, until no longer pink, about 5 minutes.

3. Stir in tomato juice and bring to simmer. Cover, reduce heat to medium-low, and simmer gently until sauce is deeply flavored, 15 to 20 minutes. Season with salt and pepper to taste.

4. Ladle turkey mixture over tortillas in baking dish and spread into even layer. Sprinkle with cheddar and remaining ½ cup onion. Bake until filling is bubbling and cheese is melted and beginning to brown, 10 to 20 minutes. Let casserole cool for 10 minutes before serving.

Notes from the Test Kitchen

Tom didn't specify amounts for the cheese or onion for the top layer; we settled on enough for the right gooey appeal and onion-y bite. We swapped the nonstick pan for a roomier Dutch oven, and we shortened the cooking time in step 3 to ensure the turkey remained tender. A mild Vidalia onion is perfect here, but a yellow onion will work.

Hurry Curry

JANICE SCHATTMAN | FORT WORTH, TEXAS

"Forget 30-minute meals, I needed 20-minute meals when the kids were growing up," writes Janice. "My husband and I are both lawyers. We had four children, and I typically got home after 6 p.m., with everyone needing to be somewhere else at 7 p.m. If I didn't have something on a plate in 20 minutes, the kids would grab fast food on the way or eat whatever was offered at their destination—usually chips and soda. This savory recipe was one of five or six weekday favorites." Janice's clever recipe makes the most of every minute and ingredient. About 10 minutes into the rice's cooking time, she dredges chicken in a quickly prepared curry spice rub, then cooks the chicken in a skillet. Next the rice (with green peas added) goes into the pan, where it picks up the flavorful browning and spice rub left behind by the chicken. She notes you could also steam spinach for a third component and dredge the leaves, rather than the rice, in the pan. Either way, it's a quick meal you'll want to make on a regular basis.

SERVES 4 TO 6

- 1½ cups water
- 1 cup basmati rice, rinsed
  Salt and pepper
- 1 cup frozen peas
- 1 tablespoon curry powder
- ½ teaspoon ground cumin
- ¼ teaspoon ground cinnamon
- 6 (4-ounce) boneless, skinless chicken thighs, trimmed
- 1 tablespoon peanut or vegetable oil
- 3 tablespoons low-sodium chicken broth
  Yogurt or sour cream, for serving

1. Bring water, rice, and ¼ teaspoon salt to boil in medium saucepan. Cover, reduce heat to low, and simmer gently until all liquid is absorbed and rice is tender, 17 to 20 minutes. Remove from heat and sprinkle peas over top (do not mix in). Cover and let sit for 10 minutes.

2. Meanwhile, combine curry powder, cumin, cinnamon, and ½ teaspoon salt. Pat chicken dry with paper towels and rub evenly with spice mixture.

3. Heat oil in large skillet over medium-high heat until just smoking. Brown chicken well on first side, 6 to 8 minutes. Flip chicken over and add broth. Cover, reduce heat to medium-low, and continue to cook until thickest part of chicken thigh registers 175 degrees on instant-read thermometer, about 10 minutes longer. Transfer chicken to serving platter and tent loosely with foil; reserve cooking liquid in skillet.

4. Add cooked rice and peas to reserved cooking liquid left in skillet and gently toss to combine. Season with salt and pepper to taste, and serve with chicken and yogurt.

Notes from the Test Kitchen

Dredging the rice in the pan after the chicken was cooked struck us as a clever way to add flavor without extra ingredients. Adding some broth to the pan with the chicken helped keep it from drying out, and we eliminated the optional spinach since we preferred to save all the flavor left in the pan by the chicken for the rice.

Greek Shrimp with Feta and Peppers

CATHERINE HEERS | SIMPSONVILLE, SOUTH CAROLINA

"My dad, who had emigrated from a poor fishing village in Greece, opened a restaurant in a Midwest town and married a local American girl who was really 'American.' Dad and all his Greek ways melted into the culture. But about four times a year, a Greek friend from a city 60 miles away would bring our favorite foods to us to share quietly in a small, private kitchen. Dad would open the packages of feta, olives, peppers, and baklava with the care of a priest. It was more than food: it was home, memories, love, and experiences only Dad could truly know and understand." The ingredients in Catherine's recipe, a Greek dish known as shrimp *saganaki*, echo those moments with her dad. Shrimp, onion, and bell peppers are cooked in tomatoes, broth, and wine, then feta and olives are added. It is salty, sweet, and brightly flavored, a sure comfort food even for those of us without Greek roots. Serve with bread or over rice.

SERVES 4 TO 6

- 2 tablespoons extra-virgin olive oil, plus extra as needed
- 1 green bell pepper, stemmed, seeded, and sliced ¼ inch thick
- 1 red bell pepper, stemmed, seeded, and sliced ¼ inch thick
- 1 yellow bell pepper, stemmed, seeded, and sliced ¼ inch thick
- 1 small onion, halved and sliced thin
- 3 garlic cloves, minced
- 1 tablespoon minced fresh oregano or 1 teaspoon dried
- 2 teaspoons minced fresh thyme or ½ teaspoon dried
- 4 medium tomatoes, cored and cut into ½-inch pieces
- ½ cup low-sodium chicken broth
- 2 tablespoons dry white wine
  Salt and pepper
- 1 pound medium shrimp (40 to 50 per pound), peeled and deveined
- 8 ounces feta, crumbled (2 cups)
- ¾ cup pitted kalamata olives, chopped
- 4 teaspoons fresh lemon juice
- 2 tablespoons chopped fresh basil

1. Adjust oven rack to middle position and heat oven to 400 degrees. Heat oil in large ovensafe skillet over medium heat until shimmering. Add bell peppers and onion and cook until softened, 5 to 7 minutes. Stir in garlic, oregano, and thyme and cook until fragrant, about 30 seconds. Stir in tomatoes, broth, and wine, bring to simmer, and cook until tomatoes are softened, about 10 minutes. Season with salt and pepper to taste.

2. Stir in shrimp and cook until beginning to turn pink, about 2 minutes. Sprinkle with feta and olives. Transfer skillet to oven and bake until shrimp are fully cooked and cheese has softened, about 5 minutes.

3. Using potholder (skillet handle will be hot), remove skillet from oven. Drizzle with lemon juice and additional extra-virgin olive oil. Sprinkle with basil and serve.

Notes from the Test Kitchen
Catherine's recipe is as visually appealing as it is flavorful. We switched from a 10-inch skillet to a roomier 12-inch and reduced the cheese from 12 ounces to a still-ample 8 ounces.

DATE AND NUT BREAD

Breads with a Story to Tell

Lovie May's Rice Muffins **82**

Cheese Muffins **84**

Minute Muffins **85**

Bubbles **86**

Double Delicious Apple Cinnamon Rolls **88**

Old Time Latvian Rolls **90**

Great-Grandma's Potato Rolls **93**

Papa Bob's Caramelized Onion Bread with Apricot Glaze **95**

Grandma Pearl's Upside-Down Tomato Pan Bread **97**

Laura's Rye Bread **98**

Date and Nut Bread **100**

Pain d'Epices **101**

Swedish Coffee Bread **102**

German New Year's Pretzel **105**

Grandma's Sweet Kuchen **107**

Christmas Stollen **108**

Lovie May's Rice Muffins

DONNA WARD | EL LAGO, TEXAS

"It was 1938 when Grandma bought her new dual-fuel cookstove, a very state-of-the-art model that burned either coal or wood. Grandma was a thrifty sort and food was never wasted. Last night's leftover cooked rice was mixed into tomorrow's chicken casserole, or, my favorite, her flavorful muffin batter," notes Donna. "She was a creative cook; sometimes she added shredded cheese, leftover bacon, or chopped ham to her batter." Though not a typical baked-good addition these days, rice was once commonly incorporated into batters. In the 17th century American South, rice plantation mistresses revamped their recipes to utilize their primary crop, and, even earlier, Europeans had been turning to rice to stretch wheat flour in times of famine. Lovie May's recipe is not all that different from those of American colonial times, and with a little cheddar and ham added it makes for a richly flavored muffin that is a real treat—certainly not to be reserved only for when you are watching the budget! "When natural gas was finally piped to her small, rural Missouri town," writes Donna, "she continued to bake these muffins in her brand new 1952 gas range. Now I am a grandmother, I bake them for my family, and they are every bit as good as Grandma's."

MAKES 10 MUFFINS

- 1 **cup all-purpose flour**
- 1 **tablespoon sugar**
- 1½ **teaspoons baking powder**
- ½ **teaspoon salt**
- ⅔ **cup whole milk**
- 1 **large egg**
- 2 **tablespoons unsalted butter, melted and cooled**
- 1 **cup cooked rice**
- 4 **ounces thinly sliced deli ham, cut into ¼-inch pieces**
- 3 **ounces cheddar cheese, shredded (¾ cup)**

1. Adjust oven rack to middle position and heat oven to 425 degrees. Lightly grease and flour 10 cups of 12-cup muffin tin.

2. Whisk flour, sugar, baking powder, and salt together in large bowl. In separate bowl, whisk milk, egg, and melted butter together, then stir in rice, ham, and cheese. Gently fold milk mixture into flour mixture until just combined (do not overmix).

3. Portion batter into prepared muffin cups. Bake until golden brown and toothpick inserted into center comes out clean, about 20 minutes, rotating tin halfway through baking.

4. Let muffins cool in tin for 10 minutes. Remove muffins from tin and let cool slightly before serving. Serve warm.

Notes from the Test Kitchen

Though the yield seemed a bit odd to us at first, we realized a recipe requiring about 1 cup of leftover rice was convenient, and 10 muffins were enough to serve 4 to 6 (these muffins are best eaten the day they are made). Donna said adding bacon, ham, or cheese was optional; we thought a few additions were a must. To ensure that the muffins didn't stick to the pan, we both greased and floured the tins. Feel free to use leftover or precooked rice (sold as Ready Rice in supermarkets).

Cheese Muffins

JASMIN BARON | LIVONIA, NEW YORK

Given this recipe's title, you might first imagine savory muffins made with cheddar, Parmesan, or maybe even blue cheese, none of which would be that unusual. So the fact that Jasmin's recipe turns to cottage cheese is surprising, but, along with the sour cream and melted butter, it makes her muffins ultra-moist. "My Grandma Baron passed away in 2005 at the age of 95," writes Jasmin. "The child of German immigrants, she raised 10 children in a rural village on the prairies and was well known for her cooking. My Aunt Joylyn retrieved a large folder full of Grandma's recipe cards and handwritten cooking notes after Grandma was moved to a nursing home, and she has since passed these recipes on to me. Many of these recipes bring back childhood memories of Grandma's kitchen, where there was always the smell of a fresh pot of coffee and something good baking in the oven. Simple and delicious, many of the recipes use seasonal, local ingredients, and are almost always frugal. This recipe, simply titled 'Cheese Muffins,' was tucked into the folder on a scrap of paper. It's incredibly simple and could probably be dressed up with herbs and spices of one's choosing, but it stands on its own as a memory of a simpler time." We liked Jasmin's idea of adding an herb, so we incorporated scallions, which complement the savory flavors and lend a hint of color and freshness to these muffins.

MAKES 12 MUFFINS

- 2 **cups all-purpose flour**
- 2 **teaspoons sugar**
- 1 **teaspoon baking powder**
- 1 **teaspoon salt**
- 1 **teaspoon pepper**
- 2 **cups cottage cheese**
- ½ **cup sour cream**
- 8 **tablespoons (1 stick) unsalted butter, melted and cooled**
- 2 **large eggs**
- 2 **scallions, sliced thin**

1. Adjust oven rack to middle position and heat oven to 375 degrees. Lightly grease 12-cup muffin tin.

2. Whisk flour, sugar, baking powder, salt, and pepper together in large bowl. In separate bowl, whisk cottage cheese, sour cream, melted butter, eggs, and scallions together. Gently fold cottage cheese mixture into flour mixture until just combined (do not overmix).

3. Portion batter into prepared muffin cups. Bake until golden brown and toothpick inserted into center comes out clean, 25 to 35 minutes, rotating tin halfway through baking.

4. Let muffins cool in tin for 10 minutes. Remove muffins from tin and let cool slightly before serving. Serve warm.

Notes from the Test Kitchen

We loved the creative use of ingredients in this recipe, but we did make a few tweaks, cutting back on the sour cream and sugar to create a slightly drier, more savory muffin to complement the pepper and scallions, and we upped the salt.

Minute Muffins

CAROL SWAIN LEWIS | POPLAR BLUFF, MISSOURI

While these muffins can't literally be made in a minute, Carol's recipe is as good as it gets, taking just about that long to mix the batter together and pop the pan in the oven. The recipe, what you might call "a lazy man's biscuit," also stands out because it calls for neither eggs nor butter, but instead relies on a combination of buttermilk and mayonnaise to create richness. "My mother taught accounting at the local high school, and though she had worked all day, she always prepared dinner for my brother, my father, and me," writes Carol. "I remember when she got this recipe. What a time-saver it was! We had minute muffins often, and the various herbs and such that Mom added made it seem to me as if she were the best cook ever!" Though the submitted recipe was for a simple, plain muffin batter, we added garlic and rosemary, probably one of the many flavor additions Carol's mother discovered, and they make her muffins a wonderful savory accompaniment to almost any meal, particularly soup or pasta.

MAKES 8 MUFFINS

- 2   cups all-purpose flour
- 1   tablespoon baking powder
- 1   teaspoon salt
- 1   cup buttermilk
- ¼   cup mayonnaise
- 1   garlic clove, minced
- 1½ teaspoons minced fresh rosemary or
     ½ teaspoon dried

1. Adjust oven rack to middle position and heat oven to 375 degrees. Grease 8 cups of 12-cup muffin tin.

2. Whisk flour, baking powder, and salt together in large bowl. In separate bowl, whisk buttermilk, mayonnaise, garlic, and rosemary together. Gently fold buttermilk mixture into flour mixture until just combined (do not overmix).

3. Portion batter into prepared muffin cups. Bake until golden brown and toothpick inserted into center comes out clean, 18 to 25 minutes, rotating tin halfway through baking.

4. Let muffins cool in tin for 10 minutes. Remove muffins from tin and let cool slightly before serving. Serve warm.

Notes from the Test Kitchen

The simplicity of this recipe makes it perfect for weeknights, and it can be endlessly varied with different add-ins; our inclusion of rosemary and garlic is just one great option. The original recipe made a dozen small muffins, but we decided to make eight larger muffins instead, just right for sharing with a few dinner guests.

Bubbles

CAROLYN RENNER | WEATHERFORD, TEXAS

Before today's yeasty doughnut holes there were drop doughnuts, made from a simple yeastless batter that could be prepared quickly from only a handful of ingredients. Carolyn's recipe is right in keeping with those old-fashioned versions. Doughnuts in the United States go back to the Dutch settlers, but, unlike the typical ring-shaped doughnuts, no rolling or stamping of dough is required for drop doughnuts. Spoonfuls are simply dropped into hot oil, meaning that these fritterlike treats can be on the table in minutes. Carolyn's Bubbles—appropriately named, given drop doughnuts such as these look like bubbles of fried dough—are interesting because she uses evaporated milk for the liquid component, which adds a unique richness to the batter, and her suggested addition of apples provides wonderful texture and a hit of freshness. Says Carolyn of her recipe: "We didn't get these as often as we would have liked, but they were very scrumptious!" The dough itself isn't very sweet (she adds no sugar), so serving them with a little maple syrup for dipping as she suggests is the perfect finishing touch.

MAKES 16 DROP DOUGHNUTS

- 2 **cups all-purpose flour**
- 2 **teaspoons baking powder**
- 1 **teaspoon salt**
- ¾ **cup evaporated milk**
- 2 **large eggs**
- 1 **apple, peeled, cored, and shredded (optional)**
  Vegetable oil
  Maple syrup, for serving

1. Whisk flour, baking powder, and salt together in large bowl. Whisk milk, eggs, and apple (if using) together in medium bowl. Fold milk mixture into flour mixture until just combined (do not overmix).

2. Add oil to large saucepan until it measures 1 inch deep. Heat oil over medium-high heat until it registers 375 degrees on instant-read thermometer. Using two spoons, gently drop golf ball–size portions of batter (about 3 tablespoons each) into hot oil. Fry, stirring gently, until doughnuts are crisp and deeply browned, about 3 minutes, adjusting heat as necessary to maintain oil at 375 degrees.

3. Using slotted spoon, transfer fried doughnuts to large paper towel–lined plate. Repeat with remaining batter. Serve warm with syrup.

Notes from the Test Kitchen

These fried treats couldn't have been simpler to make, and we loved her variation that incorporated apples (we found that shredded apples incorporated most easily). We slightly modified her procedure by mixing the dry and wet ingredients separately first before mixing the two together for a more uniformly combined mixture. We also increased the amount of liquid slightly for a wetter dough that gave us lighter doughnuts. Be careful not to overbeat the batter, as it will make the Bubbles tough.

Double Delicious Apple Cinnamon Rolls

BARBARA ESTABROOK | RHINELANDER, WISCONSIN

After a single bite of one of Barbara's cinnamon rolls, there's no going back. The filling has not only the usual cinnamon and brown sugar but also applesauce, which adds a hint of sweetness. Then there's the glaze—a combination of honey, brown sugar, cinnamon, almonds, and butter—which covers the bottom of the rolls. Top them off with a white frosting and these rolls really are "double delicious." Barbara writes, "The origin of my recipe is from a 1960s church-published cookbook. I liked a recipe a parishioner contributed called Apple-Taffy Rolls. Instead of filling the rolls with apple butter, I used unsweetened applesauce that I made by covering peeled apple slices with water and cooking them on low until they were soft, then I mashed them. The honey glaze with almonds was my own idea. My children loved the fact that the rolls were frosted on the top and had a honey-nut glaze on the bottom—they called them 'double delicious!'" Barbara sent us a simplified recipe, which called for prepared chunky applesauce, an option we preferred since it makes her recipe a little bit quicker.

MAKES 12 ROLLS

GLAZE
- ⅓ cup honey
- ⅓ cup packed light brown sugar
- 4 tablespoons (½ stick) unsalted butter, melted and cooled
- ¼ teaspoon ground cinnamon
- ½ cup almonds, chopped

ROLLS
- 1 cup whole milk, warmed (110 degrees)
- 2 large eggs
- 4–4½ cups all-purpose flour
- ⅓ cup granulated sugar
- 1 envelope (2¼ teaspoons) instant or rapid-rise yeast
- 1½ teaspoons salt
- 6 tablespoons (¾ stick) unsalted butter, cut into ½-inch pieces and softened, plus 2 tablespoons melted butter for brushing
- 1 cup unsweetened chunky applesauce
- ⅔ cup packed brown sugar
- 2 teaspoons ground cinnamon

FROSTING
- 3 tablespoons unsalted butter, softened
- 3 tablespoons whole milk
- ¼ teaspoon almond extract
- 1½ cups confectioners' sugar

1. FOR THE GLAZE: Lightly grease 13 by 9-inch baking dish. Combine honey, brown sugar, melted butter, and cinnamon, then spread mixture over bottom of prepared baking dish. Sprinkle with almonds.

2. FOR THE ROLLS: Whisk milk and eggs together in liquid measuring cup. Combine 4 cups flour, granulated sugar, yeast, and salt in stand mixer fitted with dough hook. With mixer on low speed, slowly add milk mixture and let dough come together, about 2 minutes. Increase mixer speed to medium-low and knead until dough is smooth and elastic, about 6 minutes.

3. With mixer on medium-low speed, slowly add butter, one piece at a time, every 15 seconds. Scrape down sides of bowl and continue to knead dough on medium-low speed until dough forms very soft ball, 10 to 15 minutes longer. If after 6 minutes dough seems very sticky, add remaining ½ cup flour, 2 tablespoons at a time, until dough clears sides of bowl but sticks to bottom. Place dough in large, lightly greased bowl and cover with greased plastic wrap. Let rise in warm place until doubled in size, about 2 hours.

4. Meanwhile, microwave applesauce in bowl, stirring occasionally, until thickened and it measures ½ cup, about 10 minutes. Stir in brown sugar and cinnamon and let cool to room temperature.

5. Turn dough out onto lightly floured counter and roll into 18-inch square. Following photos, brush melted butter over dough, then spread applesauce filling over dough, leaving 1-inch border along top edge. Loosen bottom edge of dough from counter using bench scraper (or metal spatula), and roll dough up into tight log. Pinch seam closed and roll log seam side down. Pat ends of log to even them.

6. Slice log into 12 even rolls using serrated knife. Arrange rolls, cut side down, in prepared baking dish on top of glaze. Wrap tightly with greased plastic wrap. Let rise in warm place until rolls have nearly doubled in size and are pressed against one another, about 1 hour. (Alternatively, refrigerate rolls for up to 16 hours; let rolls sit at room temperature until they have nearly doubled in size, 1 to 1½ hours, before continuing.)

7. Adjust oven rack to middle position and heat oven to 350 degrees. Unwrap rolls and bake until golden and puffed, 25 to 30 minutes. Let rolls cool in baking dish for 5 minutes. Flip rolls out onto wire rack set over sheet of parchment paper (for easy cleanup) and let cool completely, about 1 hour.

8. FOR THE FROSTING: Beat butter, milk, and almond extract in medium bowl with electric mixer on medium-high speed until smooth, about 2 minutes. Reduce mixer speed to medium-low, slowly add confectioners' sugar, and beat until incorporated and smooth, about 5 minutes. Increase mixer speed to medium-high and beat until light and fluffy, about 5 minutes longer. Arrange cooled rolls on serving platter, glazed side down, spread with frosting, and serve.

Notes from the Test Kitchen

As soon as we iced these cinnamon rolls, they were gone. We did make a few changes, including cooking down the applesauce to make the filling a little less watery, and we cut back on the almond extract in the frosting. Chunky applesauce will give the filling nice pieces of apple, but smooth applesauce will also work.

MAKING DOUBLE DELICIOUS APPLE CINNAMON ROLLS

1. Brush the square of dough with butter, then spread the filling over the top, leaving a 1-inch border along the top edge.

2. Carefully roll the dough into a tight log, making sure to maintain an even thickness throughout.

3. Pinch the seam together to secure. Roll the log over so that it is seam side down and pat the ends to even them.

4. Using a serrated knife, slice the log into 12 even rolls and arrange them, cut side down, in the prepared baking dish.

Old Time Latvian Rolls

DAN COPP | MURFREESBORO, TENNESSEE

"If there's anything I remember about my grandmother, it is the alluring aroma of her Latvian rolls emanating from the oven. These delectable rolls have become a thing of legend in my family, and only a few of us have knowledge of the recipe. Like most family recipes, my grandmother's rolls have a story. On October 22, 1944, at the height of the Second World War, my grandparents fled Daugaupolis, Latvia, as it was being invaded by Soviet troops, leaving behind all their possessions. After dodging artillery shells and flying bullets, trekking 180 miles on foot to evade the advancing Soviet army, spending several years in a refugee camp, and enduring the death of their three-year-old son, my grandparents—now penniless refugees—sailed to America in 1952, where they began new lives in Terre Haute, Indiana. Although Soviet officials confiscated all of my grandmother's material possessions in Latvia, the one thing they couldn't take from her was her knack for cooking and the recipe for rolls she grew up eating." Her rolls are, for the most part, a typical Eastern European recipe: a rich, soft, sweet white flour bread dough that can be fashioned into either a loaf or rolls. However, the vanilla in Dan's grandmother's recipe is an interesting inclusion since Latvian rolls are often identified with caraway or saffron (neither of which you will find in this recipe). The vanilla, a flavoring you're more likely to find in more cakelike breads such as babka or kulich (a Russian Easter bread), must be Dan's grandmother's own touch.

MAKES 12 ROLLS

- 1¾ cups water, warmed (110 degrees)
- ½ cup evaporated milk, warmed (110 degrees)
- 5–5½ cups all-purpose flour
- ⅓ cup sugar
- 1 envelope (2¼ teaspoons) instant or rapid-rise yeast
- 2 large egg yolks
- 2 tablespoons unsalted butter, melted and cooled
- 2 teaspoons salt
- ¼ teaspoon vanilla extract
- 1 large egg beaten with 1 tablespoon water, for brushing

1. Combine water and milk in liquid measuring cup. Combine 4 cups flour, sugar, and yeast in stand mixer fitted with dough hook. With mixer on low speed, slowly add milk mixture and let dough come together, about 2 minutes (dough will be very loose).

2. Remove bowl from mixer, cover with greased plastic wrap, and let rise in warm place until doubled in size, about 1 hour. Gently fold dough over several times using dough scraper or large rubber spatula, then re-cover and let rest for 20 minutes; repeat process of folding and resting twice more.

3. Whisk egg yolks, melted butter, salt, and vanilla together in liquid measuring cup. Return bowl of dough to stand mixer. Add 1 cup more flour and mix dough on low speed until combined, about 2 minutes. Slowly add egg mixture and mix until combined, about 2 minutes.

4. Increase mixer speed to medium-low and knead until dough is smooth and elastic, about 8 minutes. If after 4 minutes dough seems very sticky, add remaining ½ cup flour, 2 tablespoons at a time, until dough clears sides of bowl but sticks to bottom.

5. Grease rimmed baking sheet. Turn dough out onto clean counter and stretch it into 15-inch log. Following photos, cut log into 12 equal pieces and cover with greased plastic wrap. Working with one piece of dough at a time, round dough into smooth, taut rolls and arrange on prepared baking sheet, spaced at least 2 inches apart.

6. Mist rolls with vegetable oil spray, cover loosely with plastic wrap, and let rise in warm place until nearly doubled in size and dough barely springs back when poked with knuckle, 45 to 75 minutes.

7. Adjust oven rack to middle position and heat oven to 400 degrees. Brush rolls with beaten egg mixture and bake until deep golden brown, about 15 minutes, rotating baking sheet halfway through baking. Let rolls cool on baking sheet for 15 minutes before serving. Serve warm or at room temperature.

Notes from the Test Kitchen
Though these fluffy, oversized, rich dinner rolls took some time to prepare, the results made the work more than worth it. Dan's grandmother's original recipe was a solid one, but it made incredibly large 6-inch rolls, so we cut the size back to make an even dozen rolls that are still generously sized.

ROUNDING DOUGH FOR DINNER ROLLS

1. After stretching the dough into in an even log, use a dough scraper (or knife) to divide the dough into even pieces, as directed in the recipe.

2. Drag each piece of dough in small circles over a clean counter, using a cupped hand, until the dough feels firm and round. It should feel like the dough is spinning underneath your hand, but not turning over.

Great-Grandma's Potato Rolls

KURT LICHTENSTEIN | NORTH EAST, MARYLAND

"Fifty-plus years ago my great-grandmother would supervise the making of her rolls for all the family fancy dinners," Kurt tells us. "She was in her nineties then and a daughter had to do the actual cooking. Three or four families would attend the dinners—there would be 30 to 40 people, adults and children—and the rolls would usually disappear first." And it's no wonder: These yeast rolls are simple to make yet are supremely soft and richly flavored. Adding mashed potatoes to dinner rolls might be unique to some folks, but the technique actually has quite a long history. Potatoes, after all, have been a staple in North America since the 18th century, and their versatility for both cooking and baking applications was quickly discovered. Among the earliest original American cookbooks was *A New System of Domestic Cookery*, published in 1807, and in it you'll find a recipe called "Potatoe Rolls." Its ingredients are surprisingly similar to those in Kurt's great-grandmother's recipe, though she adds sugar for a hint of sweetness, an addition that makes her rolls irresistible.

MAKES 16 LARGE ROLLS

- 2 **cups whole milk, warmed (110 degrees)**
- 11 **tablespoons vegetable shortening, melted and cooled**
- 1 **cup mashed potatoes**
- ½ **cup sugar**
- 2 **large eggs**
- 7–8 **cups all-purpose flour**
- 1 **envelope (2¼ teaspoons) instant or rapid-rise yeast**
- 1½ **teaspoons salt**

1. Whisk milk, melted shortening, mashed potatoes, sugar, and eggs together in liquid measuring cup. Combine 7 cups flour, yeast, and salt in stand mixer fitted with dough hook. With mixer on low speed, slowly add milk mixture and let dough come together, about 2 minutes.

2. Increase mixer speed to medium-low and knead until dough is smooth and elastic, about 8 minutes. If after 4 minutes dough seems very sticky, add remaining 1 cup flour, 2 tablespoons at a time, until dough clears sides of bowl but sticks to bottom.

(Continued on page 94)

3. Turn dough out onto lightly floured counter and knead by hand to form smooth, round ball. Place dough in large, lightly greased bowl and cover with greased plastic wrap. Let rise in warm place until doubled in size, 1 to 1½ hours.

4. Grease two 9-inch round cake pans. Turn dough out onto clean counter and stretch it into 24-inch log. Following photos on page 91, cut log into 16 equal pieces and cover with greased plastic wrap. Working with one piece of dough at a time, round dough into smooth, taut rolls. Following photos at right, arrange 8 rolls in each prepared cake pan, placing one roll in middle and others around it.

5. Lightly press on rolls so they just touch each other. Mist rolls with vegetable oil spray, cover loosely with plastic wrap, and let rise in warm place until nearly doubled in size and dough barely springs back when poked with knuckle, 45 to 75 minutes.

6. Adjust oven rack to lower-middle position and heat oven to 350 degrees. Bake rolls until golden brown, 25 to 30 minutes, rotating pans halfway through baking. Let rolls cool in pans for 15 minutes. Run small knife around edge of rolls to loosen, then turn out onto wire rack to cool further, if desired. Serve warm or at room temperature.

Notes from the Test Kitchen

Our tasters gobbled up these addictive dinner rolls. We did make a few changes to the original recipe to make it more foolproof. We reduced the oven temperature and extended the cooking time to avoid burning the tops of the rolls. We also found that letting the rolls rise until they tripled in size, as called for in the original, was too large for the pan so we let them rise only until doubled, and they were still amply large. Giving a range for the amount of flour accommodated for the variability among mashed potatoes. You can use homemade mashed potatoes or any kind of prepared mashed potatoes from the supermarket. Be sure your mashed potatoes are warm and have a loose but not soupy texture; otherwise, they will cause the dough to be too wet.

MAKING POTATO ROLLS

1. Arrange 8 rolls in each greased 9-inch cake pan, placing one roll in the middle and the others around it.

2. After the baked rolls have cooled in the pans for 15 minutes, run a small knife around the edge, and turn them out onto a wire rack.

Papa Bob's Caramelized Onion Bread with Apricot Glaze

CATHERINE WILKINSON | DEWEY, ARIZONA

"As a young child in the Depression, my late father-in-law had very little to eat and what he did have wasn't cooked very well because his parents were so busy trying to make ends meet. This led to a lifetime of searching out interesting ingredients and learning how to cook them or bake with them well. He was an amazing, inventive cook. One food he was enamored with was Vidalia onions, and he would order bags from a 'secret' source in Georgia every spring. He worked on this bread recipe for quite a while, ignoring the teasing from his family about his weird 'onion bread.' But we all soon stopped laughing when he gave us a taste!" Part tea bread, part savory loaf, Papa Bob incorporates warm spices and sautéed onions into the dough, then glazes the baked loaves with a savory-sweet mixture of more onions, apricot preserves, and sherry vinegar. It's perfect with brunch or breakfast eggs, or even as a midday snack.

MAKES TWO 8-INCH LOAVES

18	tablespoons (2¼ sticks) unsalted butter, softened
4	Vidalia onions, chopped fine
1½	teaspoons salt
2½	cups all-purpose flour
2	teaspoons baking soda
½	teaspoon ground nutmeg
½	teaspoon ground cinnamon
¼	teaspoon ground cloves
2	cups sugar
4	large eggs
½	cup apricot preserves or jam
¼	cup sherry vinegar

1. Melt 2 tablespoons butter in large skillet over medium heat. Add onions and ½ teaspoon salt and cook until softened and lightly browned, 8 to 10 minutes. Remove from heat; measure out and reserve 2 tablespoons cooked onions separately for glaze.

2. Adjust oven rack to lower-middle position and heat oven to 350 degrees. Grease two 8½ by 4½-inch loaf pans. Whisk flour, baking soda, nutmeg, cinnamon, cloves, and remaining 1 teaspoon salt together in bowl.

3. In large bowl, beat sugar and remaining 16 tablespoons butter together with electric mixer on medium speed until light and fluffy, 3 to 6 minutes. Beat in eggs, one at a time, until combined, about 30 seconds, scraping down bowl and beaters as needed. Beat in remaining cooked onions until combined, about 30 seconds. Reduce mixer speed to low and slowly add flour mixture until combined, about 30 seconds.

4. Give batter final stir with rubber spatula to make sure it is thoroughly combined. Scrape batter into prepared pans and smooth tops. Bake until golden brown and toothpick inserted into center comes out clean, about 1 hour, rotating pans halfway through baking.

5. Let loaves cool in pans for 10 minutes. Meanwhile, bring reserved cooked onions, apricot preserves, and vinegar to simmer in saucepan and cook until thickened and reduced to ½ cup, about 10 minutes. Remove loaves from pans, brush warm glaze over top, and let cool on wire rack for at least 1 hour before serving.

Notes from the Test Kitchen
We loved the inventiveness of this recipe. We hardly changed a thing about it, only increasing the salt a bit for a little more savory balance.

Grandma Pearl's Upside-Down Tomato Pan Bread

MERRY GRAHAM | NEWHALL, CALIFORNIA

"Tucked away in Grandma's wooden box there is a crumbled faded treasure, a recipe for Upside-Down Tomato Cake," writes Merry. "Our summers and holidays were filled with alluring aromas from her oven. I actually had several of her recipes to choose from, all of which she baked with what the harvest brought in from their 40-acre prune ranch in San Jose, California. So why did I pick Grandma Pearl's Upside-Down Tomato Pan Bread? Simple; this fluffy moist pan bread intrigues me! It can be served with salads, soups, stews, chilis, poultry, or meat. It is beautiful because the tomatoes caramelize and show off just like an upside-down pineapple cake."

MAKES ONE ROUND LOAF

- ½ cup olive oil
- 1 pint cherry tomatoes, quartered
- 1 tablespoon sugar
- 2 teaspoons minced fresh oregano or ½ teaspoon dried
- 1½ teaspoons salt
- 2 cups all-purpose flour
- ¼ cup Parmesan cheese, grated, plus extra for serving
- 1 tablespoon baking powder
- ¼ cup chopped fresh basil
- 1 cup whole milk
- 3 large eggs
- 2 teaspoons grated fresh lemon zest and 1 tablespoon fresh lemon juice

1. Adjust oven rack to middle position and heat oven to 375 degrees. Heat 3 tablespoons oil in 12-inch ovensafe nonstick skillet over medium-high heat until shimmering. Add tomatoes, 1 teaspoon sugar, 1 teaspoon oregano, and ¼ teaspoon salt to skillet and cook, stirring gently, until softened and lightly browned, 5 to 7 minutes. Remove skillet from heat.

2. Whisk flour, Parmesan, baking powder, 1 tablespoon basil, remaining 2 teaspoons sugar, remaining 1¼ teaspoons salt, and remaining 1 teaspoon oregano together in large bowl. In separate bowl, whisk milk, eggs, lemon zest, lemon juice, and remaining 5 tablespoons oil together. Gently fold milk mixture into flour mixture until just combined (do not overmix).

3. Spread cooked tomatoes into even layer in skillet. Dollop batter evenly over tomatoes and spread into even layer, covering tomatoes completely. Return skillet to medium-high heat and cook until batter just begins to brown around edge, about 2 minutes. Transfer skillet to oven and bake until top is golden brown, 25 to 30 minutes.

4. Using potholder (skillet handle will be hot), remove skillet from oven. Let bread cool in skillet for 5 minutes. Run small knife around edge of bread to loosen from pan. Place inverted serving platter (or cutting board) over top and gently flip bread onto platter using potholders (or towels). Sprinkle with remaining 3 tablespoons basil and additional Parmesan. Slice bread into wedges and serve warm or at room temperature.

Notes from the Test Kitchen

This focaccia-like, sweet-savory bread is one of a kind. The original recipe was a little too sweet for us, so we cut the sugar back from ¼ cup to 1 tablespoon, and we upped the oil (we opted to use all olive oil instead of both vegetable and olive oil). We also added Parmesan to the batter in addition to using it to top the bread. Browning the batter on the stovetop for a short period of time helped develop more flavor and visual appeal.

Laura's Rye Bread

JO ANNE LIGHTFOOT | SCHAUMBURG, ILLINOIS

"Each bite of this bread takes me right back to Grandma's farm kitchen in New Gottland, Kansas. This was the only bread we ate at her house, and slices were served with dinner and at lunch, which was served midafternoon, usually as bologna and cheese sandwiches. Mom only made the bread occasionally for us, so it retained its treat status for our family. Unlike beefsteak rye, this is light and tender, pleasantly sweet, and devoid of any fruit or seeds. The smell as it bakes is divine, and a warm slice fresh out of the oven, slathered with butter, is mandatory. It is wonderful toasted with butter, cheese, or peanut butter. The heels even make great bread crumbs. Grandma received this recipe from her sister Laura. For me, it will always be Grandma's rye bread. I have this bread on hand at all times, and it always makes me think of the good times at Grandma's kitchen table as well."

MAKES TWO 8-INCH LOAVES

2¼	cups boiling water
1	cup rye flour
¼	cup sorghum or mild molasses
¼	cup packed brown sugar
2	tablespoons vegetable shortening or unsalted butter, melted and cooled, plus 2 tablespoons melted butter for brushing
5–5½	cups all-purpose flour
1	envelope (2¼ teaspoons) instant or rapid-rise yeast
1	teaspoon salt

1. Whisk water, rye flour, sorghum, sugar, and melted shortening in liquid measuring cup and let cool until just warm (about 110 degrees). Combine 5 cups all-purpose flour, yeast, and salt in stand mixer fitted with dough hook. With mixer on low speed, slowly add water-rye mixture and let dough come together, about 2 minutes.

2. Increase mixer speed to medium-low and knead until dough is smooth and elastic, about 8 minutes. If after 4 minutes dough seems very sticky, add remaining ½ cup flour, 2 tablespoons at a time, until dough clears sides of bowl but sticks to bottom.

3. Turn dough out onto lightly floured counter and knead by hand to form smooth, round ball. Place dough in large, lightly greased bowl and cover with greased plastic wrap. Let rise in warm place until doubled in size, 1 to 1½ hours.

4. Grease two 8½ by 4½-inch loaf pans. Turn dough out onto lightly floured counter, divide into two equal pieces, and cover with greased plastic wrap. Following photos, press one piece of dough into 9-inch square. Roll dough into tight log and pinch seam closed. Place loaf, seam side down, in prepared pan. Repeat with remaining piece of dough.

5. Mist loaves with vegetable oil spray, cover loosely with plastic wrap, and let rise in warm place until nearly doubled in size and dough barely springs back when poked with knuckle, 45 to 75 minutes.

6. Adjust oven rack to lower-middle position and heat oven to 350 degrees. Brush loaves with melted butter, then lightly spray with water. Bake until golden brown and center of loaf registers 200 degrees on instant-read thermometer, 40 to 50 minutes, rotating pans halfway through baking. Let loaves cool in pans for 15 minutes. Remove loaves from pans and let cool completely on wire rack before serving.

Notes from the Test Kitchen

This appealing loaf offers a mild rye flavor that won plenty of fans in the test kitchen, but it made three loaves so we scaled it down to make just two (a reasonable amount to polish off while still fresh). However, we felt that the rye flavor needed a boost, so we left it at its original amount, which lent a little more flavor but still kept it at that mild appealing level that makes Laura's recipe unique. For an accurate measurement of water, bring a teakettle to a boil, then measure 2¼ cups.

SHAPING LAURA'S RYE BREAD

1. Press the dough into a 9-inch square using your hands.

2. Roll the dough up into a tight log.

3. Pinch the seam together to secure.

4. Fit the dough, seam side down, into a greased 8½ by 4½-inch loaf pan.

Date and Nut Bread

MARY CANNATARO | CHICAGO, ILLINOIS

"I still have the recipe card my mom gave me when I first got married, and the card was her original, dated 3-26-56," Mary tells us. "Every time our church had a bake sale, they would call up my mom and request her to make many loaves of this. We would wrap them in plastic wrap and tie them with a curling ribbon according to the season. They sold out immediately every time. We sometimes would buy back a loaf ourselves if we did not make extra so we could have it when we got home!" This bread definitely makes a great gift, with its fun shape that comes from being baked in cans. Her bread has balanced sweetness, and soaking the dates in baking soda and water ensures they're tender. "This bread will always remind me of my mom, who passed away 10 years ago, and it has been a hit with anyone I have ever given it to." We tend to agree with Mary that it's just not the same if you don't bake it in a can, but the recipe works fine using loaf pans (see below for instructions).

MAKES THREE SMALL LOAVES

2½	cups pitted whole dates, chopped fine
2	cups boiling water
2	teaspoons baking soda
2	large eggs
2	teaspoons vanilla extract
4	cups all-purpose flour
1½	teaspoons salt
1¾	cups sugar
6	tablespoons (¾ stick) unsalted butter or vegetable shortening, softened
1	cup walnuts, chopped

1. Adjust oven rack to middle position and heat oven to 350 degrees. Thoroughly wash, dry, grease, and flour three 28-ounce tomato or vegetable cans with tops removed but bottoms still intact.

2. Combine dates, water, and baking soda in medium bowl. Cover and let sit until dates have softened, about 30 minutes. Whisk in eggs and vanilla until combined.

3. Whisk flour and salt together in bowl. In large bowl, beat sugar and butter together with electric mixer on medium speed until light and fluffy, 3 to 6 minutes. Beat in date mixture until combined, about 30 seconds, scraping down bowl and beaters as needed. Reduce mixer speed to low and slowly add flour mixture until combined, about 30 seconds. Stir in walnuts until combined.

4. Give batter final stir with rubber spatula to make sure it is thoroughly combined. Scrape batter evenly into prepared cans and smooth tops. Place cans on rimmed baking sheet and bake until golden brown and toothpick inserted into center comes out clean, about 1 hour, rotating baking sheet halfway through baking.

5. Let loaves cool in cans for 10 minutes. Run small knife around edge of loaves to loosen from cans. Remove bread from cans and let cool completely on wire rack before serving.

Notes from the Test Kitchen

Mary called for 4 tablespoons of shortening; we upped the amount for a more tender loaf and gave the option of using butter. You can bake this recipe in six 14.5-ounce cans or two 8½ by 4½-inch loaf pans. Divide the batter among greased, floured cans or pans and bake as directed. For smaller cans, reduce baking time to about 45 minutes.

Pain d'Epices

JEANNIE COOPERMAN | SANBORNTON, NEW HAMPSHIRE

"My mother came over from Brittany in 1923 when she was just 20 years old. She had no connections in this country, but she had studied English, so she thought she would be able to manage. She had a terrible time at first because she couldn't understand American English. Fortunately, she had met someone on the ship who helped her get a job as a nanny to a nice family. This recipe was from her aunt. My mother and her four brothers had been orphaned, so her aunt gave up her teaching career in Paris to raise them. She was a very good cook who always made sure that pain d'epices was in the house, and my mother followed this same practice. When I raised my own family, I often kept pain d'epices, by then called 'marmalade cake,' on hand." Though Jeannie titles her recipe Pain d'Epices, her family definitely put their own spin on this traditional French baked good. A classic recipe will include rye flour and a generous mix of spices (the name is often translated "gingerbread"), neither of which are included here. Nevertheless, her recipe was clearly inspired by tradition, as pain d'epices incorporates a significant amount of honey. The bread is often served with a slather of marmalade, and Jeannie's recipe cleverly incorporates orange marmalade right into the batter itself.

MAKES TWO 8-INCH LOAVES

- 2 cups whole milk
- ½ cup orange marmalade
- ½ cup honey
- 4 cups all-purpose flour
- 2 cups sugar
- 1 teaspoon baking soda
- 1 teaspoon salt

1. Adjust oven rack to middle position and heat oven to 350 degrees. Grease two 8½ by 4½-inch loaf pans.

2. Bring milk, marmalade, and honey to gentle simmer in saucepan over medium heat, stirring often, until marmalade has melted. Remove from heat and let cool until just warm (about 110 degrees).

3. Whisk flour, sugar, baking soda, and salt together in large bowl. Gently fold milk mixture into flour mixture until just combined (do not overmix).

4. Scrape batter into prepared pans and smooth tops. Bake until golden brown and toothpick inserted into center comes out clean, about 1 hour, rotating pans halfway through baking.

5. Let loaves cool in pans for 15 minutes. Remove loaves from pans and let cool completely on wire rack before serving.

Notes from the Test Kitchen

The orange-honey flavor of this sweet loaf made it hard to resist. The original recipe had too much batter for a single loaf pan, so we adapted it to yield two loaves. Jeannie called for resting the batter for three hours before baking. We found that this step didn't make any difference in texture or flavor, so we baked it right after mixing.

Swedish Coffee Bread

WILL LAMPE | POMPTON PLAINS, NEW JERSEY

"My grandmother, May Broady Lampe, was born in 1894 and made everything she cooked from scratch. Breakfast was always my favorite meal: scrambled eggs, bacon, coffee, and this wonderful Swedish Coffee Bread, baked fresh that morning and still warm from the oven. I'd take a thick slice and butter it. The combination of warm bread, cardamom, and cinnamon made for a wonderful treat." In Sweden, baking an assortment of breads and sweets is a Christmastime tradition, and this just slightly sweet, braided loaf, usually served with tea or strong coffee, is one of the many favorites. Cardamom has been a favored spice among Scandinavians since Viking times, so it's not surprising that its warm, complex flavor is one highlight of this buttery, rich bread. Will's grandmother's recipe also includes cinnamon, which serves as a nice complement. And while many braided Swedish coffee bread recipes bake the dough free-form (much like a loaf of challah), this version calls for baking the braided dough in a loaf pan. "It's even good the next day, sliced and toasted," notes Will. "My sister makes this recipe using her bread machine, and says it makes it very easy. However you make it, this bread is amazing!"

MAKES TWO 8-INCH LOAVES

1½	cups whole milk
½	cup water
½	cup plus 2 tablespoons sugar
6	tablespoons vegetable shortening or unsalted butter, plus 2 tablespoons melted butter for brushing
2	teaspoons ground cardamom
1	tablespoon salt
2	large eggs
6½–7	cups all-purpose flour
4	teaspoons instant or rapid-rise yeast
1½	teaspoons ground cinnamon

1. Bring milk, water, ½ cup sugar, shortening, cardamom, and salt to gentle simmer in saucepan over medium heat, stirring often. Whisk to melt any remaining pieces of shortening, then remove from heat and let cool until just warm (about 110 degrees). Whisk in eggs.

2. Combine 6½ cups flour and yeast in stand mixer fitted with dough hook. With mixer on low speed, slowly add milk mixture and let dough come together, about 2 minutes.

3. Increase mixer speed to medium-low and knead until dough is smooth and elastic, about 8 minutes. If after 4 minutes dough seems very sticky, add remaining ½ cup flour,

(Continued on page 104)

2 tablespoons at a time, until dough clears sides of bowl but sticks to bottom.

4. Turn dough out onto lightly floured counter and knead by hand to form smooth, round ball. Place dough in large, lightly greased bowl and cover with greased plastic wrap. Let rise in warm place until doubled in size, about 1 hour. Punch dough down and let rise again for 30 minutes.

5. Grease two 8½ by 4½-inch loaf pans. Turn dough onto lightly floured counter, divide into two equal pieces, and cover with greased plastic wrap. Following photos, divide and roll one piece of dough evenly into three, 18-inch-long ropes. Braid ropes together and pinch ends to secure. Nestle braid into prepared pan, tucking under pinched ends. Repeat with remaining piece of dough.

6. Cover loaves with greased plastic wrap and let rise until nearly doubled in size and dough barely springs back when poked with knuckle, 45 to 75 minutes.

7. Adjust oven rack to middle position and heat oven to 425 degrees. Brush loaves with melted butter and sprinkle with remaining 2 tablespoons sugar and cinnamon. Bake for 5 minutes, then reduce oven temperature to 350 degrees and continue to bake until golden brown and center of loaf registers 200 degrees on instant-read thermometer, 30 to 35 minutes longer, rotating pans halfway through baking.

8. Let loaves cool in pans for 15 minutes. Remove loaves from pans and let cool completely on wire rack before serving.

Notes from the Test Kitchen

This braided loaf is a real looker, and the fact Will's grandmother used a loaf pan was a new twist to us (the majority of the recipes we found made free-form loaves). We scaled the recipe down to make just two loaves rather than four since we wanted to polish all of it off while fresh, and in lieu of harder-to-find cardamom seeds, we came up with an equivalent amount of ground cardamom.

BRAIDING SWEDISH COFFEE BREAD

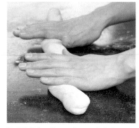
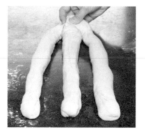
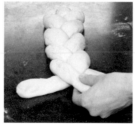

1. Divide the dough into 3 equal pieces and roll each piece into an even 18-inch rope.

2. Line the 3 ropes up side by side and pinch the top ends together to seal.

3. Take the dough rope on the right and lay it over the center rope. Take the dough rope on the left and lay it over the center rope. Repeat until the ropes of dough are entirely braided. Pinch the ends together.

4. Transfer the loaf to a greased loaf pan, tucking ends underneath.

German New Year's Pretzel

LINDA SCHENK | MILAN, OHIO

"Although this is not an original family recipe," writes Linda, "it has been a traditional favorite of our family for as long as I can remember. Every New Year's it was important to my father that we have the Feddersen Bakery's German New Year's Pretzel with our holiday meal. It is believed the New Year's pretzel will bring good luck throughout the New Year." The traditional German New Year's pretzel is a far cry from the familiar supermarket bagged hard pretzels or the large soft pretzels you get at a ballpark; it's a yeasted coffee cake that has been shaped into a pretzel and brushed with a sweet glaze. In Germany and in areas in the United States where a large number of German immigrants settled, you'll find that this bread is a traditional gift that symbolizes good luck and fortune, just as Linda notes. "This recipe was first published in Ohio's *Sandusky Register* newspaper in 1945, and the Grahl family who ran the Feddersen Bakery decided to produce the pretzels at New Year's time. The pretzels have been a popular holiday tradition in this area ever since. In 2007, the original baker, Mr. Thomsen, passed away, and the bakery closed. The family did not want the recipe to be lost so it was published in the *Sandusky Register* once again. The Grahl family allowed others to keep the tradition and recipe alive for many years to come."

MAKES 2 LARGE LOAVES

DOUGH

- 1 cup whole milk, warmed (110 degrees)
- 3 large eggs
- ⅓ cup water, warmed (110 degrees)
- 4 tablespoons (½ stick) unsalted butter, melted and cooled
- 6–6½ cups all-purpose flour
- ½ cup granulated sugar
- 2 envelopes (4½ teaspoons) instant or rapid-rise yeast
- 2 teaspoons salt
- 1 teaspoon ground mace
- 1 large egg beaten with 1 tablespoon water, for brushing

GLAZE

- 1¾ cups confectioners' sugar
- ¼ cup whole milk
- ¼ teaspoon almond extract (optional)
- Pinch salt

(Continued on page 106)

1. FOR THE DOUGH: Whisk milk, eggs, water, and melted butter together in liquid measuring cup. Combine 6 cups flour, granulated sugar, yeast, salt, and mace in stand mixer fitted with dough hook. With mixer on low speed, slowly add milk mixture and let dough come together, about 2 minutes.

2. Increase mixer speed to medium-low and knead until dough is smooth and elastic, about 8 minutes. If after 4 minutes dough seems very sticky, add remaining ½ cup flour, 2 tablespoons at a time, until dough clears sides of bowl but sticks to bottom.

3. Turn dough out onto lightly floured counter and knead by hand to form smooth, round ball. Place dough in large, lightly greased bowl and cover with greased plastic wrap. Let rise in warm place until doubled in size, 1 to 1½ hours.

4. Line two rimmed baking sheets with parchment paper. Turn dough out onto lightly floured counter, divide into two equal pieces, and cover with greased plastic wrap. Roll one piece of dough into 36-inch rope, about 1¼ inches thick, then transfer to prepared baking sheet and shape into large pretzel following photos. Repeat with remaining piece of dough.

5. Cover pretzels with greased plastic wrap and let rise in warm place until nearly doubled in size and dough barely springs back when poked with knuckle, 45 to 75 minutes.

6. Adjust oven racks to upper-middle and lower-middle positions and heat oven to 350 degrees. Brush pretzels with beaten egg mixture and bake until deep golden brown and centers of pretzels register 200 degrees on instant-read thermometer, 30 to 35 minutes,

switching and rotating baking sheets halfway through baking. Let pretzels cool on baking sheets for 15 minutes.

7. FOR THE GLAZE: Whisk confectioners' sugar, milk, almond extract (if using), and salt together in bowl. Brush glaze evenly over warm pretzels. Transfer glazed pretzels to wire rack and let cool completely before serving.

Notes from the Test Kitchen

We loved the tradition behind this bread, and the subtle, unusual flavor from mace made it a real winner. We made a few tweaks to make the recipe more manageable. The dough in the original was more batterlike and very tricky to roll out, so we increased the flour by a fair amount to make it easier. Linda's glaze was simply cornstarch and water; we opted to use an egg wash for a golden sheen followed by a glaze with confectioners' sugar, which we found in other similar recipes.

FORMING A PRETZEL

1. After rolling the dough into an even 36-inch rope, transfer the rope to a parchment-lined baking sheet. Cross and twist the ends of the dough to form a large pretzel shape.

2. Tuck the ends under the dough at about the 5 o'clock position and the 7 o'clock position to secure.

Grandma's Sweet Kuchen

GAIL LIGHTNER | LEXINGTON, KENTUCKY

Kuchen covers a variety of breads and cakes in Germany, and Gail's recipe, somewhere between cake and bread, nicely fits in the group. "Grandma Justice raised her children during the first half of the 20th century in southern Ohio. Bread baking day began Saturdays at 4 a.m., producing six loaves of plain bread and one pan of kuchen. Indents in the dough received a sweet custard mixture forming pools of egg-y sweetness, then cinnamon sugar was sprinkled on top, along with dots of butter, and finally it was baked with the loaves. The last of Grandma's children, Aunt Dot, is 95. She has lived in Grandma's house for 25 years. On Christmas Eve 2006 one of her children and I stayed with her, and on Christmas morning I made kuchen. As we savored the warm, yeasty delight later that Christmas Day, we remembered Grandma."

SERVES 10 TO 12

1⅔	cups water, warmed (110 degrees)
2	tablespoons vegetable shortening or unsalted butter, melted and cooled
4½–5	cups all-purpose flour
½	cup plus 2 tablespoons sugar
1	envelope (2¼ teaspoons) instant or rapid-rise yeast
1½	teaspoons salt
2½	cups whole milk
2	large eggs
1	teaspoon vanilla extract
2	teaspoons ground cinnamon
4	tablespoons (½ stick) unsalted butter, cut into ½-inch pieces

1. Whisk water and melted shortening together in liquid measuring cup. Combine 4½ cups flour, 1 tablespoon sugar, yeast, and salt in stand mixer fitted with dough hook. With mixer on low speed, slowly add water mixture and let dough come together, about 2 minutes.

2. Increase mixer speed to medium-low and knead until dough is smooth and elastic, about 8 minutes. If after 4 minutes dough seems very sticky, add remaining ½ cup flour, 2 tablespoons at a time, until dough clears sides of bowl but sticks to bottom.

3. Turn dough out onto lightly floured counter and knead by hand to form smooth, round ball. Place dough in large, lightly greased bowl and cover with greased plastic wrap. Let rise in warm place until doubled in size, 1 to 1½ hours.

4. Grease 13 by 9-inch baking pan. Press dough into prepared baking pan, cover with greased plastic wrap, and let rise in warm place until nearly doubled in size and dough barely springs back when poked with knuckle, 45 to 75 minutes.

5. Adjust oven rack to middle position and heat oven to 375 degrees. Whisk milk, eggs, vanilla, and ½ cup more sugar together in liquid measuring cup. Press shallow indentations into dough with finger, spaced 2 inches apart. Slowly pour custard over top, allowing excess to flow over side of dough and settle in bottom of pan. Sprinkle with remaining 1 tablespoon sugar and cinnamon, then dot with butter. Bake until custard is set and center of bread registers 200 degrees on instant-read thermometer, 25 to 30 minutes.

6. Let bread cool in pan for at least 30 minutes. Serve slightly warm or at room temperature.

Christmas Stollen

JOANNE E. TOWNSEND | MONTAGUE, MICHIGAN

In Germany, holiday baking is pretty much defined by Christmas stollen, a yeast-risen dough packed with nuts, citrus zest, and rum-soaked dried fruits. It can take days to prepare. Loaves are liberally coated with butter and sugar, which means they not only taste great but also keep well. Stollen goes all the way back to the 15th century, and the oldest versions are typically dense and heavy. Joanne's recipe has a lot of appeal because it incorporates all the traditional add-ins, yet the bread itself is a modern, lighter take. She also prefers to wrap the bread around a single layer of the fruit-and-nut filling, rather than incorporate these ingredients throughout the loaf like most stollen recipes. "I'm half-German, half-Dutch, and I watched a great German baker make this bread/dessert," she writes. "He would give a loaf to my family at Christmas, and when I married and moved away, I read about its history and came up with my own version. It's not Christmas without it, and I make many so I can share them for a special treat. Once you make this, I am sure you'll make it again, and if you're of German descent, it may become a tradition in your families!" Make sure to have a few toothpicks on hand to help hold the seam shut during baking.

MAKES TWO LARGE STOLLEN

FILLING

- ¾ cup candied fruit mix
- ⅓ cup raisins
- ⅓ cup currants
- ⅓ cup candied cherries, halved
- ¼ cup rum
- ⅔ cup slivered almonds

DOUGH

- 11 tablespoons unsalted butter, melted and cooled, plus 5 tablespoons melted butter for brushing
- 3 large eggs
- ½ cup whole milk, warmed (110 degrees)
- ½ cup water, warmed (110 degrees)
- ½ teaspoon almond extract
- ½ teaspoon lemon extract
- 6½–7 cups all-purpose flour
- ½ cup plus 2 tablespoons granulated sugar
- 1 tablespoon grated lemon zest
- 1 envelope (2¼ teaspoons) instant or rapid-rise yeast
- 1 teaspoon salt
  Confectioners' sugar, for dusting

1. FOR THE FILLING: Combine candied fruit mix, raisins, currants, cherries, and rum in large bowl, cover, and refrigerate for at least 12 hours, or up to 1 day. Stir in almonds.

2. FOR THE DOUGH: Mix 11 tablespoons melted butter, eggs, milk, water, almond extract, and lemon extract together in liquid measuring cup. Combine 6½ cups flour, ½ cup granulated sugar, lemon zest, yeast, and salt in stand mixer fitted with dough hook. With mixer on low speed, slowly add milk mixture and let dough come together, about 2 minutes.

3. Increase mixer speed to medium-low and knead until dough is smooth and elastic, about 8 minutes. If after 4 minutes dough seems very sticky, add remaining ½ cup flour,

2 tablespoons at a time, until dough clears sides of bowl but sticks to bottom.

4. Turn dough out onto lightly floured counter and knead by hand to form smooth, round ball. Divide dough into two equal pieces and cover with greased plastic wrap. Roll one piece of dough into 10 by 8-inch rectangle, about ¼ inch thick, with short side facing you. Following photos, sprinkle half of candied fruit mixture over top half of dough, leaving ¾-inch border around edge. Brush top edge with water, then fold bottom half of dough over filling and press on edge firmly to seal.

5. Rotate fruit-filled dough so short side faces you, then reroll into 10 by 8-inch rectangle, about ½ inch thick. Brush with one-third of the melted butter and sprinkle with 1 tablespoon granulated sugar. Fold left and right sides of dough into middle, overlapping them slightly. Press seam together and secure it with toothpicks, then pat ends of loaf to even them. Repeat with remaining piece of dough, remaining dried fruit mixture, another one-third of the melted butter, and remaining 1 tablespoon granulated sugar.

6. Transfer loaves, seam side up, to parchment-lined rimmed baking sheet, spaced 2 inches apart. Brush loaves with more melted butter, cover loosely with plastic wrap, and let rise in warm place until nearly doubled in size and dough barely springs back when poked with knuckle, 45 to 75 minutes.

7. Adjust oven rack to middle position and heat oven to 350 degrees. Bake loaves until golden brown and centers of loaves register 200 degrees on instant-read thermometer, about 45 minutes, rotating baking sheet halfway through baking.

8. Brush freshly baked loaves with remaining melted butter and dust liberally with confectioners' sugar until well coated. Let loaves cool on baking sheet for 15 minutes. Transfer loaves to wire rack, remove toothpicks, and let cool completely before serving.

Notes from the Test Kitchen

Joanne's lighter version of stollen was a welcome change to the common leaden loaves, and the fact that it required only one rise meant it didn't take days to prepare. She didn't specify an amount of flour; we found that 6½ to 7 cups was about right. Though Joanne, as specified in most old-fashioned recipes, shaped the loaves to represent the baby Jesus in swaddling clothes, we simplified the process so that the loaves would come together like making a burrito, with the sides and ends folded over. You can find candied cherries in deli containers at most supermarkets in the same aisle as the nuts.

SHAPING CHRISTMAS STOLLEN

1. After rolling the dough into a rectangle, sprinkle half of the filling over the top half of the dough, leaving a ¾-inch border around the edge.

2. Brush the top edge of the dough with water, then fold the bottom half over the filling and press to seal. Rotate so the new short side faces you.

3. After rerolling the filled dough into a 10 by 8-inch rectangle, fold the left and right thirds to the middle and overlap.

4. Press the seam together and secure it with toothpicks. Pat the ends of the loaf to even them.

BLACK CURRANT TIRAMISU

Cakes Plain and Simple

Pennsylvania Dutch Shoofly Cake 112

Grandma Lillian's Raisin Cake 114

Nonna's Breakfast and Dessert Farina Cake 115

Tomato Soup Cake 116

Cafeteria Lady Cake 118

German Plum Cake 119

Mom's Marble Cake 120

Scripture Cake 122

Cookie Top Cake 125

Mudder's Fresh Apple Cake 126

Nora Lee's Ambrosia Cake 127

Butternut-Pecan Cake with Cranberry–Cream Cheese Frosting 129

Prince of Wales Cake 131

Grated Bread and Chocolate Cake 133

Black Currant Tiramisu 136

Pennsylvania Dutch Shoofly Cake

ANGELA SPENGLER | CLOVIS, NEW MEXICO

You've probably heard of shoofly pie, an old-fashioned classic made with a sweet, simple filling of molasses, sugar, butter, and water and a crumb topping (the filling is what allegedly earned the pie its name, as the sugar attracted flies). So it's probably not surprising that Angela's recipe is a close cousin to the pie. Both have strong Amish-country roots, and, like the pie, this cake features a big, bold molasses flavor and a crumb topping. "The Pennsylvania Dutch are a very prominent part of the culture of the Lancaster area of central Pennsylvania," writes Angela. "Many expressions, traditions, and, of course, food of the Amish have made their way from the Pennsylvania Dutch community out to the rest of us (or, as the Amish say, 'to the English'). Shoofly Cake is a very common dessert in my hometown. I never realized that it was actually a very local specialty until moving outside of Pennsylvania. My grandmother made a delicious shoofly cake and my aunt still frequently graces the sideboard with one for a birthday celebration. It is homey, distinct, and so moist. I grew up eating this treat and consider myself fortunate to have done so."

SERVES 15 TO 18

- 4 cups all-purpose flour
- 1 cup sugar
- 1 tablespoon baking soda
- ½ teaspoon salt
- 16 tablespoons (2 sticks) unsalted butter, cut into chunks and softened
- 2 cups water
- 1¼ cups molasses

1. Adjust oven rack to middle position and heat oven to 350 degrees. Grease 13 by 9-inch baking pan.

2. Whisk flour, sugar, baking soda, and salt together in large bowl. Add butter and cut into flour mixture using fork (or two butter knives) until evenly distributed and mixture is moist and crumbly; measure out and reserve 1 cup crumb mixture for topping.

3. Bring water and molasses to simmer in saucepan and cook, stirring often, until molasses is dissolved, 1 to 2 minutes. Let molasses mixture cool slightly, then stir into flour mixture until just combined.

4. Scrape batter into prepared pan, smooth top, and gently tap pan on counter to settle batter. Sprinkle reserved crumb mixture over batter and bake until light golden brown and toothpick inserted into center comes out with a few moist crumbs attached, 30 to 40 minutes, rotating pan halfway through baking. Let cake cool completely in pan, about 2 hours, before serving.

Notes from the Test Kitchen

Angela called for baking molasses, an ingredient that early recipes also specified and is sold by Amish purveyors (these purveyors also offered "eating molasses"). To get around having to make a special order, we switched to regular unsulfured mild (light) molasses (we also tested robust, dark molasses, which gave us a good, but less preferred cake). We liked the contrasting texture of the crumb topping but cut back a little from the 2 cups Angela used.

Grandma Lillian's Raisin Cake

ROSE M. GRIFFITH | PITTSBURGH, PENNSYLVANIA

"It was the morning before the Fourth of July and everyone was preparing for our Griffith family picnic," Rose recounts. "The smells from Grandma's kitchen wafted out through the open window as I reached the back door. I shut my eyes and took a deep, longing breath of the aroma of fresh baked cake. Opening my eyes, I saw Grandpa walk by the screened porch door and see me waiting there in my pink gingham shirt and solid pink shorts. 'Here comes Trouble, Mum,' he called. 'Better hide the cake!' I opened the door and came inside to be enveloped in a rib-crushing hug. This holiday was memorable because most other times Grandma was a stickler for waiting for the party before anyone could eat anything. I don't know what she saw in my eyes when I walked in that time, but, without a word, she cut me the corner piece and served it up. It was still warm and the raisins nearly melted in my mouth. The cake was always moist and the right amount of sweet. I still don't like raisins in any food except cake."

SERVES 15 TO 18

3	cups water
1½	cups raisins
4	cups all-purpose flour
1	tablespoon baking soda
1	teaspoon baking powder
1	teaspoon ground cinnamon
1	teaspoon ground nutmeg
½	teaspoon salt
⅛	teaspoon ground cloves
8	tablespoons vegetable shortening or unsalted butter
2	cups sugar
1	cup walnuts, chopped

1. Adjust oven rack to middle position and heat oven to 350 degrees. Grease 13 by 9-inch baking pan. Bring 2 cups water and raisins to boil in saucepan and cook, stirring occasionally, until raisins are softened and mixture measures 2 cups, about 5 minutes; set aside to cool slightly.

2. Whisk flour, baking soda, baking powder, cinnamon, nutmeg, salt, and cloves together in medium bowl. In large bowl, beat shortening and sugar together with electric mixer on medium speed until light and fluffy, 3 to 6 minutes. Reduce mixer speed to low and beat in one-third of flour mixture, followed by remaining 1 cup water. Repeat with half of remaining flour mixture and cooled raisin mixture. Beat in remaining flour mixture until just combined. Fold in walnuts.

3. Give batter final stir with rubber spatula to make sure it is thoroughly combined. Scrape batter into prepared pan, smooth top, and gently tap pan on counter to settle batter. Bake until golden brown and wooden skewer inserted into center comes out with a few moist crumbs attached, about 45 minutes, rotating pan halfway through baking. Let cake cool completely in pan, about 2 hours, before serving.

Notes from the Test Kitchen
We loved the old-fashioned simplicity of this recipe. We made only a few minor tweaks, cutting back on the cloves by ¼ teaspoon and adding a little salt for balance. If you want to dress it up a bit, you can dust this cake with confectioners' sugar.

Nonna's Breakfast and Dessert Farina Cake

MARY CANNICI | CLEARWATER BEACH, FLORIDA

"This recipe immigrated to this country from Sicily when Nonna was a little girl and her family came to Ellis Island," writes Mary. "It has been a part of the family, living in our recipe books, ever since. Ridiculously easy to make, it is always well received at any potluck, breakfast, or dinner table, equally enjoyed by the elderly, the newest babies, and everyone in between." Mary's grandmother's recipe is a cinnamon-dusted, puddinglike dessert that gets creaminess from ricotta, a slight heft from farina (a finely ground cereal grain), and richness from several eggs, which also help it set up into a nicely sliceable cake. Her recipe was likely inspired by two traditional Italian spoon desserts: semolina pudding, a dish similar to Nonna's recipe minus the ricotta (semolina is a grain more coarsely ground than farina), and ricotta pudding, also very similar to Nonna's, minus the grain. Mary notes that her Nonna enjoyed this dessert even when she was nearing 100 years old.

SERVES 15 TO 18

- 4 **cups whole milk**
- 1¼ **cups sugar**
- 8 **tablespoons (1 stick) unsalted butter, cut into chunks**
- 1 **cup farina**
- 2 **cups whole-milk ricotta cheese**
- 2 **teaspoons vanilla extract**
- 6 **large eggs, lightly beaten**
- 1 **teaspoon ground cinnamon**

1. Adjust oven rack to middle position and heat oven to 350 degrees. Grease 13 by 9-inch baking pan.

2. Bring milk, sugar, and butter to simmer in large saucepan and cook, stirring often, until butter is melted and sugar is dissolved, 1 to 2 minutes. Slowly whisk in farina until smooth. Off heat, stir in ricotta and vanilla. Let mixture cool slightly, then stir in beaten eggs until combined.

3. Scrape batter into prepared pan and smooth top. Sprinkle top with cinnamon and bake until toothpick inserted into center comes out clean, about 30 minutes, rotating pan halfway through baking. Let cake cool in pan for 10 minutes, then serve warm.

Notes from the Test Kitchen

This was the sort of soft and sweet, simple dessert we all agreed would go over well with children and adults alike. We didn't need to change much at all about Mary's recipe. To avoid the risk of curdling, we made sure to let the batter cool slightly before stirring in the eggs. Though Mary suggested serving it warm or cold, our tasters much preferred it warm.

Tomato Soup Cake

SANDRA PATENAUDE | LOWELL, MASSACHUSETTS

Using condensed soup in a quick casserole is a familiar shortcut; canned soup in a cake, however, is a lost technique. The subtle sweet-savory tomato flavor is a perfect complement to the spices here, and with cream cheese frosting, this cake is a sure winner. Tomato-based desserts from the 19th century (like one 1869 recipe we found for a bread pudding with canned tomatoes) were perhaps the inspiration for this recipe. It's hard to confirm who first thought of using condensed soup in a cake, but there's convincing evidence the idea came from the Campbell Soup Company. And as Sandra notes, "It's a great spice cake and no one knows the secret ingredient!"

SERVES 15 TO 18

CAKE

- 3 cups all-purpose flour
- 1 tablespoon baking powder
- 1 teaspoon baking soda
- 1 teaspoon ground cinnamon
- 1 teaspoon ground cloves
- 1 teaspoon ground nutmeg
- 1 (11-ounce) can condensed tomato soup
- ¾ cup water
- 3 large eggs
- 1¼ cups granulated sugar
- 16 tablespoons vegetable shortening or unsalted butter, cut into chunks and softened

FROSTING

- 1 (8-ounce) package cream cheese, softened
- 4 teaspoons whole milk
- 1 teaspoon vanilla extract
- 4 cups confectioners' sugar

1. FOR THE CAKE: Adjust oven rack to middle position and heat oven to 375 degrees. Grease 13 by 9-inch baking pan, then line bottom with parchment paper.

2. Whisk flour, baking powder, baking soda, cinnamon, cloves, and nutmeg together in bowl. In separate bowl, whisk tomato soup, water, and eggs together.

3. In large bowl, beat granulated sugar and shortening together with electric mixer on medium speed until light and fluffy, 3 to 6 minutes. Reduce mixer speed to low and beat in one-third of flour mixture, followed by half of soup mixture. Repeat with half of remaining flour mixture and remaining soup mixture. Beat in remaining flour mixture until just combined.

4. Give batter final stir with rubber spatula to make sure it is thoroughly combined. Scrape batter into prepared pan, smooth top, and gently tap pan on counter to settle batter. Bake until golden brown and toothpick inserted into center comes out with a few moist crumbs attached, 30 to 35 minutes, rotating pan half-way through baking. Let cake cool completely in pan, about 2 hours.

5. FOR THE FROSTING: Beat cream cheese, milk, and vanilla together in large bowl with electric mixer on medium-high speed until smooth, 2 to 4 minutes. Reduce mixer speed to medium-low, slowly add confectioners' sugar, and beat until smooth, 4 to 6 minutes. Increase mixer speed to medium-high and beat until frosting is light and fluffy, 4 to 6 minutes. Spread frosting evenly over top of cake and serve.

Notes from the Test Kitchen

We didn't need to change a thing. Do not use low-fat cream cheese; it can cause the frosting to separate and will be too thin to properly spread.

Cafeteria Lady Cake

BRENDA KELLER | UHRICHSVILLE, OHIO

"Over 40 years ago my mother asked what kind of cake I wanted for my birthday, 'yellow or chocolate?' I replied, 'I want cake like the cafeteria lady makes.' Neither yellow nor chocolate, the Cafeteria Lady Cake was dense with grated apples, raisins, and nuts, with a glaze that enveloped every crumb with moistness. The only problem was that my mother had no idea what I was talking about. My birthday cake was yellow with homemade buttercream and pink flower decorations. Upon returning to school, I passed through the cafeteria line and informed the 'cafeteria lady' that my mom made good birthday cake but not as good as her cake. She laughed and said she would have to give my mom lessons. Before the end of the week the cafeteria lady gave me a sheet of yellow paper. She said to give it to my mom so she could make me a cake next year. I have made the cake often. Nothing beats the "Cafeteria Lady Cake."

SERVES 15 TO 18

CAKE

- 3 cups all-purpose flour
- 1 teaspoon baking soda
- 1 teaspoon ground cinnamon
- ½ teaspoon salt
- 2 cups sugar
- 1½ cups vegetable oil
- 2 large eggs
- 1 teaspoon vanilla extract
- 3 apples, peeled and grated
- 1 cup walnuts, chopped
- 1 cup raisins

GLAZE

- ½ cup buttermilk
- 8 tablespoons (1 stick) unsalted butter, cut into chunks
- 1 cup sugar
- 1 teaspoon vanilla extract
- ½ teaspoon salt

1. FOR THE CAKE: Adjust oven rack to middle position and heat oven to 325 degrees. Grease 13 by 9-inch baking pan.

2. Whisk flour, baking soda, cinnamon, and salt together in large bowl. In separate bowl whisk sugar, oil, eggs, and vanilla together until sugar is mostly dissolved. Stir sugar mixture into flour mixture until just combined. Fold in apples, walnuts, and raisins.

3. Scrape batter into prepared pan, smooth top, and gently tap pan on counter to settle batter. Bake until golden brown and toothpick inserted into center comes out with a few moist crumbs attached, 50 to 60 minutes, rotating pan halfway through baking. Let cake cool in pan for 10 minutes.

4. FOR THE GLAZE: Meanwhile, bring buttermilk, butter, sugar, vanilla, and salt to simmer in saucepan, and cook, stirring often, until butter is melted and sugar is dissolved, 1 to 2 minutes. While cake is still warm, poke holes all over top with wooden skewer. Slowly pour glaze evenly over cake. Let cake sit until cooled completely and glaze has been absorbed, about 2 hours. Serve.

Notes from the Test Kitchen

Brenda's recipe called for 3 to 4 cups grated apples; we settled on 3 apples as the right amount. Make sure to grate the apples on the large holes of a box grater.

German Plum Cake (Deutscher Pflaumenkuchen)

BARBARA LANKE | PITTSBURGH, PENNSYLVANIA

"My Grandmother Grossie learned to cook from her mother, my great-grandmother, Louisa Johanna Lichauer, who raised 12 children after arriving in Pittsburgh from Bavaria in 1880 with her husband, Johann, a carpet weaver. Recipes were passed to her daughters by observation. Ingredients were memorized, as were the measurements. Dessert was a luxury, so when the plums were ripe, everyone eagerly anticipated *pflaumenkuchen*, which was *eine festlickeit* ('a treat')!" Common throughout Germany and Austria, pflaumenkuchen is a yellow cake topped with plums and perhaps followed by a sprinkling of sugar or a streusel topping (Barbara's grandmother opted for a cinnamon streusel). Barbara notes about her family's recipe, "Pflaumenkuchen conveys love of family from one generation to the next, and the next, and the next."

SERVES 9

TOPPING
- ¾ **cup sugar**
- ½ **cup all-purpose flour**
- 1 **teaspoon ground cinnamon**
- 4 **tablespoons (½ stick) unsalted butter, cut into chunks and softened**

CAKE
- 1½ **cups all-purpose flour**
- ⅓ **cup sugar**
- 2 **teaspoons baking powder**
- ½ **teaspoon salt**
- 4 **tablespoons (½ stick) unsalted butter, cut into small chunks**
- ½ **cup buttermilk**
- 1 **large egg**
- ½ **teaspoon vanilla extract**
- 2 **pounds ripe Italian plums, halved and pitted**
  Heavy cream, for serving

1. FOR THE TOPPING: Pulse sugar, flour, and cinnamon together in food processor until combined. Scatter butter over top and pulse until mixture resembles coarse crumbs, about 10 pulses. Let sit at room temperature until needed.

2. FOR THE CAKE: Adjust oven rack to middle position and heat oven to 425 degrees. Grease 8-inch square cake pan.

3. Process flour, sugar, baking powder, and salt in food processor until combined. Scatter butter over top and process until mixture resembles coarse crumbs, about 10 pulses. Transfer mixture to bowl. In separate bowl, whisk buttermilk, egg, and vanilla together. Stir buttermilk mixture into flour mixture until just combined.

4. Scrape batter into prepared pan, smooth top, and gently tap pan on counter to settle batter. Arrange plums, skin side down, on top of batter. Sprinkle topping over plums. Bake until golden brown and toothpick inserted into center comes out with a few moist crumbs attached, about 30 minutes, rotating pan halfway through baking. Let cake cool in pan for 10 minutes. Drizzle individual portions with heavy cream and serve warm.

Notes from the Test Kitchen
We made only a few tweaks to Barbara's grandmother's recipe, adjusting the topping because we found the original a little dry. This recipe works best with ripe Italian plums. If substituting red or black plums, use an equal weight of plums, but cut them into eighths.

Mom's Marble Cake

DAWN WRIGHT | RAYMOND, WASHINGTON

"As a child, I was not allowed into my Polish mother's kitchen. Her kitchen was her sanctuary, and this cake was her crown jewel. It won repeated prizes at county fairs and local cook-offs," notes Dawn, a fact that isn't too surprising once you've had a taste. Most often, marble cakes are a combination of chocolate and plain pound cake batters, but Dawn's mother's recipe, with whipped egg whites folded in and plenty of baking powder, has a great light and airy texture. And because she uses unsweetened chocolate, the flavor of the chocolate portion is pure and rich. "I was also not allowed to have the batter," Dawn adds about the days when her mother made this cake. "But I would sneak some, and if I was very good, I might get to have the spoon or spatula. What heaven that was! I remember the light, sweet batter, and the smell of the kitchen when it baked, and the look of pride when the grand prize ribbons were displayed in the house for the family to see. My mother died right after I graduated from high school. I sifted through Mom's recipes, marveling at her abilities in the kitchen. Many years later, as a young wife, it dawned on me that I didn't have to just look, I might try to bake too!"

SERVES 12

- 2 ounces unsweetened chocolate, chopped
- 1 cup water
- 1¾ cups granulated sugar
- ¼ teaspoon baking soda
- 2 cups all-purpose flour
- 1 tablespoon baking powder
- 1 teaspoon salt
- 7 large eggs, separated, room temperature
- ½ cup vegetable oil
- 2 teaspoons vanilla extract
- ½ teaspoon cream of tartar
  Confectioners' sugar, for dusting

1. Adjust oven rack to lowest position and heat oven to 375 degrees. Following photos on page 121, line bottom of 16-cup tube pan with parchment paper but do not grease.

2. Microwave chocolate, ¼ cup water, and ¼ cup granulated sugar in large bowl, stirring often, until melted and smooth, 1 to 2 minutes. Stir in baking soda and let mixture cool to room temperature, 15 to 20 minutes.

3. Whisk flour, baking powder, salt, and remaining 1½ cups granulated sugar together in large bowl. Whisk separated egg yolks, oil, vanilla, and remaining ¾ cup water together in separate bowl, then stir into flour mixture until just combined.

4. In another large bowl, whip separated egg whites and cream of tartar together with electric mixer on medium-low speed until foamy, about 1 minute. Increase mixer speed to medium-high and continue to whip egg whites to stiff peaks, 2 to 4 minutes.

5. Fold one-third of whipped egg whites into batter until almost no white streaks remain. Fold in remaining whipped egg whites until just incorporated. Transfer half of batter to bowl with cooled chocolate mixture and fold to combine.

6. Scrape yellow batter into prepared pan, then top with chocolate batter. Run butter knife through batter to create swirls, then smooth top. Wipe any drops of batter off sides of pan and gently tap pan on counter to settle batter. Bake for 15 minutes, then reduce oven temperature to 325 degrees and continue to bake until golden brown and wooden skewer inserted into center comes out clean, about 45 minutes, rotating pan halfway through baking.

7. Invert tube pan over large metal kitchen funnel or neck of sturdy bottle (or, if your pan has "feet" that rise above top edge of pan, simply let cake rest upside down). Let cake cool completely, upside down, about 2 hours.

8. Run small knife around edge of cake to loosen. Gently tap pan upside down on counter to release cake. Peel off parchment, then turn cake right side up onto serving platter. Dust cake with confectioners' sugar and serve.

Notes from the Test Kitchen

The lightness of Dawn's cake made it all too easy for tasters to eat more than one slice. We added a parchment-paper liner to the bottom of the tube pan to make sure the cake didn't stick, and instead of adding the batter to the pan in four layers, as Dawn's recipe called for, we added it in two to make this step simpler, and we were still able to create the right marbled effect.

MAKING MOM'S MARBLE CAKE

1. To ensure that the cake can be easily removed from the pan once baked, start by cutting a piece of parchment paper into a ring that just fits inside the tube pan, then place the parchment in the bottom of the pan.

2. After preparing both the yellow and chocolate batters, pour the yellow batter into the prepared pan, then top it with the chocolate. Run a butter knife through the batter to create swirls, then smooth the top.

Scripture Cake

CAMILLA SAULSBURY | NACOGDOCHES, TEXAS

"My maternal grandfather (we called him 'Father') was an Episcopal priest. He also happened to be an incredible baker," Camilla writes. "Of all the goodies he made, his Scripture Cake stood head and shoulders above all the rest. I have the yellowed piece of frayed paper, written in the hand of his grandmother, with the original recipe he used." The concept of Scripture Cake likely came from a church group, and published recipes began appearing in the 1890s in magazines like *Harper's Bazaar*. The idea was that slices of Scripture Cake could be sold by churches as a way to raise money, and instead of selling cake with a standard-issue copy of the recipe listing its ingredients and method, ingredients would be referenced by Bible verses. So instead of calling for six eggs, for example, the recipe listed six Job 39:14. Anyone who wanted to make the cake at home would have to know that this verse reads, "Which leaveth her eggs in the earth, and warmeth them in dust." Some Bible verses are more vague than others, so Scripture Cakes, while consistently a spiced pound cake, often varied on some ingredient details, such as the types of dried fruit or nuts added. Camilla's family recipe is also interesting because it starts in a cold oven, a 20th century technique used to save money on gas. Camilla writes, "Father made a few additions to the cake (cardamom, ginger, and coriander) after he and my grandmother traveled to the Holy Land in the early 1960s. My family has been making Scripture Cake at Christmas and Easter, and throughout the year, for 40 years. My mother added the thick, lemon-y glaze, inspired by the Meyer lemon tree we had in our backyard."

SERVES 12

CAKE

- 2½ cups all-purpose flour
- 2 teaspoons baking powder
- 2 teaspoons ground cinnamon
- 1½ teaspoons ground cardamom
- 1½ teaspoons ground ginger
- 1 teaspoon ground coriander
- 1 teaspoon salt
- 16 tablespoons (2 sticks) unsalted butter, cut into chunks and softened
- 2 cups packed dark brown sugar
- 1 cup granulated sugar
- ¼ cup olive oil
- 6 large eggs, room temperature
- 1 cup evaporated milk
- ⅔ cup golden raisins
- ⅔ cup dried figs, chopped
- ½ cup salted pistachios, chopped
- ½ cup sliced almonds, toasted

GLAZE

- 1¾ cups confectioners' sugar
- 3 tablespoons whole milk
- 1 tablespoon fresh lemon juice
- ½ cup salted pistachios, chopped (optional)

(Continued on page 124)

1. **FOR THE CAKE:** Grease 16-cup tube pan. Whisk flour, baking powder, cinnamon, cardamom, ginger, coriander, and salt together in bowl.

2. In large bowl, beat butter, brown sugar, granulated sugar, and oil together with electric mixer on medium speed until light and fluffy, 3 to 6 minutes. Beat in eggs, one at a time, until combined, about 30 seconds.

3. Reduce mixer speed to low and beat in one-third of flour mixture, followed by ½ cup evaporated milk. Repeat with half of remaining flour mixture and remaining ½ cup evaporated milk. Beat in remaining flour mixture until just combined. Fold in raisins, figs, pistachios, and almonds.

4. Give batter final stir with rubber spatula to make sure it is thoroughly combined. Scrape batter into prepared pan and smooth top. Wipe any drops of batter off sides of pan and gently tap pan on counter to settle batter. Adjust oven rack to lower-middle position and place cake on rack. Heat oven to 325 degrees and bake until wooden skewer inserted into center comes out with a few moist crumbs attached, 1½ to 2 hours, opening oven door only to rotate pan halfway through baking.

5. Let cake cool in pan for 10 minutes. Run small knife around edge of cake to loosen, then flip it out onto wire rack. Turn cake right side up and let it cool completely, about 2 hours.

6. **FOR THE GLAZE:** Whisk confectioners' sugar, milk, and lemon juice together in bowl and let sit until thickened, about 25 minutes. Drizzle glaze over top and sides of cake and sprinkle with pistachios (if using). Let glaze set before serving, about 25 minutes.

Notes from the Test Kitchen

Reading old versions of this recipe was like trying to crack a code, and we loved that this version relied on the old-fashioned cold-oven technique (we tried baking it in a preheated oven and it wasn't the same). Camilla's original recipe produced a cake that was a little heavy, so we cut back a bit on the flour as well as the butter, and we upped the oven temperature by 25 degrees and added more baking powder to get the cake to rise higher. We also tweaked the ingredients in her glaze so there was just enough drizzle over the cake for an appealing, decorative finish.

Cookie Top Cake

LINDA DEBENEDETTO | COLUMBIA, SOUTH CAROLINA

Linda's recipe may look and taste like a plain pound cake at first (and a good one at that), but one bite of its top crust, which has the buttery-crisp texture of a sugar cookie, and you'll realize it's like no other pound cake you've ever had. The cookie top seems to happen almost magically. There is nothing unusual about the way Linda makes the batter or pours it into the pan, but we have a hunch the cookie top is a result of the significant amount of baking powder she adds to the batter (by comparison, a traditional pound cake does not include any baking powder at all, and newer recipes might add only up to 1 teaspoon). Linda's great-grandmother taught her to cook, and "soon I will teach my granddaughter," Linda writes. "I am looking forward to her having such a warm and fuzzy memory of me too. As for the Cookie Top Cake, I have yet to find anything like it." Serve this cake with fresh berries and whipped cream.

SERVES 12

3	cups all-purpose flour
4½	teaspoons baking powder
½	teaspoon salt
1	cup heavy cream
5	large eggs
1	teaspoon almond extract
2¾	cups sugar
20	tablespoons (2½ sticks) unsalted butter, cut into chunks and softened

1. Adjust oven rack to middle position and heat oven to 350 degrees. Grease 16-cup tube pan.

2. Whisk flour, baking powder, and salt together in bowl. In separate bowl, whisk cream, eggs, and almond extract together. In large bowl, beat sugar and butter together with electric mixer on medium speed until light and fluffy, 3 to 6 minutes. Beat in cream mixture until combined, about 1 minute. Reduce mixer speed to low and slowly beat in flour mixture, in three additions, until just combined. Increase mixer speed to high and beat until smooth, about 3 minutes. (Batter will be very thick.)

3. Give batter final stir with rubber spatula to make sure it is thoroughly combined. Scrape batter into prepared pan and smooth top. Wipe any drops of batter off sides of pan and gently tap pan on counter to settle batter. Bake until golden brown and wooden skewer inserted into center comes out with a few moist crumbs attached, 50 to 60 minutes, rotating pan halfway through baking.

4. Let cake cool in pan for 10 minutes. Run small knife around edge of cake to loosen, then flip it out onto wire rack. Turn cake right side up and let it cool completely, about 2 hours, before serving.

Notes from the Test Kitchen

For easier shopping, we swapped out the self-rising flour in Linda's recipe for all-purpose flour, and upped the baking powder and salt to accommodate our change. We reduced the baking time from 70 minutes to 50 to 60 minutes, as the longer cooking time darkened the top of the cake too much.

Mudder's Fresh Apple Cake

MELANIE MCCASKILL | GERMANTOWN, TENNESSEE

For Melanie, and probably for most folks who grew up with parents and/or grandparents who loved to cook, "great old recipes are treasured memories. They evoke a smell and taste that take you back to your childhood." This recipe for a moist spice cake studded with pecans and chunks of apple is one that does just that for Melanie. "For as long as I can remember, my husband Jack's mother (Mudder) made this cake. I have taught my daughter Megan Page how to make this cake. Three generations of delicious love. Even though Mudder is no longer here, her fresh apple cake continues to make ongoing generations happy. Memories of gatherings past and present are just an added bonus. Is there anything better than family and wonderful food?"

SERVES 12

- 2½ cups all-purpose flour
- 2 teaspoons baking powder
- 1 teaspoon baking soda
- 1 teaspoon salt
- 1 teaspoon ground cinnamon
- ½ teaspoon ground nutmeg
- 2 cups sugar
- 1 cup vegetable oil
- 3 large eggs, room temperature
- 1 teaspoon vanilla extract
- 2 Granny Smith apples, peeled, cored, and cut into ¼-inch pieces
- 1 cup pecans, chopped

1. Adjust oven rack to middle position and heat oven to 350 degrees. Grease 16-cup tube pan.

2. Whisk flour, baking powder, baking soda, salt, cinnamon, and nutmeg together in bowl. In large bowl, beat sugar, oil, eggs, and vanilla together with electric mixer on medium speed until thick and glossy, about 2 minutes. Reduce mixer speed to low and slowly beat in flour mixture, in 3 additions, until just combined. Fold in apples and pecans.

3. Give batter final stir with rubber spatula to make sure it is thoroughly combined. Scrape batter into prepared pan and smooth top. Wipe any drops of batter off sides of pan and gently tap pan on counter to settle batter. Bake until wooden skewer inserted into center comes out with a few moist crumbs attached, 50 to 60 minutes, rotating pan halfway through baking.

4. Let cake cool in pan for 10 minutes. Run small knife around edge of cake to loosen, then flip it out onto wire rack. Turn cake right side up and let it cool completely, about 2 hours, before serving.

Notes from the Test Kitchen

We love baked apples with plenty of warm spices and nuts, so Melanie's recipe, which brings it all together in cake form, wasn't a hard sell for us. We didn't change a thing about her recipe.

Nora Lee's Ambrosia Cake

JANICE ELDER | CHARLOTTE, NORTH CAROLINA

"Just as certain as Santa bounding down the chimney with a new doll, I knew Christmas meant my mother would make her annual Ambrosia Cake," Janice writes. According to Greek mythology, ambrosia was the food of the gods, but it also has a more terrestrial connection. By the late 19th century, ambrosia was the name given to a popular American dessert, a sweet fruit salad typically made with oranges and shredded coconut, and nuts and other tropical fruits might be added. Janice's buttermilk pound cake, which incorporates orange zest, pecans, dates, and coconut and is drizzled with an orange syrup, was clearly inspired by the original American classic.

SERVES 12

CAKE

3½	cups all-purpose flour
1	teaspoon baking soda
½	teaspoon salt
½	cup buttermilk, room temperature
2	tablespoons grated fresh orange zest (2 oranges)
16	tablespoons (2 sticks) unsalted butter, cut into chunks and softened
2	cups sugar
4	large eggs, room temperature
1	cup pecans, chopped
1	cup pitted dates, chopped
1	cup sweetened shredded coconut

SYRUP

½	cup sugar
6	tablespoons orange juice

1. FOR THE CAKE: Adjust oven rack to lower-middle position and heat oven to 300 degrees. Grease 16-cup tube pan. Whisk flour, baking soda, and salt together in bowl. In separate bowl, combine buttermilk and orange zest.

2. In large bowl, beat butter and sugar together with electric mixer on medium speed until light and fluffy, 3 to 6 minutes. Beat in eggs, one at a time, until combined, about 30 seconds.

3. Reduce mixer speed to low and beat in one-third of flour mixture, followed by half of buttermilk mixture. Repeat with half of remaining flour mixture and remaining buttermilk mixture. Beat in remaining flour mixture until just combined. Fold in pecans, dates, and coconut.

4. Give batter final stir with rubber spatula to make sure it is thoroughly combined. Scrape batter into prepared pan and smooth top. Wipe any drops of batter off sides of pan and gently tap pan on counter to settle batter. Bake until wooden skewer inserted into center comes out with a few moist crumbs attached, 1 to 1½ hours, rotating pan halfway through baking. Let cake cool in pan for 10 minutes.

5. FOR THE SYRUP: Meanwhile, bring sugar and orange juice to gentle simmer in saucepan and cook, stirring often, until sugar is dissolved, 1 to 2 minutes. Run small knife around edge of cake to loosen, then flip it out onto wire rack. Turn cake right side up and poke top and sides with wooden skewer. Brush warm syrup all over cake. Let cake cool completely, about 2 hours, before serving.

Notes from the Test Kitchen

We liked the sweet orange flavor Janice's syrup lent, but it didn't soak into the cake as we had expected, so we reduced the amount and brushed it over the cake's top and sides instead.

Butternut-Pecan Cake with Cranberry–Cream Cheese Frosting

JUDY ARMSTRONG | PRAIRIEVILLE, LOUISIANA

"As a young child, I recall following my grandfather around in his garden 'to help' plant, weed, and pick vegetables. If I was especially well behaved, he would allow me to hold the reins of Dora, the mule, as they plowed the dirt and made new rows for new plants. I lovingly recall wise advice, gentle smiles, and loud laughs from when I spent my summer mornings side by side with my grandfather. We would pick the fresh vegetables, place them gently in the bushel basket, and bring them to my grandmother to prepare." Among the many things Judy's grandmother made was this rich butternut cake, Judy tells us. It is like a marriage between zucchini bread and carrot cake, with butternut squash baked into layers of a spice cake, flecked with cinnamon chips, pecans, and cranberries, and iced with a cream cheese frosting. By adding Grand Marnier to both the cake and the icing, and decorating the cake with halved pecans, cranberries, and fresh squash blossoms, Judy's grandmother turned her cake into a real special-occasion treat.

SERVES 8 TO 10

CAKE

- 1 (1-pound) peeled and seeded butternut squash half, cut into 1-inch chunks
- 5 large eggs
- 2 tablespoons orange liqueur, such as Grand Marnier
- 2 tablespoons cane syrup
- 2 tablespoons grated fresh ginger
- 1 teaspoon ground nutmeg
- ½ teaspoon ground cloves
- 1 (18.5-ounce) package yellow cake mix
- 1⅔ cups cinnamon chips
- 1 cup pecans, chopped
- ⅔ cup dried cranberries
- 1 tablespoon all-purpose flour

FROSTING

- 2 (8-ounce) packages cream cheese, softened
- 16 tablespoons (2 sticks) unsalted butter, cut into chunks and softened
- 1 tablespoon orange liqueur, such as Grand Marnier
- 4 cups confectioners' sugar
- 2 cups pecan halves, 1 cup chopped
- ⅔ cup dried cranberries, chopped
- 3 fresh squash blossoms (optional)

1. FOR THE CAKE: Adjust oven racks to upper-middle and lower-middle positions and heat oven to 350 degrees. Following photos on page 130, grease and flour three 9-inch round cake pans and line bottoms with parchment paper.

(Continued on page 130)

2. Microwave squash, covered, in bowl until tender, about 6 minutes. Process squash, eggs, orange liqueur, cane syrup, ginger, nutmeg, and cloves in food processor until smooth, about 30 seconds, scraping down sides of bowl as needed. Transfer squash mixture to large bowl and stir in cake mix until just combined. Toss cinnamon chips, pecans, and cranberries with flour in separate bowl, then fold into batter.

3. Divide batter evenly between prepared pans, smooth tops, and gently tap pans on counter to settle batter. Bake until golden brown and toothpick inserted into center comes out with a few moist crumbs attached, about 20 minutes, switching and rotating pans halfway through baking.

4. Let cakes cool in pans for 10 minutes. Run small knife around edge of cakes to loosen, then flip out onto wire racks. Peel off parchment, turn cakes right side up, and let cool completely before frosting, about 2 hours.

5. FOR THE FROSTING: Beat cream cheese, butter, and orange liqueur together in large bowl with electric mixer on medium-high speed until smooth, 2 to 4 minutes. Reduce mixer speed to medium-low, slowly add confectioners' sugar, and beat until smooth, 4 to 6 minutes. Increase mixer speed to medium-high and beat until frosting is light and fluffy, 4 to 6 minutes. In separate bowl, combine chopped pecans and cranberries. Fold half of pecan mixture into frosting.

6. Line edges of cake platter with strips of parchment to keep platter clean while assembling cake. Place one cake layer on platter. Spread ½ cup frosting over top, right to edge of cake. Repeat with one more cake layer and

½ cup more frosting. Place remaining cake layer on top and press lightly to adhere. Frost cake with remaining frosting and sprinkle top and sides with remaining pecan mixture. Garnish cake with remaining 1 cup pecan halves and squash blossoms (if using). Remove parchment strips from platter before serving.

Notes from the Test Kitchen

The original recipe called for roasting the butternut squash to soften it; we switched to the microwave for faster results. You can find cinnamon chips near the chocolate chips in the baking section at your local grocery store. Do not use low-fat cream cheese here, as it can cause the frosting to separate and become too thin to spread properly when icing the cake. You can substitute 1 tablespoon maple syrup plus 1 tablespoon molasses for the cane syrup.

PREPARING CAKE PANS

1. After greasing the sides and bottom of a cake pan, sprinkle it with flour, then shake and rotate to coat evenly with the flour; shake out any remaining flour.

2. Fit a trimmed piece of parchment paper into the pan. Grease the paper again, if called for in the recipe.

Prince of Wales Cake

SHIRLEY MURDOCK | ROLL, ARIZONA

While Shirley submitted a layer cake recipe for this pedigreed spice cake, in the memory Shirley shares here, she prepared it as cupcakes. "In 1943 at age 12, I made these cupcakes when my mother and I went to see my brother, who was in the Navy Air Corps. I carefully packed the cupcakes on top of some bananas in a little duffle bag. During a train delay, a man tripped and fell on top of my precious bag, squashing the cupcakes into the bananas. My brother and his buddies thought they were wonderful, anyway." Shirley connects this cake to Edward, Prince of Wales (born in 1894 and eventually crowned King Edward VIII), noting the cake was created for him when he visited the EP Ranch in Pekisko, Alberta, Canada, a property he first visited in 1919 and eventually bought. However, we found evidence of the cake's existence long before 1919, so it likely wasn't an original by the ranch. Various stories and newspaper articles suggest that Prince of Wales Cake could have been created and named for one of several princes of Wales, going all the way back to Edward, born in 1537, who became King Edward VI. The earliest recipes were for a dark spice layer cake, and later variations alternated layers of spice cake with white cake. Frostings varied among recipes: A 1921 version called for buttercream with raisins and nuts, another from 1932 called for caramel icing, and others used cream cheese, like Shirley's recipe. Whatever the story might be, what counts most is that this version, with raisin-studded layers of spice cake and a cream cheese frosting, is a recipe you'll want to make again and again.

SERVES 8 TO 10

CAKE

- 3½ cups cake flour
- 2 teaspoons baking powder
- 2 teaspoons baking soda
- 2 teaspoons ground cinnamon
- 1 teaspoon ground cloves
- 1 teaspoon ground nutmeg
- 1 cup buttermilk
- 4 large eggs
- 2 tablespoons molasses
- 20 tablespoons (2½ sticks) unsalted butter, cut into chunks and softened
- 2 cups granulated sugar
- ½ cup raisins

FROSTING

- 3 (8-ounce) packages cream cheese, softened
- 16 tablespoons (2 sticks) unsalted butter, cut into chunks and softened
- 3 tablespoons sour cream
- 2 teaspoons vanilla extract
- ¼ teaspoon salt
- 3 cups confectioner's sugar

(Continued on page 132)

1. FOR THE CAKE: Adjust oven rack to middle position and heat oven to 350 degrees. Grease and flour two 9-inch round cake pans, then line bottoms with parchment paper following photos on page 130.

2. Whisk flour, baking powder, baking soda, cinnamon, cloves, and nutmeg together in bowl. In separate bowl, whisk buttermilk, eggs, and molasses together.

3. In large bowl, beat butter and granulated sugar together with electric mixer on medium speed until light and fluffy, 3 to 6 minutes. Reduce mixer speed to low and beat in one-third of flour mixture, followed by half of buttermilk mixture. Repeat with half of remaining flour mixture and remaining buttermilk mixture. Beat in remaining flour mixture until just combined. Fold in raisins.

4. Give batter final stir with rubber spatula to make sure it is thoroughly combined. Divide batter evenly between prepared pans, smooth tops, and gently tap pans on counter to settle batter. Bake until toothpick inserted into center comes out with a few moist crumbs attached, about 30 minutes, rotating pans halfway through baking.

5. Let cakes cool in pans for 10 minutes. Run small knife around edge of cakes to loosen, then flip out onto wire racks. Peel off parchment, turn cakes right side up, and let cool completely before frosting, about 2 hours.

6. FOR THE FROSTING: Beat cream cheese, butter, sour cream, vanilla, and salt together in large bowl with electric mixer on medium-high speed until smooth, 2 to 4 minutes. Reduce mixer speed to medium-low, slowly add confectioners' sugar, and beat until smooth, 4 to 6 minutes. Increase mixer speed to medium-high and beat until frosting is light and fluffy, 4 to 6 minutes.

7. Line edges of cake platter with strips of parchment to keep platter clean while frosting cake. Following photos, slice each cake into two even layers with long serrated knife. Place one of bottom cake layers on platter. Spread 1 cup of frosting over cake, right to edges. Repeat with two more cake layers and 2 cups more icing. Place remaining cake layer on top and press lightly to adhere. Frost cake with remaining frosting, then remove parchment strips from platter and serve.

Notes from the Test Kitchen

Since Shirley's recipe was open-ended in terms of presentation, we decided that baking two 9-inch rounds, which we then sliced horizontally to create four thin layers, gave this cake an elegance that fit its name. The cake in the original recipe was a tad dry, so we upped the butter and went down on the flour, and we reduced the oven temperature by 25 degrees to ensure it didn't dry out. Do not use low-fat cream cheese here, as it can cause the frosting to separate and become too thin to spread properly when icing the cake.

MAKING THIN LAYERS FOR CAKE

1. Find the middle of each cake round with a ruler, then mark the middle at several points around the cake using a small knife.

2. Using the marks as a guide, score the entire edge of the cake with a long serrated knife. Continue to run the knife around the cake several more times, slowly cutting inward, to slice the layers apart.

Grated Bread and Chocolate Cake

LISA KEYS | MIDDLEBURY, CONNECTICUT

"I come from a long line of frugal cooks. Nothing, especially food, was ever thrown away. I am sure this cake was created to use up leftovers like day-old bread and so I often refer to it as just that, 'The Leftover Cake.' My mom and my grandmother had a hundred and one uses for day-old Italian bread, but I think this cake is the most interesting." Using grated bread in place of flour is certainly a creative (and not entirely uncommon) old-fashioned use for day-old bread. Yet Lisa's family recipe—a batter that incorporates almond flour, grated chocolate, and red wine and is baked into two rounds that are cut horizontally to make four layers, then brushed with amaretto liqueur and iced with chocolate whipped cream—is most certainly fit for a special occasion. "It was only during the Christmas holidays that the liqueur was used, in order to make the cake a little extra special."

SERVES 8 TO 10

CAKE

- 2 cups almond flour
- 2 tablespoons all-purpose flour
- ½ cup dry plain bread crumbs
- 1 ounce semisweet chocolate, grated
- 1 teaspoon baking powder
- 9 large egg whites
- 1½ cups confectioners' sugar
- ¼ cup dry red wine
- 2 tablespoons fresh lemon juice

FROSTING

- 2 cups heavy cream, chilled
- ¼ cup granulated sugar
- 2 tablespoons Dutch-processed cocoa powder

- ¼ cup amaretto or other almond-flavored liqueur
- ½ ounce semisweet chocolate, grated

1. FOR THE CAKE: Adjust oven rack to middle position and heat oven to 350 degrees. Grease and flour two 9-inch round cake pans, line bottoms with parchment paper, and grease paper following photos on page 130. Whisk almond flour, all-purpose flour, bread crumbs, chocolate, and baking powder together in bowl.

2. In large bowl, whip egg whites with electric mixer on medium-low speed until foamy, about 1 minute. Increase mixer speed to medium-high and whip whites to soft, billowy mounds, 1 to 2 minutes. Reduce mixer speed to low and gradually whip in confectioners' sugar, about 30 seconds. Return mixer speed to medium-high and continue to whip whites until glossy and stiff peaks form, 1 to 3 minutes longer.

3. Gently whisk wine and lemon juice into whipped egg whites by hand. Add one-third of flour mixture, then fold to combine until a few streaks of flour remain. Add and fold in remaining flour mixture, in two additions, until incorporated.

(Continued on page 135)

4. Divide batter evenly between prepared pans, smooth tops, and gently tap pans on counter to settle batter. Bake until light golden brown and cakes feel firm and spring back when touched, about 20 minutes, rotating pans halfway through baking.

5. Let cakes cool in pans for 10 minutes. Run small knife around edge of cakes to loosen, then flip out onto wire racks. Peel off parchment, turn cakes right side up, and let cool completely, about 2 hours.

6. FOR THE FROSTING: Whip cream, granulated sugar, and cocoa together in large bowl with electric mixer on medium-low speed until frothy, about 1 minute. Increase mixer speed to high and continue to whip until cream forms stiff peaks, 1 to 2 minutes longer.

7. Line edges of cake platter with strips of parchment to keep platter clean while frosting cake. Following photos on page 132, slice each cake into two even layers with long serrated knife. Place one of bottom cake layers on platter. Brush with 1 tablespoon amaretto and spread ⅔ cup whipped cream over top, right to edges. Repeat with two more cake layers, 2 tablespoons more amaretto, and 1⅓ cups more whipped cream. Place remaining cake layer on top and press lightly to adhere. Brush with remaining 1 tablespoon amaretto. Frost cake with remaining whipped cream and sprinkle top with chocolate. Remove parchment strips from platter before serving.

Notes from the Test Kitchen

Lisa's recipe called for ground almonds or almond flour. Since grinding whole almonds to flour without turning them to almond butter can be tricky, we stuck with store-bought flour (which you can find at most upscale groceries and in the health food section of most supermarkets). Using store-bought bread crumbs meant we didn't have to wait around for a loaf of bread to stale. We also shortened the baking time to ensure that the cake didn't dry out. While Lisa's family included the amaretto for special occasions only, we felt that this cake was a special-occasion dessert, so we made it a part of the recipe. This cake can overbake quickly, so check often for doneness once it begins to show color. Using plain (not seasoned) store-bought bread crumbs, which have a fine texture, makes the crumbs easy to incorporate into the batter.

GRATING CHOCOLATE

Use a rasp-style grater or the small holes of a box grater to achieve finely grated chocolate.

Black Currant Tiramisu

ANTHONY DIANTONIO | SEA ISLE CITY, NEW JERSEY

When it comes to tiramisu, the image we've always pictured is the classic Italian dessert of marsala- and espresso-soaked ladyfingers layered in a baking dish with mascarpone and grated chocolate. Then we found Anthony's recipe; he swaps the baking dish for a springform pan for a more cakelike version. Out goes the mascarpone (Italian-style cream cheese) in favor of a mixture of American cream cheese, whipped cream, and ricotta, and he stirs in a little syrup made from black currant jam for a subtle fruit flavor. He then sandwiches amaretti cookies and more syrup between two layers of the cheese mixture. In addition to including the ladyfingers in the layering, Anthony uses them to surround the exterior for an elegant presentation. "This is the first dessert my wife, Angelina, made for me," Anthony tells us. "We now make it together and experiment with different flavors. Angelina's family has shared this recipe for more than 100 years. This recipe was brought over from Italy, tucked away in her Nonna's head. Her Nonna and aunts have made different versions over the years. Tiramisu means 'pick me up' in Italian. I think my wife made it for me as she was picking me up, or should I say roping me in! Easy to make and the outcome is unbelievable. The first time my wife remembers making this recipe was at age three. Angelina would stand on a chair and help cook with her Nonna and aunts. Through the years Angelina's fondest memories have been in the kitchen with her family. Now Angelina is teaching her soon to be three-year-old daughter, Antonella, the techniques. It is a different chair but still the wonderful aromas and great times in the kitchen!"

SERVES 12

- ¾ cup black currant preserves
- ⅓ cup fresh lemon juice (2 lemons)
- ⅓ cup water
- 2 (8-ounce) packages cream cheese, softened
- 1 cup whole-milk ricotta cheese
- ½ cup sugar
- 1 cup heavy cream, chilled
- 48–60 soft ladyfingers (8 ounces)
- 12 amaretti cookies, crushed fine (½ cup)

1. Microwave preserves in bowl, stirring occasionally, until melted, about 1 minute. Whisk in lemon juice and water. Measure out and reserve ½ cup of mixture for filling.

2. In large bowl, beat cream cheese, ricotta, and sugar together with electric mixer on medium speed until light and fluffy, 3 to 6 minutes. Beat in reserved ½ cup of syrup until combined, about 30 seconds.

3. In separate large bowl, whip heavy cream with electric mixer on medium-low speed until frothy, about 1 minute. Increase mixer speed

to high and continue to whip until cream forms stiff peaks, 1 to 2 minutes longer.

4. Fold one-third of whipped cream into cream cheese mixture until almost no white streaks remain. Fold in remaining whipped cream until just incorporated.

5. Grease 9-inch springform pan. Following photos, arrange one-third of ladyfingers around sides of prepared pan with flat sides facing inward. Arrange half of remaining ladyfingers, flat side facing up, over bottom of pan, trimming them as needed to fill in any gaps. Gently brush with ¾ cup more syrup.

6. Spread half of filling into prepared pan and smooth into even layer. Arrange remaining ladyfingers evenly over top, trimming to fit as needed. Brush with remaining syrup and sprinkle with crushed amaretti cookies. Spread remaining filling over top and smooth into even layer.

7. Wrap tightly with plastic wrap and refrigerate until filling is set, at least 8 hours, or up to 1 day. Remove sides of pan, carefully slide tiramisu onto cake platter, and serve.

Notes from the Test Kitchen
After making this elegant dessert the first time, we realized that we actually had enough to make two tiramisus, so we scaled back the ingredients to make just one and streamlined the method to make it simpler to assemble. Anthony layered in whole amaretti cookies, but we found that crushed cookies were easier to distribute evenly and also easier to eat. We liked the black currant flavor so much that we added more of it to the cheese mixture. Refrigerating the tiramisu for a full day ensured that it was set and easy to slice.

MAKING BLACK CURRANT TIRAMISU

1. Arrange the ladyfingers along the interior and bottom of the prepared pan, trimming and packing them gently to ensure that no open spaces remain.

2. Being careful not to disturb the cookies, gently brush them with ¾ cup syrup.

3. Spread half of the filling into the ladyfinger-lined pan, smooth into an even layer, then arrange the remaining ladyfingers over the top. Trim the ladyfingers as needed to fill in any gaps.

4. Brush flat layer of ladyfingers with the remaining syrup, then sprinkle evenly with the crushed amaretti cookies. Pour the remaining filling over the top and smooth into an even layer. Wrap tightly and refrigerate.

GENUINE DANISH KLEINER

A Legacy of Cookies

Rosa Franklin Cookies 140

Scrumptious Orange Bites 141

Estelle's Black Walnut Chocolate Pixies 143

Anise Refrigerator Cookies 144

Svenska Pinners 145

Peppernuts 146

Church Cookies 148

Mildred Toogood's Lebkuchen 149

Cathedral Windows 150

Blarney Stones 152

Chapel Squares 155

The Bishop's Bars 157

Genuine Danish Kleiner 158

Rosa Franklin Cookies

BRIAN BRUST AND ROBIN GIVENS | LYNCHBURG, VIRGINIA

"The story of the Rosa Franklin cookie has been passed along generation to generation by the bakers and cooks here at Sweet Briar College, Virginia," write Brian and Robin, the sous chef and head baker, respectively, at Sweet Briar. "It is said that Rosa Franklin was the housekeeper for Dean Mary Ely Lyman in 1946. Dean Lyman asked Rosa if she would prepare some sweets to have with afternoon tea for a few faculty members that she invited to her house on campus. Rosa made a meringue cookie with pecans (the Rosa Franklin), and also a chocolate macaroon. The recipes for both of these cookies were never written down until years later. Like many of the dishes prepared at Sweet Briar, recipes were passed down from cooks and bakers to other staff members. These two cookies became favorites at catered events and were meant to be served exclusively at special occasions. To this day the Rosa Franklin is still the most requested cookie at all of our special functions."

MAKES ABOUT 2 DOZEN COOKIES

1	large egg white
2	teaspoons vanilla extract
1	cup packed light brown sugar
⅛	teaspoon baking soda
2	cups pecans, chopped

1. Adjust oven rack to middle position and heat oven to 300 degrees. Line rimmed baking sheet with parchment paper.

2. Whip egg white and vanilla together with electric mixer on medium-low speed until foamy, about 1 minute. Increase mixer speed to medium-high and whip whites to soft, billowy mounds, about 1 minute. Gradually whip in sugar and baking soda and continue to whip until mixture is lightened and smooth, about 2 minutes. Fold in pecans.

3. Drop tablespoon-size portions of batter onto prepared sheet, spaced about 1 inch apart.

Bake cookies until lightly browned, 10 to 12 minutes, rotating sheet halfway through baking. Turn off oven and let cookies cool in oven for 10 minutes. Remove cookies from oven and let cool on sheet for 10 minutes. Transfer cookies to wire rack and let cool completely before serving.

Notes from the Test Kitchen

The original recipe did not specify a set cooking time, suggesting only to bake the cookies until they were light brown, so we nailed down a baking time. Though reluctant to alter a tradition, we found that pecan halves made the cookies difficult to eat; chopped pecans proved much better. The original recipe yielded 28 cookies but didn't give a size for the cookies; we liked tablespoon-size portions, which gave us 24 cookies that could conveniently fit on one baking sheet. Make sure to leave them in the turned-off oven for 10 minutes; this helps avoid stickiness.

Scrumptious Orange Bites

JEAN THOMPSON | SAINT PAUL, MINNESOTA

"I first tasted these cookies at a summer job when I was in college," notes Jean. "They were so good we would sneak into the pantry and grab a handful whenever the cook wasn't around. She got so annoyed with us she finally locked them up and we had to make our own." One bite and you'll understand why Jean and her fellow coworkers couldn't resist these cakey, sweet cookies infused with orange flavor and studded with pecans, dates, and butterscotch chips. "My kids enjoyed hearing the story of me sneaking cookies and getting into trouble. But alas, I misplaced the recipe for about 25 years and could only describe the flavor of the orange-caramelly goodness. Just recently I found the recipe with some old photos, written in my sturdy young handwriting. Now they are my kids' favorite cookies!"

MAKES ABOUT 4 DOZEN COOKIES

- 1⅓ cups all-purpose flour
- 1 teaspoon salt
- ¾ teaspoon baking soda
- 1½ cups pitted whole dates, chopped
- 8 tablespoons (1 stick) unsalted butter
- ½ cup packed light brown sugar
- 1 teaspoon grated fresh orange zest plus ½ cup orange juice
- 2 large eggs
- 1 cup butterscotch chips
- 1 cup pecans, chopped
- Confectioners' sugar, for dusting

1. Adjust oven racks to upper-middle and lower-middle positions and heat oven to 375 degrees. Line two rimmed baking sheets with parchment paper. Whisk flour, salt, and baking soda together in bowl.

2. Bring dates, butter, brown sugar, orange zest, and orange juice to simmer in saucepan and cook until mixture has thickened slightly and measures 2 cups, about 5 minutes. Transfer mixture to large bowl and let cool to room temperature, about 30 minutes.

3. Whisk eggs into cooled date mixture, one at a time, until combined. Fold in flour mixture until just combined, then fold in butterscotch chips and pecans. Drop generous tablespoon-size portions of dough onto prepared baking sheets, spaced about 2 inches apart. Bake cookies until edges are set and beginning to brown, but centers are still soft and puffy, about 10 minutes, switching and rotating sheets halfway through baking.

4. Let cookies cool on sheets for 10 minutes, then transfer to wire rack and let cool completely. Repeat with remaining dough using cooled, freshly lined baking sheets. Lightly dust cooled cookies with confectioners' sugar before serving.

Notes from the Test Kitchen
We'd never encountered a cookie like this, and we didn't change the recipe at all.

Estelle's Black Walnut Chocolate Pixies

ABIGAIL CARLIN | WEXFORD, PENNSYLVANIA

Like a lot of grandmothers, Abigail's was one who loved to keep her family's sweet tooth happy with a steady stream of baked goods. "Several years ago, when she and my grandfather sold their home, I eagerly went through her recipe box, looking for one thing in particular: black walnut chocolate cookies. They were chocolaty, chewy, with gorgeously crackled tops striped white with powdered sugar. They had always been my father's favorites, and it seemed unthinkable that the recipe had been lost. But I couldn't find it, and no one else seemed to have it either. Then, this spring, when I was getting ready for my wedding, we began to plan a cookie table to accompany the cake. While we were pawing through the recipe box, my mother stopped to read one ancient, generically titled, handwritten note card for 'Chocolate Pixies.' I don't know why it caught her eye. It was the black walnut recipe! One bite was enough to bring all those memories rushing back. Unmistakable. Grandma and Papa are both over 90, and their health prevents them from coming to my wedding. But I'm going to have Black Walnut Chocolate Pixies on the cookie table. I'll be thinking of Grandma every bite."

MAKES ABOUT 5 DOZEN COOKIES

4	ounces unsweetened chocolate, chopped
4	tablespoons (½ stick) unsalted butter
2	cups all-purpose flour
½	cup black walnuts or walnuts, chopped fine
2	teaspoons baking powder
½	teaspoon salt
2	cups granulated sugar
4	large eggs
½	cup confectioners' sugar

1. Microwave chocolate and butter in large bowl, stirring often, until melted and smooth, 1 to 3 minutes; let cool slightly. In separate bowl, whisk flour, walnuts, baking powder, and salt together.

2. Slowly whisk granulated sugar into cooled chocolate mixture until combined. Whisk in eggs, one at a time, until combined. Fold in flour mixture until just combined. Cover and refrigerate until firm, about 2 hours.

3. Adjust oven racks to upper-middle and lower-middle positions and heat oven to 300 degrees. Line two rimmed baking sheets with parchment paper. Spread confectioners' sugar in shallow dish. Working with 1 tablespoon of dough at a time, roll dough into balls, then roll in confectioners' sugar to coat.

4. Transfer balls to prepared sheets, spaced about 2 inches apart. Bake cookies until edges are set, but centers are still soft and puffy, 18 to 20 minutes, switching and rotating sheets halfway through baking. Let cookies cool on sheets for 10 minutes, then transfer to wire rack and let cool completely before serving. Repeat with remaining dough using cooled, freshly lined baking sheets.

Notes from the Test Kitchen

It's hard to beat a chewy chocolate cookie, and it doesn't hurt that these cookies are also real lookers. We did make one tweak, baking the cookies a little bit longer than specified in Abigail's original recipe.

Anise Refrigerator Cookies

SUE SHOOK | CHESTERTON, INDIANA

"This is a recipe my grandmother made at Christmastime every year. It is one of the ones I have that she wrote out on a recipe card. And one of the few my mother gave me years ago. The card is fragile now, the writing is faded, and it's worth the world to me. Sometimes, I seem to remember, she would crush the anise seed using her Swedish mortar and pestle but not always. This is a simple recipe that brings back memories of both my grandmother and Christmas in our house." As Sue notes, there is nothing overly complicated about this recipe, which is what makes it so appealing. These not-too-sweet, crisp cookies, with just anise seeds for a subtle licorice flavor, are a sure winner with any crowd, great for serving with coffee or tea or as a simple dessert or afternoon snack.

MAKES ABOUT 3 DOZEN COOKIES

1¾	cups all-purpose flour
1	teaspoon baking powder
1	teaspoon anise seeds
¼	teaspoon salt
1	cup sugar
8	tablespoons vegetable shortening, softened
1	large egg

1. Whisk flour, baking powder, anise seeds, and salt together in bowl. In large bowl, beat sugar and shortening together with electric mixer on medium speed until light and fluffy, 3 to 6 minutes. Beat in egg until combined, about 30 seconds, scraping down bowl and beaters as needed. Reduce mixer speed to low and slowly add flour mixture until just combined.

2. Transfer dough to clean counter and roll into 9-inch log, about 1½ inches in diameter. Wrap dough tightly in plastic wrap and refrigerate until firm, about 1 hour.

3. Adjust oven racks to upper-middle and lower-middle positions and heat oven to 400 degrees. Line two rimmed baking sheets with parchment paper.

4. Slice dough into ¼-inch-thick rounds and transfer to prepared sheets, spaced about 1½ inches apart. Bake cookies until edges are lightly browned, 10 to 12 minutes, switching and rotating sheets halfway through baking.

5. Let cookies cool on sheets for 3 minutes, then transfer to wire rack to cool completely before serving.

Notes from the Test Kitchen

A pure and simple recipe like this one can't hide any flaws; we could tell after one test it was a winner. We didn't see the need to change much about the original recipe. Sue didn't specify a thickness for the cookie or a length for the log, so we followed the test kitchen's basic refrigerator cookie measurements.

Svenska Pinners

PAMELA BARRETT | QUEEN CREEK, ARIZONA

"My earliest childhood memories of Christmas were of eating these cookies. My mother's parents came here from Sweden in the early 1900s. Mom was born here in 1918 and was the third of seven children, so they had to have immigrated before 1915. This was one of her mother's Christmas cookie recipes she brought with her from Sweden. When done correctly they are like a shortbread cookie only better, with the slight sweetness and crunch from the egg white and walnut topping. My mother used both margarine and butter in the recipe and almond or vanilla extract depending on what she had on hand. No matter how she made them, my five brothers, one sister, and I loved them. Mom had about six Christmas cookies she would make every year, but by far this was our favorite. She would literally make 20 to 30 dozen of these cookies and put them in tins and hide them so we wouldn't eat them all before Christmas."

MAKES ABOUT 3 DOZEN COOKIES

- 2¾ cups all-purpose flour
- Pinch salt
- 24 tablespoons (3 sticks) unsalted butter, cut into chunks and softened
- ¾ cup plus 1 teaspoon sugar
- 1 large egg, separated
- 1 teaspoon almond extract or vanilla extract
- ½ cup black walnuts or walnuts, chopped fine

1. Line rimmed baking sheet with parchment paper. Whisk flour and salt together in bowl.

2. In large bowl, beat butter and ¾ cup sugar together with electric mixer on medium speed until light and fluffy, 3 to 6 minutes. Beat in egg yolk and almond extract until combined, about 30 seconds. Reduce mixer speed to low and slowly add flour mixture until just combined.

3. Transfer dough to prepared sheet and press into 10 by 8-inch rectangle, about ½ inch thick. Using floured fork, press tines into dough across rectangle to make washboard design. Lightly beat egg white with remaining 1 teaspoon sugar in small bowl, then brush over dough. Sprinkle with walnuts, lightly pressing on nuts to adhere. Wrap dough with plastic wrap and refrigerate until firm, about 30 minutes.

4. Adjust oven racks to upper-middle and lower-middle positions and heat oven to 350 degrees. Line two rimmed baking sheets with parchment paper. Slide parchment with chilled dough onto cutting board, and cut dough into 2 by 1-inch rectangular cookies. Transfer cookies to prepared sheets, spaced about 1½ inches apart.

5. Bake cookies until lightly browned and set, 20 to 25 minutes, switching and rotating sheets halfway through baking. Let cookies cool on sheets for 1 minute, then transfer to wire rack and let cool completely before serving.

Notes from the Test Kitchen

Tasters agreed, these cookies are the perfect shortbread-like treat for an afternoon snack. All we really needed to do was clarify Pamela's directions for forming and cutting the cookies.

Peppernuts

MARLYS HUGHES | HASTINGS, MINNESOTA

"My grandma made these for holidays," Marlys tells us of these fun bite-size spice cookies, which are a holiday tradition in various European countries, including Denmark, Germany, and Belgium. Traditionally, peppernuts, or pepper nuts, contained ground nuts and black pepper, hence their name, though today's recipes (including Marlys's) often contain neither. "We loved going to her house and sneaking into the coffee cans full of these little treats. They are wonderful with coffee, tea, or for stuffing into your pocket and sneaking outside to eat." They're also a perfect holiday gift.

MAKES ABOUT 10 CUPS MINI COOKIES

3½	cups all-purpose flour
½	teaspoon baking soda
½	teaspoon ground cinnamon
½	teaspoon salt
⅓	cup water
1	teaspoon instant espresso or instant coffee
1	teaspoon vanilla extract
1	teaspoon anise extract
¼	teaspoon maple extract
16	tablespoons (2 sticks) unsalted butter, cut into chunks and softened
⅔	cup granulated sugar
⅓	cup molasses
2	tablespoons maple syrup
	Confectioners' sugar

1. Whisk flour, baking soda, cinnamon, and salt together in medium bowl. In separate bowl, combine water, instant espresso, vanilla, anise extract, and maple extract.

2. In large bowl, beat butter, granulated sugar, molasses, and maple syrup together with electric mixer on medium speed until combined, 3 to 6 minutes. Slowly beat in water mixture until combined, about 30 seconds. Reduce mixer speed to low and slowly add flour mixture until just combined. Cover and refrigerate until firm, about 1 hour.

3. Adjust oven racks to upper-middle and lower-middle positions and heat oven to 325 degrees. Line two rimmed baking sheets with parchment paper. Transfer dough to lightly floured counter and divide into 12 equal pieces.

4. Working with one piece of dough at a time, roll into ½-inch-thick rope and cut rope crosswise into ½-inch lengths. Transfer cookies to prepared sheets, spaced about ½ inch apart.

5. Bake until golden brown, about 15 minutes, switching and rotating sheets halfway through baking. Let cookies cool completely on sheets for 10 minutes, then transfer to platter. Repeat with remaining dough using cooled, freshly lined baking sheets. Lightly dust cooled cookies with confectioners' sugar before serving.

Notes from the Test Kitchen

We just couldn't stop snacking on these little treats. The original recipe made a huge amount of cookies (something like 30 cups), so we cut back to make enough to package up as a dozen or so holiday gifts. We went up a little on the proportion of cinnamon, and we settled on the upper end of Marlys's baking time of 10 to 15 minutes, as we liked the cookies on the crispy side.

Church Cookies

ERMA YODER | MILLERSBURG, INDIANA

"This recipe was handed down through the generations of my husband's Amish grandmothers, then to me by his mother, who still makes them at 96 years of age. We can trace the recipe back to his great-grandmother at least. When I got married, I soon learned that 'cookie' was defined first and foremost as Church Cookies. These cookies were traditionally made to pass around to the children during the lengthy Amish church services, hence the name. In fact, when I got the recipe they were called 'Gma Cookies,' for the Pennsylvania Dutch rendering of church." One bite of these huge, cakey glazed vanilla cookies and you'll understand why they were the perfect treat for keeping the children occupied!

MAKES ABOUT 2 DOZEN LARGE COOKIES

COOKIES

4	cups all-purpose flour
2	teaspoons baking powder
1	teaspoon baking soda
½	teaspoon salt
1⅔	cups granulated sugar
16	tablespoons (2 sticks) unsalted butter, cut into chunks and softened
2	large eggs
1½	teaspoons vanilla extract
1	cup whole milk

GLAZE

1⅓	cups confectioners' sugar
2	tablespoons whole milk
¼	teaspoon vanilla extract

1. FOR THE COOKIES: Whisk flour, baking powder, baking soda, and salt together in bowl. In large bowl, beat sugar and butter together with electric mixer on medium speed until light and fluffy, 3 to 6 minutes. Beat in eggs, one at a time, and vanilla until combined, about 30 seconds, scraping down bowl as needed.

2. Reduce mixer speed to low and slowly add one-half of flour mixture, followed by milk. Add remaining flour mixture until just combined.

3. Transfer dough to clean counter and divide into two equal pieces. Press each piece of dough into 4-inch disk, wrap tightly in plastic wrap, and refrigerate until firm, 3 to 4 hours.

4. Adjust oven racks to upper-middle and lower-middle positions and heat oven to 350 degrees. Line two rimmed baking sheets with parchment paper.

5. Working with one piece of dough at a time, roll dough out on well-floured counter to even ¼-inch thickness. Stamp out cookies using 4-inch round cookie cutter and transfer to prepared sheets, spaced about 2 inches apart.

6. Bake cookies until center is set and edges are just beginning to turn brown, 10 to 12 minutes, switching and rotating sheets halfway through baking. Let cookies cool on sheets for 10 minutes, then transfer to wire rack to cool completely before glazing, about 1 hour. Repeat with remaining dough using cooled, freshly lined sheets.

7. FOR THE GLAZE: Whisk sugar, milk, and vanilla together in bowl. When cookies are cool, spread 1 teaspoon glaze over each cookie. Let glaze set for 30 minutes before serving.

Notes from the Test Kitchen

Erma's recipe made almost 75 cookies; we scaled it down to make a manageable amount. Adding salt balanced the sweetness, and rolling the cookies out thinner gave them just the right texture.

Mildred Toogood's Lebkuchen

ED HIMELBLAU | SAN LUIS OBISPO, CALIFORNIA

"My grandmother, Mildred Toogood, made this light, cake-like version of *lebkuchen* year-round, not just at Christmas." Lebkuchen, a traditional German Christmas treat with roots that go back to medieval times, is comparable to cakey iced gingerbread but is more intensely spiced and has a subtle citrus accent. As Ed implies, there are both soft and hard versions, though the soft version, like his grandmother's recipe, is more common. "In my grandmother's hands the recipe yielded a much lighter product than the dense, gingerbread-like lebkuchen I've seen in bakeries. I've always enjoyed this recipe for its pairing of lemon with the warm spices. Mildred grew up on a farm near the Mississippi River in Minnesota and recalled the lebkuchen her mother made and stored in a tin box on a mantel near the dining room table. During my childhood visits to my grandmother's house I always looked forward to that tin box!"

MAKES ABOUT 2 DOZEN BARS

BARS

- 4 tablespoons (½ stick) unsalted butter
- 4 tablespoons vegetable shortening
- 3 cups all-purpose flour
- 1 tablespoon ground cinnamon
- 1 teaspoon baking soda
- 1 teaspoon ground cardamom
- ¾ teaspoon ground ginger
- ½ teaspoon salt
- 1 cup granulated sugar
- 1 cup light molasses
- 2 large eggs
- 1 teaspoon grated fresh lemon zest

GLAZE

- 1½ cups confectioners' sugar
- 3 tablespoons whole milk
- 1 tablespoon fresh lemon juice

1. FOR THE BARS: Adjust oven rack to lower-middle position and heat oven to 325 degrees. Line 13 by 9-inch baking pan with foil lengthwise and widthwise, letting excess hang over edges. Grease foil. Melt butter and shortening together in microwave, about 2 minutes; let cool slightly.

2. Whisk flour, cinnamon, baking soda, cardamom, ginger, and salt together in bowl. In large bowl, whisk granulated sugar, molasses, eggs, and lemon zest together, then whisk in cooled butter mixture until combined. Stir in flour mixture until just combined.

3. Scrape batter into prepared pan and smooth top. Bake bars until toothpick inserted into center comes out clean, 40 to 45 minutes, rotating pan halfway through baking.

4. Let bars cool completely in pan, about 2 hours. Remove bars from pan using foil and cut into squares.

5. FOR THE GLAZE: Whisk confectioners' sugar, milk, and lemon juice together in bowl until smooth, then spread evenly over bars. Let glaze set for 30 minutes before serving.

Notes from the Test Kitchen

We made just a few changes to Ed's grandmother's recipe. We found that 25 minutes of cooking wasn't sufficient so we upped the baking time. We also reduced the ginger slightly, and instead of cutting and glazing the bars while warm, we waited until they were cooled for tidier looking results. To make the glaze easier to spread, we upped the amount of milk by a tablespoon or two.

Cathedral Windows

CHRIS LANZ | COUPEVILLE, WASHINGTON

By rolling a combination of colored mini marshmallows, nuts, and a melted chocolate mixture into a log, then chilling and slicing the log crosswise, you get these festive treats known variously as Cathedral Windows, Church Window Cookies, and Mosaic Cookies. As far as we can tell, recipes first appeared in the late 1960s, spreading mainly through newspapers. They are a snap to make and a fun, kid-friendly addition to any holiday cookie spread. "Mom always made sure [my sister and I] received a tray of goodies from her, and she embraced my two young stepdaughters in this same tradition by giving each of them their own plate of treats every year. In 2008, when the youngest showed up with a big tray of Cathedral Windows she had made for my mother's memorial reception, I immediately saw how wise and generous my mother truly was."

MAKES ABOUT 4 DOZEN COOKIES

- 1 cup bittersweet chocolate chips
- 8 tablespoons (1 stick) unsalted butter
- 1 large egg, beaten
- 1 cup confectioners' sugar
- 1 (10.5-ounce) package colored mini marshmallows
- ½ cup pecans, walnuts, or almonds, toasted and chopped fine
- ½ cup unsweetened finely shredded coconut

1. Microwave chocolate and butter in large bowl, stirring often, until melted and smooth, 1 to 3 minutes; let cool slightly.

2. Combine egg and 2 tablespoons of cooled chocolate mixture (to temper), then whisk mixture into remaining chocolate mixture. Stir in confectioner's sugar, marshmallows, and pecans until combined.

3. Following photos, transfer half of chocolate mixture to large sheet of plastic wrap and form into rough 12-inch log, about 2 inches in diameter. Wrap log tightly and gently roll back and forth to form uniform cylinder. Twist ends to help log keep its shape and freeze until firm, about 2 hours. Repeat with remaining chocolate-marshmallow mixture.

4. Spread coconut evenly over large plate. Working with one log at a time, roll in coconut until evenly coated, then slice into ½-inch-thick cookies and serve.

Notes from the Test Kitchen

Chris's recipe was easy to follow, though we simplified it by melting the chocolate in the microwave instead of a double boiler. Chris notes the logs can be kept frozen, well wrapped, for up to 4 months. Once sliced, the cookies can be stored in an airtight container in the refrigerator for up to 3 days.

FORMING CATHEDRAL WINDOWS

1. Form half of the chocolate-marshmallow mixture into a 12-inch log, about 2 inches thick, on a sheet of plastic wrap.

2. Wrap the log tightly in the plastic wrap. Holding the ends of the plastic wrap, roll the log away from you to form a tight cylinder.

Blarney Stones

CHERIE SECHRIST | RED LION, PENNSYLVANIA

"My most vivid childhood memories are of our family food events. Even though our family was scattered as much as 100 miles apart in areas of Pennsylvania, we all came together three times a year. One was for corn day, when we would pick, husk, cook (in a big iron kettle over a fire), cut, cool, bag, and freeze several hundred dozen ears of corn and then split them among the family members. The other summer event was making chow chow (a pickle relish). The recipe I'm sharing here comes from the annual Cookie Baking Day. This always took place on Black Friday, the day following Thanksgiving. I have lost count of the many varieties of cookies that were always stirred up that day. Since we normally baked 80 to 100 dozen all in one day, some were mixed ahead of time by various family members. One of my favorites was the Blarney Stone bar cookies." Recipes for Blarney Stones have a long history that goes all the way back to the early 1900s. The oldest versions were for pieces of dark fruit or fruited spice cake, served either plain or frosted green, while later recipes called for frosting squares or fingers of white or yellow cake, then either rolling the cake in peanuts, green candies, or green coconut, or decorating them with citron. Cherie's family recipe opts for the frosted yellow cake fingers rolled in peanuts variation (she frosts just three sides for simplicity). We actually found similar recipes going by the name Giant's Causeway Cakes, named after an impressive geological formation of interlocking stone columns of varying heights, also in Ireland. But whichever name you might think is a better fit, these unique cookies are sure to be a fun addition to your baking repertoire.

MAKES ABOUT 2 DOZEN (4 BY 1-INCH) COOKIES

COOKIES

- 2 cups all-purpose flour
- 1 tablespoon baking powder
- ¼ teaspoon salt
- 2 cups granulated sugar
- 5 large eggs, separated, room temperature
- 2 teaspoons vanilla extract

FROSTING

- 2½ cups unsalted roasted peanuts, chopped
- 3 cups confectioners' sugar
- 16 tablespoons (2 sticks) unsalted butter, cut into chunks and softened
- ½ teaspoon almond extract
- 1 teaspoon vanilla extract

1. **FOR THE COOKIES:** Adjust oven rack to middle position and heat oven to 300 degrees. Line 13 by 9-inch baking pan with foil lengthwise and widthwise, letting excess hang over edges. Grease foil.

2. Whisk flour, baking powder, and salt together in bowl. In large bowl, beat granulated sugar and egg yolks together with electric mixer on medium speed until uniform and creamy, 3 to 5 minutes. Mix in vanilla until combined, about 30 seconds. Reduce mixer speed to low and slowly add flour mixture until just combined (mixture will be very dry and crumbly). Thoroughly clean and dry beaters.

3. In clean, large bowl, whip egg whites with electric mixer on medium-low speed until foamy, about 1 minute. Increase mixer speed to medium-high and whip whites to stiff peaks, 1 to 2 minutes.

4. Fold one-third of whipped egg whites into crumbs to moisten. Fold in remaining whites until combined (batter will look lumpy and foamy). Scrape batter into prepared pan and smooth top. Bake until light golden brown, about 30 minutes, rotating pan halfway through baking.

5. Let cool in pan for 10 minutes. Remove from pan using foil, transfer to wire rack, and let cool completely, about 1 hour. Cut into 4 by 1-inch cookies.

6. **FOR THE FROSTING:** Spread peanuts in shallow dish for rolling. Beat confectioners' sugar, butter, almond extract, and vanilla together in large bowl with electric mixer on low speed until combined, about 1 minute. Increase mixer speed to medium and beat until light and fluffy, 3 to 6 minutes.

7. Following photos, spread generous tablespoon of frosting evenly over top and sides of each cookie, then roll in peanuts to coat. Serve.

Notes from the Test Kitchen

We thought these bars were a great way to add variety to the usual holiday cookie assortment. Cherie's original recipe baked the bars in an ungreased pan, which led to sticking, so we decided to use a greased foil sling for easier removal. Cherie suggested thinning the frosting with half-and-half if needed, but we found it was easy to spread without it.

MAKING BLARNEY STONES

1. Spread a generous tablespoon of the frosting evenly over the top and sides of each cookie.

2. Roll the frosted cookie in the chopped peanuts.

Chapel Squares

JEANNE HOLT | MENDOTA HEIGHTS, MINNESOTA

"Is it a sin to go to church on Sunday and say a prayer that Grandma had made Chapel Squares for the Sunday dinner dessert? If so, I transgressed many times during my formative years," writes Jeanne. "But I really loved those golden-crusted, almond-laced apple squares and I was absolutely positive that if God had tried just one little bite he would totally understand and approve." With a sweet apple filling balanced by dried sour cherries and rich almond paste, sandwiched between flaky pastry crust and topped with a light glaze, these bars could certainly be described as divine. It doesn't hurt that they have a clever name; Jeanne's family changed it from Cherry Apple Squares to Chapel Squares since they were typically an after-church treat. Serving them today takes Jeanne a step back in time. "Images of Grandma, busily working in the kitchen, come to mind, along with memories of a dining room table packed so full with family that you had to keep those elbows in or risk spilling some of your dinner in your lap, and most importantly the sounds of family sharing stories and laughter."

MAKES ABOUT 24 SQUARES

CRUST

- ½ cup whole milk
- 2 large eggs, separated, whites lightly beaten
- 2½ cups all-purpose flour
- 2 tablespoons granulated sugar
- ½ teaspoon salt
- 11 tablespoons vegetable shortening, cut into ½-inch pieces and chilled
- 5 tablespoons unsalted butter, cut into ¼-inch pieces and chilled

FILLING

- ¾ cup dried sour cherries
- 4 teaspoons water
- 4 Haralson or Granny Smith apples, peeled, cored, and sliced thin
- 2 Fireside or Golden Delicious apples, peeled, cored, and sliced thin
- ⅔ cup granulated sugar
- ½ teaspoon ground cinnamon
- ⅛ teaspoon salt
- 4 ounces almond paste, cut into ¼-inch pieces

GLAZE

- 1¼ cups confectioners' sugar
- 3 tablespoons whole milk
- ¼ teaspoon almond extract

1. FOR THE CRUST: Whisk milk and egg yolks together in bowl. Process flour, granulated sugar, and salt in food processor until combined. Scatter shortening over top and process until mixture resembles coarse cornmeal, about 10 seconds. Scatter butter pieces over top and pulse until mixture resembles coarse crumbs, about 10 pulses. Transfer mixture to large bowl.

2. Sprinkle milk mixture over flour mixture. Stir and press dough together, using stiff rubber spatula, until dough sticks together. Transfer dough to clean counter and divide into two equal pieces. Place each piece of dough on sheet of plastic wrap and flatten into 4-inch square. Wrap each piece tightly in plastic wrap and refrigerate for 1 hour.

(Continued on page 156)

3. FOR THE FILLING: Adjust oven rack to lowest position and heat oven to 400 degrees. Microwave cherries and water in covered bowl until steaming, about 1 minute. Let sit until cherries have softened and cooled to room temperature, about 30 minutes. Combine softened cherries and water, apples, granulated sugar, cinnamon, and salt in large bowl; set aside.

4. Let dough soften at room temperature for 10 minutes. Following photos, roll one dough square between two large sheets of parchment paper into 19 by 14-inch rectangle. Remove top piece of parchment. Loosely roll dough around rolling pin, then gently unroll dough over 18 by 13-inch nonstick rimmed baking sheet. Gently fit dough into sheet and sprinkle with almond paste. Drain apple mixture thoroughly, then spread over dough-lined sheet. Cover with plastic wrap and refrigerate until needed.

5. Roll remaining dough square between two large sheets of parchment into 19 by 14-inch rectangle. Remove top piece of parchment. Loosely roll dough around rolling pin and gently unroll it over filling. Trim, fold, and crimp edges of dough together using fork.

6. Cut 1-inch-long vents in top crust at 2 inch intervals, then brush with beaten egg whites. Bake bars for 10 minutes, then reduce oven temperature to 350 degrees and continue

to bake until juices are bubbling and crust is golden brown, 40 to 45 minutes, rotating sheet halfway through baking. Let bars cool in sheet for 30 minutes.

7. FOR THE GLAZE: Whisk confectioners' sugar, milk, and almond extract together in bowl until smooth, then drizzle over bars. Let bars cool until filling has set, about 2 hours, then cut into squares. Remove individual bars from sheet using spatula and serve.

Notes from the Test Kitchen
The almond paste and sour cherries made this recipe stand out from the other apple desserts. We increased the cooking time by 10 to 15 minutes so the bottom would crisp more, and we upped the milk in the glaze to get the right drizzly consistency. Jeanne called for Haralson and Fireside apples; since we couldn't find them we went with her backup varieties, Granny Smith and Golden Delicious. You will need an 18 by 13-inch rimmed baking sheet for this recipe; we prefer to use a nonstick baking sheet here, but a greased conventional baking sheet will work. You can find almond paste in the baking aisle of most grocery stores; do not use marzipan, which is slightly sweeter and smoother in consistency. These bars can be wrapped tightly in plastic wrap and stored at room temperature for up to 1 day.

MAKING CHAPEL SQUARES

1. Transfer the dough to a rimmed baking sheet using a rolling pin, then lift and press the dough into the baking sheet.

2. Dot the dough with almond paste, then spread the drained apple filling on top.

3. Top with the second rectangle of rolled-out dough, then press the edges of the two crusts together.

4. Trim the excess dough around the edge to ½ inch, tuck the edges underneath, and crimp using the tines of a fork.

The Bishop's Bars

LINDSAY WEISS | OVERLAND PARK, KANSAS

"According to my late grandma, these bars were named decades ago when a volunteer church group was eagerly awaiting a visit from their new bishop," Lindsay tells us. "When he arrived, he began the meeting by saying, 'Before we begin, let's have some coffee and the world's best bars!' From that day forward these have always been known as The Bishop's Bars." These bars are a surefire favorite, dense and rich like a blondie bar but with big, rich pockets of a chocolate filling throughout. "I enjoy eating them with a cup of coffee and thinking of their origins in a church basement many years ago!"

MAKES ABOUT 4 DOZEN BARS

COOKIE DOUGH

- 3 cups all-purpose flour
- 1½ teaspoons baking soda
  Pinch salt
- 16 tablespoons (2 sticks) unsalted butter, cut into chunks and softened
- 3 cups packed brown sugar
- 3 large eggs
- 1 tablespoon vanilla extract
- 1½ cups quick-cooking oats

FILLING

- 2 cups bittersweet chocolate chips
- 1 (14-ounce) can sweetened condensed milk
- 2 tablespoons unsalted butter
  Pinch salt

1. FOR THE COOKIE DOUGH: Adjust oven rack to middle position and heat oven to 350 degrees. Line 18 by 13-inch rimmed baking sheet with foil.

2. Whisk flour, baking soda, and salt together in bowl. In large bowl, beat butter and sugar together with electric mixer on medium speed until light and fluffy, 3 to 6 minutes. Beat in eggs, one at a time, and vanilla until combined, about 30 seconds, scraping down bowl and beaters as needed. Reduce mixer speed to low and slowly add flour mixture until just combined. Mix in oats.

3. FOR THE FILLING: Microwave all ingredients in bowl, whisking often, until melted and smooth, 1 to 3 minutes; let cool slightly.

4. Transfer two-thirds of dough to prepared sheet and press into even layer. Spread filling evenly over dough and smooth top. Break remaining dough into rough ½-inch pieces and sprinkle evenly over top. Bake bars until golden brown and set, 30 to 35 minutes, rotating sheet halfway through baking.

5. Let bars cool completely in sheet, about 2 hours, then cut into squares. Remove individual bars from sheet using spatula and serve.

Notes from the Test Kitchen

The richness of these bars certainly didn't stop our tasters from taking more than one. We did tweak a few things in Lindsay's grandma's recipe, scaling up the dough by half for better balance between dough and chocolate (they are still plenty rich). That change also helped properly fill the baking sheet. Her recipe called for chocolate chips; we settled on bittersweet because semisweet made the bars too sweet overall. Don't use a baking sheet smaller than 18 by 13 inches or the bars will be too thick and won't cook evenly. Substituting old-fashioned oats for the quick-cooking variety will yield a slightly chewier bar; avoid instant oats.

Genuine Danish Kleiner (Aegte Danske Klejner)

RUTH OKEY | COSTA MESA, CALIFORNIA

"When my great-grandmother Theodora was 12, she came to America from Denmark with her sister. She lost all her luggage on the ship over, but successfully met up with her older brother who was already living here." Theodora settled into life in her new country, later raising her own family and then seeing her grandchildren grow up. "During the Christmas holidays she often stayed with my dad (her grandson) and my mom," Ruth notes. "She taught them how to make these traditional Danish cookies." *Klejner* (kleiner) is the Danish version of a cookie that exists with slight variations all over Europe, but common to all is a diamond or rectangle shape with one end pulled through a hole in the center (just as Ruth's recipe does), and all are deep-fried. Kleiner, according to one source we found, are more cakey in texture than other European versions, which might be as thin and crisp as a fried wonton skin. The addition of cardamom is a good tip-off that this recipe is Scandinavian (it is a favorite spice among those countries), and it is also one indicator, as the recipe's name states, that this recipe is truly Danish (*aegte* means genuine or authentic). "I grew up making these with my parents. My mom made the dough and my dad fried them. I was the general assistant. Now my sister and I bring our daughters to our parents' house and we make them together. It just isn't Christmas in our family without kleiner."

MAKES ABOUT 5 DOZEN COOKIES

3¾ cups all-purpose flour

1 teaspoon baking powder

½ teaspoon salt

8 tablespoons (1 stick) unsalted butter

1½ teaspoons ground cardamom

1 cup granulated sugar

3 large eggs

¼ cup heavy cream

1 teaspoon vanilla extract

4 cups vegetable shortening or vegetable oil

Confectioners' sugar, for dusting (optional)

1. Whisk flour, baking powder, and salt together in bowl. Microwave butter and cardamom in separate bowl, stirring occasionally, until melted and fragrant, about 1 minute.

2. In large bowl, beat granulated sugar and eggs together with electric mixer on medium speed until smooth, 1 to 2 minutes. Beat in melted butter mixture, cream, and vanilla until combined, about 30 seconds, scraping down bowl and beaters as needed. Reduce mixer speed to low and slowly add flour mixture until just combined.

3. Transfer dough to clean counter and divide into four equal pieces. Place each piece of dough on sheet of plastic wrap and flatten into 4-inch square. Wrap each piece tightly in plastic wrap and refrigerate until firm, about 1 hour.

4. Line two rimmed baking sheets with parchment paper. Working with one piece of dough at a time (keep remaining dough refrigerated), roll into 12 by 10-inch rectangle, about ⅛ inch thick, on well-floured counter. Stamp out cookies using 4 by 2¾-inch diamond cookie cutter. Following photos, cut 1½-inch-long slit, lengthwise, in center of each cookie, then carefully pull tip of cookie through slit. Transfer cookies to prepared sheets and refrigerate until ready to fry.

5. Heat vegetable shortening in large saucepan over medium-high heat until it registers 350 degrees on instant-read thermometer. Carefully place about 8 cookies into hot oil and fry until golden brown on both sides, about 30 seconds per side, adjusting heat as necessary to maintain oil at 350 degrees.

6. Using slotted spoon, transfer cookies to paper towel–lined plate and sprinkle with confectioners' sugar (if using). Repeat with remaining cookies.

Notes from the Test Kitchen

This recipe was one of the biggest hits in the kitchen during our testing. Aside from the pure visual appeal, these fried cookies also have a great texture, somewhere between cake and cookie, and the touch of cardamom makes these unique among the many fried treats we've tried over the years. We cooked the cardamom briefly in butter to deepen its flavor before adding it to the dough, and we decided that some folks might like the cookies dusted with confectioners' sugar, so we made it an optional ingredient. If you don't have a diamond cookie cutter on hand, you can simply cut the dough into 4 by 3½-inch diamonds with a pizza wheel or sharp knife. You can also find kleiner/klejner cutters, also called *fattigman* cutters after the Norwegian variation, available online.

SHAPING DANISH KLEINER

1. Cut a 1½-inch-long slit in the center of each diamond-shaped cookie.

2. Pull one tip of the cookie through the slit to create a twist.

MOM'S GONE WITH THE WIND HEAVENLY PIE

Pies Worth Coming Home For

Grandma's Gooey Shoofly Pie 162

Grandmother Augsburger's Pecan Pie 163

Brown Sugar Pie 164

Single-Crust Pie Dough 166

Double-Crust Pie Dough 167

Grandma Lena's Apple Pie 168

1932 Pineapple Pie 169

Southern Sweet Potato Pecan Bread-Pudding Pie 170

Cracker Pie 173

Mom's Gone with the Wind Heavenly Pie 174

Light Bread Apple Pie 176

Hungarian Apple-Raspberry Pie 178

Roly-Boley 180

Banbury Tarts 183

Ina's Butter Tarts 185

Biggum's Fried Pies 186

Grandma's Gooey Shoofly Pie

RADELLE KNAPPENBERGER | OVIEDO, FLORIDA

"For almost 100 years, our Pennsylvania-Dutch family has made this Shoofly Pie recipe. When my 88-year-old mother, my husband, and I moved to Florida 10 years ago, we thought we lost the recipe. It wasn't until last year that my mother found it tucked between the pages of an old cookbook. We were so thrilled that I made it that very same day." With its simple spiced molasses filling, Shoofly Pie has been long associated with Amish country (notably, Europe's treacle tarts were the clear inspiration). There are two versions: wet- and dry-bottomed. The former pairs a soft filling with a crumb topping; in the latter those crumbs are mixed in for more cakelike results. Radelle's recipe is a great rendition of the crumb-topped variety, appealing not only for the visual contrast between the dark pie and light crumbs but also for its textural appeal.

SERVES 8

- 1   recipe Single-Crust Pie Dough, fitted into 9-inch pie plate and chilled (page 166)
- 1   cup all-purpose flour
- 2/3 cup packed light brown sugar
- 1/2 teaspoon ground cinnamon
- 1/4 teaspoon salt
- 1/8 teaspoon ground cloves
- 1/8 teaspoon ground ginger
- 1/8 teaspoon ground nutmeg
- 4   tablespoons (1/2 stick) unsalted butter, cut into 1/2-inch pieces and chilled
- 2/3 cup molasses
- 1   large egg yolk
- 1/2 teaspoon baking soda
- 1/2 teaspoon white vinegar
- 2/3 cup boiling water

1. Adjust oven rack to middle position and heat oven to 375 degrees. Line chilled crust with double layer of aluminum foil, covering edges to prevent burning, and fill with pie weights. Bake until pie dough looks dry and is light in color, 25 to 30 minutes. Transfer pie plate to wire rack and remove weights and foil. Increase oven temperature to 400 degrees. (Crust must still be warm when filling is added.)

2. Meanwhile, process flour, sugar, cinnamon, salt, cloves, ginger, and nutmeg in food processor until combined. Scatter butter pieces over top and pulse mixture until it resembles coarse crumbs, about 15 pulses.

3. Whisk molasses, egg yolk, baking soda, and vinegar together in medium bowl. Slowly whisk 1/3 cup boiling water into molasses mixture (to temper), then whisk in remaining 1/3 cup water; let cool slightly. Pour molasses mixture into warm pie crust and sprinkle top with crumb mixture.

4. Bake pie until toothpick inserted in center comes out with a few moist crumbs attached, about 30 minutes. Let pie cool on wire rack until filling has set, about 2 hours. Serve at room temperature.

Notes from the Test Kitchen

Radelle didn't specify a type of molasses; we opted for mild and it worked fine. We parbaked the unfilled pie crust to ensure it was perfectly cooked. For an accurate measurement of water, bring a teakettle to a boil, then measure 2/3 cup. The baked, cooled pie can be covered loosely and refrigerated for up to 1 day. You can substitute one round of store-bought pie dough for the homemade; if necessary, roll the dough round out further to an even 1/8-inch thickness before using.

Grandmother Augsburger's Pecan Pie

RICHARD YOUNG | MISSOURI CITY, TEXAS

Pecan pie is anything but lost—it has long been a Southern favorite—but Richard's grandmother's version is anything but average. While most pecan pies rely on corn syrup for sweetness, she uses a combination of corn syrup and caramelized sugar for a one-of-a-kind flavor. Richard writes: "Mary and Amos, my grandparents, moved to Sweeny, Texas, in the early 1900s in a boxcar with all their belongings and children. Amos was the local school principal and Mary was head of the school cafeteria. I remember Mary cooking okra gumbo, fried shrimp, fried chicken, deviled eggs, and many desserts. They had a large family and she always made multiple pecan pies."

SERVES 8

- 1 recipe Single-Crust Pie Dough, fitted into 9-inch pie plate and chilled (page 166)
- 1⅓ cups sugar
- ¼ cup water
- 2 tablespoons all-purpose flour
- ⅛ teaspoon salt
- 4 tablespoons (½ stick) unsalted butter, softened
- 3 large eggs
- 1 teaspoon vanilla extract
- ¾ cup light corn syrup
- 1½ cups pecans, toasted

1. Adjust oven rack to middle position and heat oven to 375 degrees. Line chilled crust with double layer of aluminum foil, covering edges to prevent burning, and fill with pie weights. Bake until pie dough looks dry and is light in color, 25 to 30 minutes. Transfer pie plate to wire rack and remove weights and foil. Reduce oven temperature to 300 degrees. (Crust must still be warm when filling is added.)

2. Meanwhile, heat ⅓ cup sugar in small saucepan over medium heat, swirling occasionally, until sugar has dissolved completely and liquid has faint golden color, 3 to 6 minutes. Reduce heat to medium-low and continue to cook, stirring occasionally, until caramel has dark amber color, 1 to 3 minutes. Off heat, slowly whisk in water until sugar is completely dissolved (mixture will bubble and steam vigorously). Let caramel cool to room temperature, about 30 minutes.

3. Whisk flour and salt together in bowl. In large bowl, beat butter and remaining 1 cup sugar together with electric mixer on medium speed until light and fluffy. Beat in eggs, one at a time, and vanilla until combined, about 30 seconds. Reduce mixer speed to low and beat in corn syrup and cooled caramel until combined, about 30 seconds. Beat in flour mixture until just combined. Fold in pecans.

4. Pour pecan mixture into warm pie crust. Bake pie until filling looks set and center jiggles slightly when pie is gently shaken, 60 to 75 minutes. Let pie cool on wire rack until filling has set, about 2 hours. Serve slightly warm or at room temperature.

Notes from the Test Kitchen

The filling in Richard's recipe curdled slightly, so we cut back on the butter, and we toasted the pecans for better texture and flavor. You can substitute one round of store-bought pie dough for the homemade; if necessary, roll the dough round out further to an even ⅛-inch thickness before using. The baked, cooled pie can be covered loosely and refrigerated for up to 1 day. Reheat the pie in a 300-degree oven for 15 minutes.

Brown Sugar Pie

AUDREY HUNTER | CHRISTIANA, TENNESSEE

"This recipe was from my grandma Kathleen Turner. It was always a favorite at Sunday dinner. I have never seen it on any restaurant menu or had it at anyone else's house. I always meant to get the recipe, but like all children, I thought I had all the time in the world. Grandma passed away five years ago, and I thought the recipe was gone for good, but someone actually found it written down. It was bare-bones without explaining how to brown butter, what kind of flour to use, etc., so I have had to ad-lib. I hope others can enjoy it as much as we did." While Audrey's grandmother's pie may appear ordinary and the ingredient list may be simple, this pie balances its caramel-like sweetness (from the brown sugar) by incorporating browned butter, which adds a subtle yet rich nuttiness. For anyone who has even a hint of a sweet tooth, this is one dessert that is truly hard to resist.

SERVES 8

- 3 tablespoons unsalted butter
- 1 cup plus 2 tablespoons packed light brown sugar
- 2 large eggs
- ¼ cup evaporated milk
- 4½ teaspoons all-purpose flour
- 1 teaspoon vanilla extract
- ⅛ teaspoon salt
- 1 recipe Single-Crust Pie Dough, fitted into 9-inch pie plate and chilled (page 166)

1. Adjust oven rack to middle position and heat oven to 350 degrees. Melt 2 tablespoons butter in saucepan over medium heat, swirling occasionally, until butter is browned and has nutty aroma, about 3 minutes; transfer to large bowl and let cool slightly.

2. Stir sugar into cooled butter until uniform. Whisk in eggs, milk, flour, vanilla, and salt until combined. Pour filling evenly into dough-lined pie plate. Cut remaining 1 tablespoon butter into 4 pieces and scatter evenly over top of pie.

3. Bake pie until browned on top and toothpick inserted into center comes out with a few moist crumbs attached, about 40 minutes. Let pie cool on wire rack until filling has set, about 2 hours. Serve at room temperature.

Notes from the Test Kitchen
Everyone in the test kitchen was surprised by how much they liked this pie. We scaled back Audrey's recipe to make one pie instead of two, and we proportionally cut back a bit on the butter topping. The baked, cooled pie can be covered loosely and refrigerated for up to 1 day. Bring to room temperature before serving. You can substitute one round of store-bought pie dough for the homemade; if necessary, roll the dough round out further to an even ⅛-inch thickness before using.

Single-Crust Pie Dough

MAKES ENOUGH FOR ONE 9-INCH PIE

1¼	cups all-purpose flour
1	tablespoon sugar
½	teaspoon salt
3	tablespoons vegetable shortening, cut into ¼-inch pieces and chilled
4	tablespoons (½ stick) unsalted butter, cut into ¼-inch pieces and chilled
4–6	tablespoons ice water

1. Process flour, sugar, and salt together in food processor until combined. Scatter shortening over top and pulse until mixture resembles coarse cornmeal, about 10 pulses. Scatter butter pieces over top and pulse mixture until it resembles coarse crumbs, about 10 pulses; transfer to large bowl.

2. Sprinkle 4 tablespoons ice water over flour mixture. Stir and press dough together, using stiff rubber spatula, until dough sticks together. If dough does not come together, stir in remaining water, 1 tablespoon at a time, until it does.

3. Turn dough onto sheet of plastic wrap and flatten into 4-inch disk. Wrap dough tightly in plastic wrap and refrigerate for at least 1 hour. Before rolling out dough, let it sit on counter to soften slightly, about 10 minutes.

4. Roll dough out to 12-inch circle, about ⅛ inch thick, on lightly floured counter. Following photos, fit dough into standard or deep-dish 9-inch pie plate, letting excess dough hang over edge. Trim, fold, and crimp edges. Freeze unbaked pie crust until firm, about 30 minutes, before filling or baking.

Notes from the Test Kitchen
The dough, wrapped tightly in plastic wrap, can be refrigerated for up to 2 days or frozen for up to 1 month. If frozen, let the dough thaw completely in the refrigerator before rolling out.

ROLLING AND FITTING SINGLE-CRUST PIE DOUGH

1. Loosely roll the dough around the rolling pin. Then gently unroll the dough over the pie plate.

2. Lift the dough around the edges and gently press it down into the corners of the pie plate.

3. Trim the dough to within ½ inch of the edge of the pie plate. Tuck the dough underneath itself to form a rim that sits above the pie plate.

4. Use the index finger of one hand and the thumb and index finger of the other to create a crimped edge.

Double-Crust Pie Dough

We found this dough worked well when making not only double-crust pies but also several other desserts in this chapter (Banbury Tarts, Ina's Butter Tarts, and Biggum's Fried Pies) that require pastry dough.

MAKES ENOUGH FOR ONE 9-INCH PIE

- 2½ cups all-purpose flour
- 2 tablespoons sugar
- 1 teaspoon salt
- 8 tablespoons vegetable shortening, cut into ½-inch pieces and chilled
- 12 tablespoons (1½ sticks) unsalted butter, cut into ¼-inch pieces and chilled
- 6–8 tablespoons ice water

1. Process flour, sugar, and salt together in food processor until combined. Scatter shortening over top and pulse until mixture resembles coarse cornmeal, about 10 seconds. Scatter butter pieces over top and pulse mixture until it resembles coarse crumbs, about 10 pulses; transfer to large bowl.

2. Sprinkle 6 tablespoons ice water over flour mixture. Stir and press dough together, using stiff rubber spatula, until dough sticks together. If dough does not come together, stir in remaining water, 1 tablespoon at a time, until it does.

3. Transfer dough to clean counter and divide into two equal pieces. Place each piece of dough onto sheet of plastic wrap and flatten into 4-inch disk. Wrap each disk tightly in plastic wrap and refrigerate for at least 1 hour before rolling.

Notes from the Test Kitchen

The dough, wrapped tightly in plastic wrap, can be refrigerated for up to 2 days or frozen for up to 1 month. If frozen, let the dough thaw completely in the refrigerator before rolling out.

MAKING A DOUBLE-CRUST PIE

When using this dough to make a double-crust pie, fit the dough for the bottom crust into the pie plate as you would for a single-crust pie (see steps 1 and 2 on page 166), add the filling, then follow these steps:

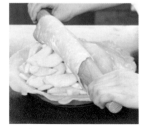

1. After rolling out and chilling the top crust, loosely roll it around the rolling pin, then gently unroll it over the filled pie crust bottom.

2. Using scissors, trim all but ½ inch of the dough overhanging the edge of the pie plate.

3. Press the top and bottom crusts together, then tuck the edges underneath.

4. Crimp the dough evenly around the edge of the pie, using your fingers. Cut vent holes in the center of the top crust with a paring knife.

Grandma Lena's Apple Pie

JILL GALLAHER | EDEN PRAIRIE, MINNESOTA

"Back in the 1940s, my grandmother owned a café in the small town of Bristol, South Dakota, called Lena's Café. One wintry day in early March 1947, the train came through town and stopped for its normal 2 p.m. break. On this stop, the passengers and the crew were allowed to get off the train and go to Lena's Café for a meal. On this particular day, the engineer and a lady sat at the counter and ordered their food and a piece of pie. When they were finished, the lady peeked around the corner into the kitchen where my grandmother, Uncle James, and Emma, the dishwasher/prep cook, were busily working. She exclaimed, 'I just had the most delicious apple pie I've ever eaten in my life!' Both Lena and James looked up and answered, 'Thank you.' James instantly recognized her as Eleanor Roosevelt, the wife of deceased President Franklin Roosevelt. My mom still makes this pie for us. It is just a simple recipe for apple pie, but it is as good today as it was back then."

SERVES 8

- 1   recipe Double-Crust Pie Dough (page 167), softened at room temperature for 10 minutes
- 1   pound Braeburn or Honeycrisp apples (2 to 3), peeled, cored, and sliced ¼ inch thick
- 1   pound Granny Smith apples (2 to 3), peeled, cored, and sliced ¼ inch thick
- 1   cup sugar
- 4½   teaspoons all-purpose flour
- 1½   teaspoons Minute tapioca
- ¼   teaspoon ground cinnamon

1. Roll one piece of dough into 12-inch circle on lightly floured counter, then fit it into 9-inch pie plate following photos on page 166, letting excess dough hang over edge; cover with plastic wrap and refrigerate for 30 minutes. Roll remaining piece of dough into 12-inch circle on lightly floured counter, then transfer to parchment-lined baking sheet; cover with plastic wrap and refrigerate for 30 minutes.

2. Adjust oven rack to middle position and heat oven to 375 degrees. Toss apples with sugar, flour, tapioca, and cinnamon in bowl, then spread into dough-lined pie plate, mounding apple mixture slightly in middle. Following photos on page 167, loosely roll second piece of dough around rolling pin, then gently unroll dough over pie. Trim, fold, and crimp edges, and cut 4 vent holes in top.

3. Bake pie until filling is bubbling and top crust is golden brown, 55 to 65 minutes. Let pie cool on wire rack until filling has set, about 3 hours. Serve slightly warm or at room temperature.

Notes from the Test Kitchen

Rather than layering the filling ingredients into the crust as Grandma Lena instructed, we found we got the best results by mixing those ingredients together before filling the crust. Her recipe called for Winesap, Jonathan, or Haralson apples, which we couldn't get our hands on; alternate options were Honeycrisp and Braeburn, which we found worked fine. The baked, cooled pie can be covered loosely and stored at room temperature for up to 1 day. To serve warm, reheat the pie in a 300-degree oven for about 15 minutes. You can substitute two rounds of store-bought pie dough for the homemade dough; if necessary, roll the dough rounds out further to 12-inch circles before using.

1932 Pineapple Pie

KRIS RUDDY | GLENDIVE, MONTANA

"This recipe was found in my grandmother's recipe box," Kris tells us about her unique pie, which has a bright, fresh-tasting filling from the combination of canned pineapple and lemon, and a graham cracker crust that is a perfect match. The filling's light texture is also unusual, somewhere between cakey and custardy, making it easy to eat a whole slice even after the most hearty of meals. Kris doesn't indicate why her grandmother dated the pie 1932, but we'd guess that it was the year she first made it. Kris notes that because her grandmother experimented a lot when cooking, "no recipe ever turned out the same as the last time she made it." Even so, you're sure to agree this pie is great every time it's made, especially if it's served with whipped cream.

SERVES 8

CRUST

- 12 whole graham crackers, broken into 1-inch pieces
- 7 tablespoons unsalted butter, melted and cooled
- 4 tablespoons sugar

FILLING

- 3 large eggs, separated, plus 1 large egg yolk, room temperature
- 1 cup sweetened condensed milk
- 1 teaspoon grated fresh lemon zest and 2 tablespoons fresh lemon juice
- ⅛ teaspoon salt
- 1 (8-ounce) can crushed pineapple, drained

1. FOR THE CRUST: Adjust oven rack to middle position and heat oven to 325 degrees. Process graham cracker pieces in food processor to fine, even crumbs, about 30 seconds. Sprinkle butter and sugar over crumbs and pulse to combine, about 3 pulses.

2. Sprinkle mixture into 9-inch deep-dish pie plate. Using bottom of measuring cup, press crumbs into even layer on bottom and sides of pie plate. Bake until crust is fragrant and beginning to brown, 13 to 18 minutes. Transfer pie plate to wire rack and let cool to room temperature. Reduce oven temperature to 300 degrees.

3. FOR THE FILLING: In large bowl, whip egg whites with electric mixer on medium-low speed until foamy, about 1 minute. Increase mixer speed to medium-high and whip whites until they are glossy and form stiff peaks, 2 to 4 minutes.

4. Whisk egg yolks, milk, lemon zest, lemon juice, and salt together in separate large bowl, then stir in pineapple. Fold one-third of whipped egg whites into pineapple mixture until a few white streaks remain. Fold in remaining whites until just incorporated.

5. Pour filling into cooled pie shell and bake until pie is golden brown and toothpick inserted into center comes out clean, 50 to 55 minutes. Let pie cool on wire rack until filling has set, about 2 hours. Serve slightly warm or at room temperature.

Notes from the Test Kitchen

We weren't sure what type of canned pineapple to use; a few tests proved crushed pineapple (drained well) worked just fine. We also tweaked the crust recipe, as the original amount of butter made it too soft, and an egg white made the texture a bit off. To ensure that the pie cooked through evenly without burning, we baked it at 300 degrees instead of 350 and cooked it a little bit longer. We also added some salt for balance.

Southern Sweet Potato Pecan Bread-Pudding Pie

MARGEE BERRY | TROUT LAKE, WASHINGTON

"My grandmother was the best when it came to making desserts," Margee writes. "Growing up we could not wait to finish our dinner when we knew she had made a special treat. She gave me a version of this recipe years ago and I think of her fondly every time I make it." If you have been searching for a pie that stands out from the crowd for a holiday spread or a potluck, this is your recipe. Prepared almost like bread pudding but in a pie plate, this recipe starts by dredging slices of toasted challah or brioche (a favorite for bread pudding) in melted butter, then in a mixture of sugar, cinnamon, and nutmeg. The slices are laid in the bottom of the pie plate, then a custard incorporating pureed sweet potatoes, cream cheese, pecans, and bourbon (naturally; this is a Southern recipe) is poured over. When baked, the bread and custard separate into layers, with the custard on the bottom and the bread on top. Served with a nutmeg-spiced whipped cream topping, this pie is guaranteed to go fast wherever you serve it.

SERVES 8

CRUST

- 8 ounces challah or brioche bread, cut into ½-inch-thick slices
- 6 tablespoons (¾ stick) unsalted butter
- ⅓ cup granulated sugar
- 1 teaspoon ground cinnamon
- ½ teaspoon ground nutmeg

FILLING

- 12 ounces sweet potatoes, peeled and cut into ½-inch pieces
- ⅔ cup granulated sugar
- 4 large eggs
- 3 ounces cream cheese, softened
- ¼ teaspoon salt
- 1 cup whole milk
- ½ cup heavy cream
- 2 tablespoons bourbon
- 1 teaspoon vanilla extract
- ¾ cup pecans, chopped

TOPPING

- ½ cup heavy cream
- 3 tablespoons turbinado or dark brown sugar
- ¼ teaspoon ground nutmeg

(Continued on page 172)

1. **FOR THE CRUST:** Adjust oven rack to middle position and heat oven to 350 degrees. Arrange bread slices directly on oven rack and toast until golden brown, about 5 minutes; transfer to plate. Reduce oven temperature to 300 degrees.

2. Grease 9-inch deep-dish pie plate. Microwave butter in shallow dish until melted, about 2 minutes. Combine sugar, cinnamon, and nutmeg in second dish. Coat one side of toast with melted butter, then dredge same side in sugar mixture. Following photo, arrange bread, sugared sides facing down, in prepared pie plate, trimming as needed to fill in gaps.

3. **FOR THE FILLING:** Microwave potatoes with ¼ cup water in covered bowl, stirring occasionally, until tender, about 7 minutes. Drain potatoes and transfer to food processor. Add granulated sugar, eggs, cream cheese, and salt, and process until smooth, about 30 seconds. Transfer potato mixture to large bowl and stir in milk, cream, bourbon, and vanilla. Pour mixture into bread-lined pie plate, smooth into even layer, and sprinkle with pecans.

4. Bake pie until center is set and pie is golden brown on top, 60 to 70 minutes. Let pie cool on wire rack for 2 hours.

5. **FOR THE TOPPING:** Whip cream, turbinado sugar, and nutmeg together in large bowl with electric mixer on medium-low speed until frothy, about 1 minute. Increase mixer speed to high and continue to whip until cream forms soft peaks, 1 to 3 minutes. Serve pie slightly warm or at room temperature with whipped cream.

Notes from the Test Kitchen

We have never come across a recipe like this one, and we all agreed we might never again; it was a shoo-in for our collection. We found that the original recipe called for more bread than we could fit in the pie plate, so we cut back a bit. It also called for processing all of the filling ingredients (except for the pecans) in the food processor, but we couldn't make them all fit into the workbowl so we stirred in most of the liquid ingredients after processing. Although the original recipe said to serve the pie chilled, we much preferred it warm. Turbinado sugar (or Sugar in the Raw) can be found in the baking aisle in most grocery stores. The baked, cooled pie can be covered loosely with plastic wrap and refrigerated for up to 1 day. Bring to room temperature before serving or, to serve warm, reheat the pie in a 300-degree oven for about 15 minutes.

MAKING A CRUST WITH BREAD

Arrange bread slices, sugared sides down, in bottom of prepared pie plate, then arrange slices around sides so that top crust points up to create a decorative edge. Trim and gently pack slices to ensure that no open spaces remain.

Cracker Pie

MERRILYN HIRSCH | RIO LINDA, CALIFORNIA

"In 1966, at 21 years old, I went to work for a wonderful woman. I had just lost my mother, and Veloy took me under her wing. Just as my mother had been, Veloy was an amazing cook and shared her delicious recipes with all of us in her office on birthdays and other special occasions. Over the years she gave me many of her family recipes, which I continue to use to this day. None are more loved by my friends and family than this one. While it resembles a pavlova, I've never seen a recipe done quite this way and have never tasted any as wonderful." While "cracker pie" may sound like a made-up name, we found recipes like Merrilyn's going back to 1900, usually called "soda cracker pie." Folding a mixture of nuts, saltines, sugar, and baking powder into whipped egg whites and baking it creates a dessert without much fuss or cost. At first, recipes called for serving the meringue on its own, but over time they started calling for topping the meringue with fruit and whipped cream, just as Merrilyn's recipe does here.

SERVES 8

- 10 saltine crackers, broken into rough pieces
- ¾ cup pecans or walnuts, chopped
- 1¼ cups sugar
- 1 teaspoon baking powder
- 3 large egg whites, room temperature
- 1 teaspoon vanilla extract
- 1 cup heavy cream, chilled
- 2 bananas, peeled and sliced thin
- 2 cups strawberries, hulled and sliced thin

1. Adjust oven rack to middle position and heat oven to 350 degrees. Grease 9-inch pie plate.

2. Pulse saltines in food processor to coarse crumbs, about 15 pulses. Transfer crumbs to small bowl and stir in pecans. Combine 1 cup sugar and baking powder in separate bowl.

3. In large bowl, whip egg whites and vanilla with electric mixer on medium-low speed until foamy, about 1 minute. Increase mixer speed to medium-high and whip whites to soft, billowy mounds, 1 to 3 minutes. Gradually whip in sugar mixture, about 1 minute. Continue to whip whites until glossy and very thick, 3 to 6 minutes. Fold in cracker mixture.

4. Spread meringue into prepared pie plate and smooth into even layer. Following photo on page 175, run finger around inside edge of pie plate to create small gap between edge of meringue and rim of plate. Bake meringue until golden brown and set, about 25 minutes. Let meringue cool completely on wire rack, about 30 minutes. (Meringue will crack and deflate after baking to form crust.)

5. Whip cream and remaining ¼ cup sugar together in large bowl with electric mixer on medium-low speed until frothy, about 1 minute. Increase mixer speed to high and continue to whip until cream forms soft peaks, 1 to 3 minutes.

6. Sprinkle bananas and strawberries into cooled meringue shell and lightly press into even layer. Spread whipped cream attractively over top. Refrigerate pie until filling and topping have set, about 1 hour, before serving.

Notes from the Test Kitchen
Tasters agreed that this summery pie was a great, refreshing change of pace. We didn't need to change a thing about this recipe.

Mom's Gone with the Wind Heavenly Pie

SANDY FARLER | BELLEVUE, WASHINGTON

"We lived in Southern California in the beautiful little town of Encino, a suburb of Los Angeles, in the 1950s. My mother was the leader of our brownie troop, and one spring, our troop was holding a bake sale in our front yard to raise money for us to go to brownie/Girl Scout camp the following summer. Mom generously baked her own creation, a delicious lemon pie (that she had always called Heavenly Pie) and added it to the selections on the sales table, carefully placing it on a bed of ice under the shade tree. Almost immediately, an extremely handsome gentleman pulled up to our neighborhood sale in his little Mercedes-Benz convertible sports car, climbed out, and proceeded to browse the delicious assortment of desserts. His eye fell upon my mom's beautiful and tempting creation, and he smiled a broad grin and immediately asked to purchase her Heavenly Pie. Mom packed up the pie and handed it to him, a blush starting at her toes and heading to her cheeks. After he drove away with his pie, Mom could barely contain her joy—our customer was not only one of our neighbors, he was also the legendary Clark Gable! So from that day forward, her pie was always referred to as Mom's Gone with the Wind Heavenly Pie!" With its meringue crust, refreshing lemony, whipped-cream-lightened filling, and topping of more whipped cream, Sandy's mother's pie fits right in with other ethereal, meringue-crusted Heavenly Pie recipes we found. They first began appearing in the 1940s and had all manner of fillings, not just lemon, and their popularity continued through the 1970s (a lemony version similar to Sandy's appears in Craig Claiborne's revised edition of the *New York Times Cook Book*, published in 1990). This fantastic version, which is light as air and truly heavenly, definitely earns its name.

SERVES 8

- 4   large eggs, separated, room temperature
- ½   teaspoon cream of tartar
- ¾   teaspoon salt
- 1½ cups sugar
- 1   tablespoon grated fresh lemon zest and 3 tablespoons fresh lemon juice
- 2   cups heavy cream, chilled

1. Adjust oven rack to middle position and heat oven to 300 degrees. Grease 9-inch deep-dish pie plate.

2. In large bowl, whip egg whites, cream of tartar, and ½ teaspoon salt with electric mixer on medium-low speed until foamy, about 1 minute. Increase mixer speed to medium-high and whip whites to soft, billowy mounds, 1 to 3 minutes. Gradually whip in 1 cup sugar, about 1 minute. Continue to whip whites until glossy and very thick, 3 to 6 minutes.

3. Spread meringue into prepared pie plate and smooth into even layer. Following photo, run finger around inside edge of pie plate to create small gap between edge of meringue and rim of plate. Bake meringue until golden brown and set, about 1 hour. Turn off oven and let meringue dry completely for 3 hours longer. Let meringue cool completely on wire rack, about 30 minutes. (Meringue will crack and deflate after baking to form crust.)

4. Meanwhile, whisk egg yolks, lemon zest, lemon juice, remaining ¼ teaspoon salt, and remaining ½ cup sugar together in medium saucepan until smooth. Cook over medium-low heat, stirring constantly, until mixture thickens slightly (about 170 degrees on instant-read thermometer), about 5 minutes. Strain curd through fine-mesh strainer into large bowl and press plastic wrap directly on surface. Refrigerate lemon curd until cooled completely, about 1 hour.

5. Whip cream in large bowl with electric mixer on medium-low speed until frothy, about 1 minute. Increase mixer speed to high and continue to whip until cream forms soft peaks, 1 to 3 minutes longer.

6. Fold half of whipped cream into cooled lemon curd until no white streaks remain. Spread lemon mixture into cooled meringue shell and smooth into even layer. Spread remaining whipped cream attractively over top and refrigerate until filling and topping have set, about 1 hour, before serving.

Notes from the Test Kitchen

This unusual pie won big fans in the test kitchen and didn't need any changing on our end. The resting times in the oven and refrigerator are crucial, otherwise the pie can be soft (not fully set) and not sliceable, or even gooey inside.

ENSURING MERINGUE BAKES EVENLY

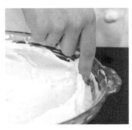

After spreading the meringue into the pie plate, run your finger around the inside edge to create a small gap between the meringue and the plate's edge. This will help the meringue rise and fall more evenly.

Light Bread Apple Pie

KENYA PURSLEY | MOSHEIM, TENNESSEE

"This recipe was my great-grandmother's and was passed to my grandmother and then on to me," writes Kenya. "I cook this dessert sometimes at work, at a small deli where most of our customers are farmers. They seem to love it." It's easy to understand why, even before you take a bite—this pie has visual appeal going for it in spades. Kenya doesn't top her casserole-style apple pie with standard crust, biscuits, or a crumble or crisp topping. Instead, she weaves strips of white bread together to create a lattice top. A cinnamon-sugar custard poured over the bread helps create a cohesive crust that is flavorful and slightly rich, yet delicate. You'll surely agree the effort is well worth it.

SERVES 12

4½	pounds Granny Smith apples (10 to 12 apples), peeled, cored, and cut into ½-inch pieces
1½	cups sugar
2	teaspoons ground cinnamon
12	slices hearty white sandwich bread
8	tablespoons (1 stick) unsalted butter, melted and cooled
1	large egg
2	tablespoons all-purpose flour
1	tablespoon whole milk
1	teaspoon vanilla extract

1. Combine apples, ¼ cup sugar, and 1 teaspoon cinnamon in large Dutch oven. Cover and cook over medium heat, stirring occasionally, until apples are almost tender but still hold their shape, about 10 minutes.

2. Drain apples thoroughly, then transfer to 13 by 9-inch baking dish and spread into even layer. Sprinkle apples with ¼ cup more sugar and let cool to room temperature, about 30 minutes.

3. Adjust oven rack to middle position and heat oven to 350 degrees. Trim crusts from each bread slice and slice bread lengthwise into four equal strips. Following photos, weave strips of bread on top of apples into lattice, trimming them as needed to fit in dish and fill in gaps.

4. Whisk remaining 1 cup sugar, melted butter, egg, flour, milk, vanilla, and remaining

1 teaspoon cinnamon together in bowl, then pour evenly over bread. Bake until bread is golden brown and crisp, 40 to 45 minutes, rotating dish halfway through baking. Let cool on wire rack for 20 minutes. Serve warm.

Notes from the Test Kitchen

Kenya's recipe called for boiling the apples until tender before adding them to the dish; for more texture and flavor, we precooked the apples (without water) until almost tender. We added some sugar along with some cinnamon for a sweeter filling. Be sure to trim and cut the bread just before weaving the lattice top to prevent the bread from cracking while weaving the strips together.

FORMING A LATTICE TOP

1. Arrange the bread strips into 12 rows (2 bread strips per row) over the filling, trimming the strips as needed to fit into the dish.

2. Weave the remaining bread strips in the opposite direction to make a lattice (about 3 strips per row). Use any leftover strips to fill in the gaps.

Hungarian Apple-Raspberry Pie

VALERIE SZLATENYI | WAKEFIELD, RHODE ISLAND

"This family recipe goes back to the early 1900s and came from Hungary with our grandparents. It originally was called a Hungarian filled cake but it's really more like a large apple pie. The use of sour cream is typical in Hungarian cooking and baking, as well as nuts and raisins. This dessert, which has graced our family tables for many years, is a huge hit with the children because of the crunchy cookie-like crust and sweetness of the raspberry jam." Valerie's grandparents' recipe is a popular Hungarian dessert known as *pité*. Though it is commonly referred to as a cake in Hungary, just as Valerie notes, it is actually more like a tart because of its bottom and top crusts and fruit filling in between (although this crust certainly does have a cakelike texture). Apple is the most popular type of pité, and the addition of berries, like the raspberries Valerie's family adds, is common. A sprinkling of bread crumbs over the fruit filling helps thicken it to just the right consistency. "With both parents gone we wanted to carry on the tradition of serving this tasty dessert but were unable to find the recipe for some years," she continues. "Our hope was my dad's only surviving 93-year-old brother, who still had a copy. When our son was little I filled a time capsule with special family memories. In it is a copy of this recipe and the names and a picture of his great-grandparents. I hope he will always cherish his heritage by making this recipe during holidays and passing it on to his future children."

SERVES 12

DOUGH

- 6 cups all-purpose flour
- 2 teaspoons baking powder
- 1½ teaspoons salt
- 2 cups sugar
- 4 large eggs
- 16 tablespoons (2 sticks) unsalted butter, cut into chunks and softened
- ½ cup sour cream
- 1½ teaspoons vanilla extract

FILLING

- 2 pounds Rhode Island Greening or Granny Smith apples (4 to 6), peeled, cored, and sliced ¼ inch thick
- 1 pound Macoun or Braeburn apples (2 to 3), peeled, cored, and sliced ¼ inch thick
- 1 teaspoon ground cinnamon
- ½ teaspoon ground nutmeg
- ½ cup dry plain bread crumbs
- ¼ cup sugar
- ½ cup raisins
- ¾ cup walnuts, chopped
- 1 (12-ounce) jar raspberry jam
- 1 tablespoon whole milk

1. **FOR THE DOUGH:** Whisk flour, baking powder, and salt together in bowl. In large bowl, beat sugar and eggs together with electric mixer on medium speed until smooth, about 1 minute. Beat in butter, sour cream, and vanilla until combined, about 1 minute, scraping down bowl

and beaters as needed. Reduce mixer speed to low and slowly add flour mixture until just combined.

2. Transfer dough to clean counter and divide into two equal pieces. Press each piece of dough into 4-inch square, wrap tightly in plastic wrap, and refrigerate until firm, 1 to 2 hours.

3. Adjust oven rack to middle position and heat oven to 350 degrees. Grease 13 by 9-inch baking dish. Roll one piece of dough into 16 by 12-inch rectangle on lightly floured counter. Following photos, loosely roll dough around rolling pin, then gently unroll dough over prepared pan. Gently ease dough into pan by lifting edge of dough with one hand while pressing into pan bottom with other.

4. FOR THE FILLING: Toss apples with cinnamon and nutmeg in bowl, then spread into dough-lined baking pan. Sprinkle evenly with bread crumbs, followed by sugar, raisins, and walnuts. Dollop jam over top, then smooth into even layer.

5. Roll remaining piece of dough into 14 by 10-inch rectangle on lightly floured counter. Loosely roll dough around rolling pin and gently unroll it over filling. Trim, fold, and crimp edges of dough together.

6. Poke vent holes in top crust at 2-inch intervals using fork, then brush with milk. Bake pie until crust is golden brown, 50 to 60 minutes, rotating pan halfway through baking. Let pie cool on wire rack until filling has set, about 2 hours. Serve slightly warm or at room temperature.

Notes from the Test Kitchen

Although this recipe seemed to have more flour than other Hungarian pité recipes we found, we liked how the filling could soak into this dough because of its cakelike texture. We liked the use of sour cream in the dough for the tenderness it lent, but we cut back on the full cup the original recipe called for to make the dough easier to work with, and at the same time we upped the butter for tenderness. We also cut back on the sugar in the filling by ¼ cup because the jam added enough sweetness on its own, and we decreased the oven temperature slightly to ensure that the top didn't overbrown. The baked, cooled pie can be covered loosely with plastic wrap and stored at room temperature for up to 1 day. To serve warm, reheat the pie in a 300-degree oven for about 15 minutes.

MAKING HUNGARIAN APPLE-RASPBERRY PIE

1. Use a rolling pin to transfer the first piece of rolled-out dough to the prepared baking pan. Lift and press the dough into the pan, letting the excess dough hang over the edge.

2. After spreading the apple mixture, bread crumbs, sugar, raisins, and walnuts over the dough, dollop the jam over the top and smooth it into an even layer.

3. After rolling out the second piece of dough, loosely roll the dough around the rolling pin, then gently unroll it over the filling.

4. Press the edges of the top and bottom crusts together. Trim the excess dough to ½ inch, tuck the edges underneath, and crimp using the tines of a fork.

Roly-Boley

JUDI ANDERSON | CHAPEL HILL, NORTH CAROLINA

"My mother's family (Boley) was from the Shenandoah Valley of Virginia. There are old English recipes similar to this called roly-poly, and I suspect they just added their own name to this over time. (They arrived in Virginia in the 1720s or so, so plenty of time for the original name to be massaged into one more memorable.) This was one of my favorites as a child, and I couldn't wait until the wild blackberries ripened on the vine so that we could enjoy this special treat. I still love it and the memories of my grandmother and my mother making it for me." The roly-poly Judi mentions is a centuries-old dessert. Early versions were made by brushing suet dough with jam, rolling it into a cylinder, wrapping it in cloth, and boiling or steaming it. Then baked versions made with flaky biscuit dough came along. Judi's family recipe strays from the modern classic because her Roly-Boley is not rolled at all. Instead, it calls for folding the dough around the filling to make individual tartlike packets, which are then served with crème anglaise. While it might be a break from tradition, the Boley family adaptation dresses up the old-fashioned roly-poly, turning it into a dessert worthy of a special occasion.

SERVES 4

CRUST

- 1½   **cups all-purpose flour**
- ½   **teaspoon salt**
- 10   **tablespoons (1¼ sticks) unsalted butter, cut into ¼-inch pieces and chilled**
- 4–6   **tablespoons ice water**

FILLING

- 2   **cups fresh blackberries**
- ⅓   **cup sugar**
- 1   **tablespoon all-purpose flour**
- 1½   **teaspoons fresh lemon juice**
- ¾   **teaspoon ground cinnamon**
- 1   **tablespoon unsalted butter, cut into 4 pieces**
- 1   **tablespoon whole milk**

CRÈME ANGLAISE

- 1   **cup whole milk**
-    **Pinch salt**
- 3   **large egg yolks**
- 2   **tablespoons sugar**
- ½   **teaspoon vanilla extract**

1. FOR THE CRUST: Process flour and salt together in food processor until combined. Scatter butter pieces over top and pulse until mixture resembles coarse cornmeal, about 15 pulses. Continue to pulse, adding water through feed tube 1 tablespoon at a time, until dough comes together and forms ball, about 10 pulses.

2. Transfer dough to clean counter and divide into four equal pieces. Wrap each piece of dough in plastic wrap and refrigerate until firm, about 1 hour. Before rolling dough out, let sit on counter to soften slightly, about 10 minutes.

3. FOR THE FILLING: Adjust oven rack to lowest position and heat oven to 350 degrees. Line rimmed baking sheet with parchment paper. Gently toss berries with sugar, flour, lemon juice, and ½ teaspoon cinnamon in bowl.

4. Roll each piece of dough into 8-inch circle on lightly floured counter. Following photos, mound one-quarter of filling in center of each dough round and dot with 1 piece of butter. Fold sides of dough over filling, being careful to leave ¼-inch border of dough around filling at base, then brush corners of pastry with water and fold top and bottom of pastry over filling. Press folds and corners gently to seal.

5. Gently transfer tarts to prepared baking sheet, spaced about 1½ inches apart. Brush with milk and sprinkle with remaining ¼ teaspoon cinnamon. Bake tarts until filling is bubbling and crust is golden brown, 55 to 60 minutes, rotating baking sheet halfway through baking. Let tarts cool on wire rack until filling has set, about 15 minutes.

6. FOR THE CRÈME ANGLAISE: Meanwhile, bring milk and salt to simmer in small saucepan over medium heat, stirring occasionally. Whisk egg yolks and sugar together in medium bowl until smooth. Whisk ½ cup of simmering milk mixture into egg yolks (to temper), then slowly whisk egg yolk mixture back into simmering milk mixture. Continue to cook sauce, whisking constantly, until thickened slightly and sauce coats back of spoon (about 175 degrees on instant-read thermometer), about 6 minutes.

7. Immediately strain sauce through fine-mesh strainer into clean bowl. Whisk in vanilla. Drizzle warm sauce over tarts and serve.

(Sauce can be cooled, covered, and refrigerated for up to 1 day. Reheat gently in small saucepan over low heat until warm before serving; do not simmer.)

Notes from the Test Kitchen

The original recipe didn't specify a type of pie crust; we settled on a sturdy all-butter tart dough, and we found that leaving a small opening in the dough when folding it over ensured that the filling didn't leak during baking. Arranging the packets so that they touched on the baking sheet, as the original recipe directed, encouraged uneven cooking and made it more difficult to serve, so we spread them out. Because we had a hard time making the original recipe's 3 to 4 cups of filling fit into four tarts, we reduced the amount. Avoid substituting store-bought pie dough for the homemade dough in this recipe.

MAKING A ROLY-BOLEY

1. Mound one-quarter of the filling in the center of one 8-inch dough round and dot with butter.

2. Fold the sides of the dough over the filling, leaving a ¼-inch border of dough around the filling at the base, brush the corners of the pastry with water, then fold over top and bottom.

Banbury Tarts

G. DAWN DELANEY | LEXINGTON, KENTUCKY

"My great-grandmother was renowned for her cooking and baking, all of which was from scratch. I was fortunate to receive her handwritten recipes from my grandmother. The recipes listed only the ingredients. Often, quantities were not even included and times and temperature were never provided. Shortly after I acquired the recipes, a family bridal shower was planned, and everyone was asked to bring baked goods to share. I decided to make her Banbury Tarts for this special occasion." G. Dawn goes on to note that although she had a little trouble with the recipe, everyone at the shower recognized her baked treats as her great-grandmother's Banbury Tarts, and the elder generation helped her iron out the recipe so that she could make them just like her great-grandmother. Even though they might not have been perfect on that first try, she says that "my Banbury Tarts were the first to disappear." The history of this pastry goes much further back than even G. Dawn's great-grandmother. The British town of Banbury has been well known for making Banbury cakes since at least the 17th century, and they are still popular today. The oldest versions wrapped pastry around a spiced raisin filling and were more like turnovers. Round, tartlike versions that were scored and broken into pieces began appearing by the 19th century, and by the early 1900s so many variations for Banbury cakes and tarts existed that a filling made from raisins, lemon peel, and egg was enough to mark the recipe as "Banbury." G. Dawn's family version turns them into small, bite-size treats, perfect for gift-giving or a party spread.

MAKES 2 DOZEN TARTS

½ cup sugar
1 large egg
½ teaspoon grated fresh lemon zest and
  2 teaspoons fresh lemon juice

½ cup raisins, chopped
1 recipe Double-Crust Pie Dough
  (page 167), softened at room temperature
  for 10 minutes

(Continued on page 184)

1. Whisk sugar, egg, lemon zest, and lemon juice together in small saucepan. Stir in raisins. Cook mixture over medium-low heat, stirring constantly, until sugar dissolves and mixture thickens, about 5 minutes. Transfer mixture to bowl and let cool completely, about 15 minutes.

2. Adjust oven rack to middle position and heat oven to 400 degrees. Line rimmed baking sheet with parchment paper. Roll one piece of dough out on lightly floured counter to even ⅛-inch thickness. Following photos, stamp out 24 rounds using 2-inch round cookie cutter and transfer to prepared baking sheet, spaced about 1 inch apart. Place 1 teaspoon of raisin mixture in center of each dough round.

3. Roll remaining piece of dough out on lightly floured counter to even ⅛-inch thickness. Stamp out 24 rounds using 2-inch round cookie cutter, and cut small X in center of each with paring knife. Brush exposed edge of dough around filling with water, top with dough rounds marked with an X, and press edges together to seal. Bake tarts until golden brown, about 20 minutes, rotating baking sheet halfway through baking.

4. Let tarts cool on baking sheet for 5 minutes, then transfer to wire rack to cool completely before serving.

Notes from the Test Kitchen

These cute little tarts disappeared quickly in the test kitchen. We found there was too much filling for the number of tarts specified in the original recipe, so we scaled the ingredients down accordingly. This recipe's success depends in large part on using a good, flaky pie dough; avoid substituting store-bought pie dough here.

MAKING BANBURY TARTS

1. Using a 2-inch round cookie cutter, stamp out 24 rounds from one piece of the dough. Transfer the rounds to the prepared baking sheet.

2. Place 1 teaspoon of the raisin mixture in the center of each round.

3. Stamp out 24 rounds from the remaining piece of dough, then cut a small X in the center of each with a paring knife.

4. Brush the exposed edge of dough around the filling with water using your finger or a pastry brush. Lay dough rounds marked with an X on top, and gently press the edges of dough together to seal.

Ina's Butter Tarts

SUSIE THOMAS | LINDEN, MICHIGAN

"This recipe originally was written out for us by my grandmother, Ina Johnston, on the back of a Liquor Control Board of Ontario order form," writes Susie. "I was born when my grandmother was 65 and already had eight grandchildren. I was the youngest girl and was fortunate enough to have spent a lot of time with her. She taught me to make pastry, pies, shortbread, and, of course, butter tarts. My grandmother was originally from Brechin, Scotland, and this recipe came to Canada with her." Butter tarts—small, flaky pastry shells with a simple yet rich filling made from butter, brown sugar, and eggs—are a favorite in Canada and are traditionally thought to have originated in that country, though a few other countries, like Scotland, have similar recipes. "They have become a must at any gathering and the most requested treat in my baking repertoire."

MAKES 3 DOZEN SMALL TARTS

1   recipe Double-Crust Pie Dough (page 167), softened at room temperature for 10 minutes

1   cup packed light brown sugar

1   large egg

2   tablespoons whole milk

1   tablespoon unsalted butter, melted

1   teaspoon vanilla extract

6   tablespoons raisins

1. Grease three 12-cup mini-muffin tins. Working with one piece of dough at a time, roll out on lightly floured counter to even $\frac{1}{16}$-inch thickness. Stamp out 18 rounds using 3-inch round cookie cutter. Fit each round into prepared muffin cups, gently lifting edge of dough with one hand while pressing into cup bottom with other (dough edges will protrude just slightly above rim). Poke holes in bottom of tart shells using fork. Refrigerate unbaked shells until firm, about 1 hour.

2. Adjust oven racks to upper-middle and lower-middle positions and heat oven to 375 degrees. Place muffin tins on two rimmed baking sheets. Bake until dough looks dry and is light in color, about 8 minutes, switching and rotating baking sheets halfway through baking.

Transfer muffin tins to wire racks and let shells cool to room temperature.

3. Whisk sugar, egg, milk, butter, and vanilla together in bowl, then transfer to liquid measuring cup. Place $\frac{1}{2}$ teaspoon raisins in each shell, then pour egg mixture over raisins until it reaches about $\frac{1}{8}$ inch from top edge (about 1 teaspoon; you may have extra egg mixture).

4. Carefully transfer tarts to oven and bake until filling is set, about 25 minutes, switching and rotating baking sheets halfway through baking. Let tarts cool in tins for 5 minutes, then transfer to wire rack and let cool completely before serving.

Notes from the Test Kitchen

The original recipe called for "shallow tart tins," but we found several recipes using more-convenient mini-muffin tins. Parbaking the crusts helped make them crisp, and docking the bottom kept them from ballooning. If you don't have three mini-muffin tins, you can bake the tart shells through step 2 in batches, transfer them to a rimmed baking sheet, then fill and bake the tarts as directed in steps 3 and 4. You can substitute two rounds of store-bought pie dough for the home-made dough; be sure to roll the dough rounds out further to an even $\frac{1}{16}$-inch thickness before using.

Biggum's Fried Pies

CAROLYN BOUNDS | SAINT LOUIS, MISSOURI

Pies are always a winner, but when you make them personal-sized and fried, they're just too good to resist. Small fruit-filled fried pies like Carolyn's have existed in America since Colonial times, and today they remain a Southern favorite, especially when paired with barbecue. Classic fried pie recipes (Carolyn's included) call for apple or peaches as the filling. Notes Carolyn: "My family loves these old-fashioned pies. I'll even mix the apple and peach together. The only problem with these pies is that they go soooo fast!"

MAKES 16 MINI HAND PIES

- 2 apples or 3 large peaches, peeled, cored or pitted, and sliced ¼ inch thick
- ½ cup sugar
- 1 tablespoon unsalted butter
- 2 tablespoons water
- 1½ teaspoons cornstarch
- 1½ teaspoons ground cinnamon
- ⅛ teaspoon ground nutmeg
- 1 recipe Double-Crust Pie Dough (page 167), softened at room temperature for 10 minutes
- 4 cups vegetable oil

1. Combine apples, ¼ cup sugar, butter, water, cornstarch, ½ teaspoon cinnamon, and nutmeg in medium saucepan. Cook over medium-low heat, stirring often, until apples soften and mixture has thickened, about 10 minutes. Off heat, mash apple mixture with potato masher into coarse paste; transfer to bowl.

2. Line rimmed baking sheet with parchment paper. Combine remaining ¼ cup sugar and remaining 1 teaspoon cinnamon in small bowl.

3. Working with one piece of dough at a time, roll out on lightly floured counter to even ⅛-inch thickness. Stamp out 8 rounds using 4-inch round cookie cutter. Place 1 tablespoon of filling in center of each dough round.

Following photos on page 46, brush edges with water, fold dough in half over filling, and crimp edges with fork to seal. Transfer hand pies to prepared baking sheet and refrigerate until firm, about 30 minutes.

4. Heat oil in large saucepan over medium-high heat until it registers 350 degrees on instant-read thermometer. Carefully place about 4 hand pies into hot oil and fry until golden brown on both sides, about 2 minutes per side, adjusting heat as necessary to maintain oil at 350 degrees.

5. Using slotted spoon, transfer hand pies to paper towel–lined plate and sprinkle with sugar and cinnamon mixture. Repeat with remaining hand pies.

Notes from the Test Kitchen
We had some trouble getting Carolyn's dough to hold together so we opted to use our own pie dough, and we cut back on the filling since the original made more than necessary. Adding a little water to the pan when cooking the filling ensured that it didn't scorch. You can substitute two rounds of store-bought pie dough for the homemade; if necessary, roll the dough rounds out further to an even ⅛-inch thickness before using.

CHOW CHOW

Putting Food By

Papa Gus's Kosher Dill Pickles 190

Baba's Bread and Butter Pickles 191

Slaked Lime Pickles 192

Grams's Pickled Peaches 196

Great-Aunt Stella's Watermelon Pickles 198

Chow Chow 199

Tomato Butter 200

Plum Catsup 202

Grandma's Tangy Rhubarb Jam 203

Papa Gus's Kosher Dill Pickles

BARBARA KIPNIS | PALM COAST, FLORIDA

"My four grandparents usually came to our house for Sunday dinner when I was a child. I dreaded the times when Grandpa H or Grandpa K, pausing their gin rummy game, would use his cane to pull me over and ask the vital question, 'Barbara, which of us makes the best dill pickles?' How could I answer and please them both? Because actually, my father made the best dill pickles! A cosmetic chemist, he had merged and modified both their recipes until he had a never-fail, simple pickle recipe that made us look forward to summer, when the freshest pickling cucumbers would be found. Dad's recipe used no preservatives, so after the pickles reached the perfect crunchy stage, the jar had to be refrigerated to slow down the progression from 'new' dill to 'sour' dill. Since our refrigerator wouldn't hold more than one gallon jug, we never made more than one jar at a time. Now retired in Florida, I can get pickling cucumbers year-round, but I still look forward to late spring, when the smallest, freshest cukes are available in the Flagler Beach Farmers' Market."

MAKES ONE 1-GALLON JAR

- 1 large bunch fresh dill
- 3½ pounds (3- to 4-inch-long) pickling cucumbers, washed, blossom ends trimmed and discarded
- 6 garlic cloves, sliced thin
- 1 teaspoon red pepper flakes
- ½ cup Morton kosher salt or ½ cup plus 3 tablespoons Diamond Crystal kosher salt
- ¼ cup white or cider vinegar

1. Thoroughly clean and dry one 1-gallon jar. Place half of dill in bottom of jar. Pack with cucumbers, garlic, and pepper flakes, then top with remaining dill.

2. Dissolve salt and vinegar into 8 cups water, then pour into jar. Place small plate inside jar on top of floating cucumbers and weight with sealed jar of water to submerge cucumbers completely in brine. (Cucumbers must be submerged completely during fermentation.)

3. Cover jar opening with clean towel and let cucumbers ferment at room temperature for 4 days, skimming surface of brine daily with large spoon. Once fermented, pickles are edible; cover jar with lid and refrigerate pickles in brine for up to 3 months.

Notes from the Test Kitchen

We loved these dill pickles for their garlicky flavor and little kick from red pepper flakes. Barbara's dad's recipe worked fine. Barbara noted that ingredients (other than the brine) could be adjusted to taste, but we liked them just as her recipe had suggested. We did, however, add ¼ cup vinegar to the brine and trim the blossom ends from the cucumbers (the bottom ends, opposite the stem) because they contain enzymes that can cause soft pickles. Make sure to purchase cucumbers small enough to fit in the jar. Discard the pickles if they become soft or slimy.

Baba's Bread and Butter Pickles

PEYTON PROCACCINI | EASTON, MARYLAND

"As long as I can remember, my dad had a garden bursting at the seams with fruits and vegetables, and there was no short supply of fresh veggies in our house. He arrived home with bushels of cucumbers one summer and announced to my mother (Baba, as she is called by her 20 grandchildren!) that he would like her to make bread and butter pickles. Well, my mother couldn't find a recipe she liked, so she created her own. She would put up quarts and quarts of these delicious pickles, and we ate them all year long. I remember as a child watching her in the kitchen and thinking the whole process to be very daunting. After I got married, however, I boldly asked for the recipe one day because I missed those delicious jars of pickles and wanted to make them myself. I have to admit I was nervous, but I was thrilled at the end to have that same wonderful taste that I remembered as a child. My dad is no longer with us, and Baba, at 84 years young, doesn't make them anymore, but my three sisters and I have carried on the tradition of presenting our friends and family with these scrumptious homemade pickles ever since."

MAKES SEVEN 1-PINT JARS

1	cup salt
6	pounds pickling cucumbers, washed, sliced crosswise ¼ inch thick, blossom ends discarded
6	onions, peeled, washed, and cut into ¼-inch rings
6	red bell peppers, washed, stemmed, seeded, and sliced ½ inch thick
6	cups sugar (2⅔ pounds)
6	cups white vinegar
⅓	cup celery seeds
⅓	cup mustard seeds
1½	teaspoons ground turmeric

1. Dissolve salt in 8 cups cold water in large container, then add 6 cups ice cubes. Submerge cucumbers, onions, and bell peppers in brine, cover, and let soak for 3 hours. Drain and rinse vegetables thoroughly, discarding any remaining ice cubes.

2. Bring sugar, vinegar, celery seeds, mustard seeds, and turmeric to boil in 12-quart pot, stirring often. Add drained vegetables, return to brief simmer, stirring occasionally, then remove from heat.

3. Following Canning 101 steps on page 195, transfer hot pickles and liquid to 7 hot, sterilized 1-pint jars, and process. Processing times depend on your altitude: 10 minutes for up to 1,000 feet, 15 minutes for 1,001 to 6,000 feet, and 20 minutes for above 6,000 feet.

Notes from the Test Kitchen

Tasters agreed, homemade bread and butter pickles beat store-bought any day. Peyton's recipe called for slicing the pickles very thick; we settled on ¼ inch. You can substitute 1½ cups Morton kosher salt or 2 cups Diamond Crystal kosher salt for the table salt; for more information on measuring salt in large quantities, see page 194. We also discarded the blossom ends from the cucumbers (the bottom ends, opposite the stem) because they contain enzymes that can cause soft pickles.

Slaked Lime Pickles

BARB KAALBERG | SUN PRAIRIE, WISCONSIN

You might imagine all pickled cucumbers are pretty much the same, but one glimpse of Barb's Slaked Lime Pickles and you'll realize that's certainly not the case. "Lime" comes into play in her recipe in two ways. First, she uses pickling lime, aka slaked lime, a food-safe powdered chemical (calcium hydroxide) that many old-fashioned recipes called for to keep pickled vegetables extra-crunchy. Then there's the color, a deep lime-green that comes from the addition of food coloring. Surprisingly, tinting pickles has quite a history. In the 19th and early 20th centuries, pickles were often tinted a bright green using copper. Cookbooks would direct cooks to throw in a copper half-pence, or to use "blue stone," which is copper sulfate. Commercial pickled and canned vegetable producers found that consumers preferred the bright color, and it also happened to conceal inferior produce. Of course, pickling with copper added is quite toxic, but it wasn't until the Pure Food and Drug Act of 1906 that copper was banned as a food additive/colorant. Nowadays, recipes (often from the South) call for adding coloring to pickles, whether it's in the form of liquid food coloring, Red Hot candies, or even Kool-Aid. Barb writes: "We looked forward to these every year. They were so crisp and sweet. The green food coloring gave them a dark green color that we found fascinating, and the crunch when you bit into them was fun!"

MAKES SIX 1-QUART JARS

- 2 **cups pickling lime (also called slaked lime)**
- 7 **pounds cucumbers, washed, sliced crosswise ¼ inch thick, blossom ends discarded**
- 10⅓ **cups sugar (4½ pounds)**
- 8 **cups cider vinegar**
- 2 **tablespoons salt**
- 1 **tablespoon pickling spice**
- 1 **teaspoon celery seeds**
- 1 **teaspoon mustard seeds**
- ¼ **teaspoon green food coloring**

1. Dissolve pickling lime in 2 gallons cold water in large container. Submerge cucumbers in lime mixture, cover, and let soak, stirring occasionally, for 24 hours.

2. Drain and rinse cucumbers thoroughly and transfer to clean, large container. Cover with cold water and let cucumbers soak for 30 minutes.

3. Drain cucumbers and transfer to large Dutch oven. Stir in sugar, vinegar, salt, pickling spice, celery seeds, mustard seeds, and food coloring. Bring mixture to boil, then reduce to simmer and cook, stirring occasionally, until pickles absorb flavors, about 35 minutes.

4. Following Canning 101 steps on page 195, transfer hot pickles and liquid to 6 hot, sterilized 1-quart jars, and process. Processing times depend on your altitude: 10 minutes for up to 1,000 feet, 15 minutes for 1,001 to 6,000 feet, and 20 minutes for above 6,000 feet.

Notes from the Test Kitchen

Barb's recipe worked fine. She didn't specify an amount of food coloring; we found that ¼ teaspoon did the trick. You can find pickling lime where other canning supplies are sold or online.

CANNING 101

Canning is a fantastic way to preserve foods you love, from jams and jellies to all manner of pickles, so that you can enjoy them throughout the year. You might hesitate to jump into canning, but it is actually a very simple and safe process, especially if you stick with water-bath canning, as we do in this book. Here is a quick overview, including the equipment you'll need and a walk-through of how to can recipes using a water bath.

EQUIPMENT

It pays to have the right equipment for canning. You don't need anything too fancy or expensive. You can typically find everything you need at a good kitchen supply or hardware store, and they often sell all-in-one canning kits to make the shopping that much easier. You'll need:

1. **A Large (18- to 21-Quart) Canning Pot** for processing and sterilizing the jars (although you can also sterilize the jars in the dishwasher).

2. **A Canning Insert with Handles** (or a rack) that fits inside the pot. Often canning pots are sold with a rack, but we prefer the canning insert, as it makes pulling the jars out of boiling water a snap.

3. **Glass Canning Jars** (aka Mason jars), which are sold with flat metal lids and threaded metal screw bands that hold the lids in place during processing.

4. **A Canning-Specific Jar Lifter,** which allows you to grasp jars very firmly and makes pulling filled jars out of a water bath much easier than using tongs.

5. **A Wide-Mouth Stainless Steel Funnel** will make pouring liquids, like jams, into jars tidy and easy.

TYPES OF SALT FOR PICKLING

When using ½ cup or more of salt in a recipe, as is called for in many pickling recipes, the type of salt you use matters. Kosher salt has a coarser crystal structure and packs fewer ounces into each cup compared with table salt. In fact, even the volume measurements between the two major brands of kosher salt—Morton and Diamond Crystal—vary significantly. Here's how they measure up:

| **1 cup table salt** | = | **1½ cups Morton kosher salt** | = | **2 cups Diamond Crystal kosher salt** |

STEP-BY-STEP WATER-BATH CANNING

1. PRESTERILIZE

The easiest way to pre-sterilize jars is to run them through your dishwasher. Alternatively, you can clean the jars using hot, soapy water, place them in your large canning pot, cover them with water, and simmer them for 10 minutes. (After removing the jars, leave the water in the pot over the heat so it will be ready for step 3.) The jars should still be hot (or warm) when it's time to fill them. To avoid damaging the lids, it is best to simmer them in a small pan of hot water over medium heat. You don't need to sterilize the bands or every piece of equipment you will be using during the process, though, if you like, you can sterilize the funnel and ladle being used to fill the jars.

2. PREPARE FOR PROCESSING, MAKE THE RECIPE, AND FILL THE JARS

Because boiling the amount of water necessary for processing takes some time, before you prepare the recipe, fill your canning pot with water and start heating it on the stovetop.

You want to make sure your recipe and the jars are both hot when it's time to can, so if your recipe takes more than 30 minutes, you can prepare it before sterilizing the jars; otherwise prepare it after sterilizing the jars. Fill the still-warm jars with the prepared recipe, leaving ½ inch of room at the top. If pickling, make sure the fruit or vegetable is fully covered by the brine/pickling liquid. Stir the contents to release air bubbles, wipe the rim of each jar clean, then put on the lids and screw on the bands until just fingertip-tight (don't completely tighten them; air in the jar needs to be able to escape).

3. PROCESS

Place the filled jars in the canning insert and lower the insert into the pot of boiling water (or lower the jars into the pot and onto the rack using a jar lifter), making sure the jars are covered by at least 1 inch of water. Process the jars for the amount of time prescribed in the recipe, making sure the water is at a rapid boil before you start the clock. Processing times vary not only based on the size of the jars you are using but also altitude. As elevation increases, water boils at lower temperatures that are less effective for canning. We specify the times for various elevations in each recipe. After the processing time is up, turn off the heat and let the jars sit in the water for 5 minutes.

4. COOL

Remove the cans from the pot using the canning insert and jar lifter (or just use a jar lifter to remove the jars if you are only using a rack) and let the jars cool on a wire rack or towel for 24 hours. During cooling, you should hear a popping noise, which is the sign that the jars are sealed airtight and the process is complete. You can check the seal by removing the bands; the lid should be taut and should adhere tightly to the rim of the jar. Store sealed jars in a cool, dark place; they will keep for at least 1 year.

Grams's Pickled Peaches

SUZANNE ALEXANDER | SOUTH POINT, OHIO

"My grandmother Helen Ackerson, whom I called Grams, had a cut-glass bowl filled with her Pickled Peaches at every family gathering and every holiday meal, whether it was turkey at Thanksgiving or ham at Easter. Thirty-five years ago, Grams served my new husband Ron her Pickled Peaches, as an accompaniment with a leg of lamb dinner, and he was in love! Ron left that meal with admiration not only for Grams's wonderful cooking, but for her recipe for Pickled Peaches," Suzanne writes. "He had great plans for our future Labor Day weekends. For years after, that holiday weekend was devoted to a bushel of just-ripe peaches, sugar, vinegar, cinnamon sticks, cloves, and canning jars. While Ron peeled the peaches, I prepared the tangy, spiced syrup. Then we cooked the peaches in the syrup, added it all to the jars, and canned them in a water bath. The results were enjoyed at our own dinners with family and friends, and also given as gifts along with the recipe so friends could start their own tradition."

MAKES FIVE 1-PINT JARS

- 5¾ cups sugar (2½ pounds)
- 1 cup white vinegar
- 3 cinnamon sticks, broken into pieces
- 2 teaspoons whole cloves
- 5 pounds ripe peaches, washed, peeled, halved, and pitted

1. Bring sugar, vinegar, cinnamon, and cloves to boil in large Dutch oven, stirring often. Stir in peaches, bring to simmer, and cook until peaches are just tender and tip of knife can be inserted into peach with little to no resistance, 6 to 10 minutes.

2. Following Canning 101 steps on page 195, transfer hot peaches and liquid to 5 hot, sterilized 1-pint jars and process. Processing times depend on your altitude: 20 minutes for up to 1,000 feet, 25 minutes for 1,001 to 3,000 feet, 30 minutes for 3,001 to 6,000 feet, and 35 minutes for above 6,000 feet.

Notes from the Test Kitchen

Suzanne's memory of her grandmother's holiday pickled peaches reminded some of our tasters of their own grandmothers' similar tradition. We thought five jars was plenty (a few for the holidays, a few for gifts), so we cut the recipe in half, and we reduced the amount of cloves in our scaled-down version for a more balanced flavor.

PEELING PEACHES AND TOMATOES

1. With a paring knife, score a small X at the base of each peach or tomato, then simmer in boiling water until the skins loosen, 30 to 60 seconds.

2. After cooling the peaches or tomatoes in ice water for 1 minute, use a paring knife to remove strips of loosened peel, starting at the X.

Great-Aunt Stella's Watermelon Pickles

BO YOUNG | GRANVILLE, NEW YORK

"Waste not, want not, my great-aunt Stella would trim watermelon rinds and pickle them in sweet brine, coloring them a vivid, watermelon green," Bo writes. "I was surprised the first time I made them to realize she dyed them to get them to be the 'right color.'" Though Bo hails from the North, pickling watermelon rind has long been a Southern tradition, a favorite for serving at barbecues or cookouts. As Bo points out, it's a great, tasty way to make use of what would otherwise just get thrown away, and a fantastic, fun snack that doesn't have to be reserved for just those times when you fire up the grill.

MAKES FIVE 1-PINT JARS

3½   pounds watermelon rind, washed and cut into 1-inch pieces (1 watermelon)
3   tablespoons salt
2¼   cups sugar
1½   cups cider vinegar
2   cinnamon sticks, broken into pieces
1   teaspoon whole cloves

1. Combine watermelon rind and salt in large container, then cover by 1 inch of water. Cover and refrigerate for at least 8 hours or up to 12 hours.

2. Drain and rinse watermelon rind thoroughly, then transfer to large Dutch oven and cover by 1 inch of water. Bring to boil over medium-high heat, then reduce to simmer and cook until rind is just tender, about 30 minutes; drain thoroughly.

3. Bring sugar, 2 cups water, vinegar, cinnamon sticks, and cloves to boil in large Dutch oven, stirring often. Add rind, bring to simmer, and cook, stirring occasionally, until rind softens and turns translucent, about 30 minutes.

4. Following Canning 101 steps on page 195, transfer hot rind and liquid to 5 hot, sterilized 1-pint jars and process. Processing times depend on your altitude: 10 minutes for up to 1,000 feet, 15 minutes for 1,001 to 3,000 feet, 20 minutes for 3,001 to 6,000 feet, and 25 minutes for above 6,000 feet.

Notes from the Test Kitchen

Those in the test kitchen who'd never had watermelon pickles quickly became fans. Bo's recipe called for cinnamon and clove oils or pickling spice. We thought the oils were an interesting touch, but since they can be hard to locate we found we could achieve a similarly flavored pickle recipe by simply using cinnamon sticks and whole cloves. Bo didn't call for food coloring like her great-aunt had done, but feel free to add a few drops of green food coloring for a fun touch.

Chow Chow

CAROLYN RENNER | WEATHERFORD, TEXAS

"If you've never had homemade chow chow alongside a heaping helping of home-cooked pinto beans, then you don't know what you've been missing," Carolyn proclaims, noting that it's "great with a big chunk of buttered home-cooked cornbread. This brings me back down to why we were born; to savor Mom's simply wonderful chow chow, pintos, and cornbread." Chow chow is still popular in the South, and enjoying it with beans and cornbread is one of the most old-fashioned ways to eat it, but it's also great for topping hot dogs and hamburgers. The name originates from China, where the term *chow chow* was applied to almost anything that was mixed or various, from pickles to turbulent waters. Jars of mixed pickles were likely kept on ships traveling to America in the 19th century, when Chinese immigrants came over to work in the gold mines and railroads. Yet pickled condiments were introduced before that from India, going by names like "Piccalilli" and "Indian Pickle" in mid 18th century cookbooks. Carolyn's recipe, with a great mix of vegetables, earns the name, and with its sweet-tart flavor and mild heat, it's a sure win for serving at cookouts and family dinners alike.

MAKES SEVEN 1-PINT JARS

- 8 green bell peppers, washed, stemmed, seeded, and chopped coarse
- 1 red bell pepper, washed, stemmed, seeded, and chopped coarse
- 6 onions, peeled, washed, and chopped coarse
- 4 cups coarsely chopped green cabbage, washed
- 2 green tomatoes, washed, cored, and chopped coarse
- 2 jalapeño chiles, washed, seeded, and chopped coarse
- 3 cups sugar
- 1 cup white vinegar
- 2 tablespoons mustard seeds
- 1 tablespoon celery seeds
- 1 tablespoon salt
- 1 teaspoon pepper
- 1 teaspoon allspice berries

1. Working in batches, process bell peppers, onions, cabbage, tomatoes, and jalapeños in food processor until coarsely chopped, about 10 seconds; transfer to 12-quart pot. Stir in sugar, vinegar, mustard seeds, celery seeds, salt, and pepper and bring mixture to boil.

2. Meanwhile, place allspice berries in double-layer cheesecloth pouch and tie securely with butcher's twine. Once mixture is boiling, add allspice pouch to pot, reduce to simmer, and cook until vegetables are tender, 20 to 30 minutes. Discard allspice pouch.

3. Following Canning 101 steps on page 195, transfer hot mixture to 7 hot, sterilized 1-pint jars and process. Processing times depend on your altitude: 5 minutes for up to 1,000 feet, 10 minutes for 1,001 to 6,000 feet, and 15 minutes for above 6,000 feet.

Notes from the Test Kitchen

We loved this recipe, especially served with grilled meats. Carolyn's directions were loose so we filled in the blanks, adding cooking times and temperatures. We didn't need to change a thing about the ingredients.

Tomato Butter

SUSAN SIMONOVICH | NORTH WALES, PENNSYLVANIA

"Tomato Butter has been a staple in Pennsylvania Dutch pantries for generations, usually served as a condiment with roast pork and beef. You can sometimes find it for sale at farm stands in the Amish country near Lancaster, Pennsylvania. This particular recipe (there are many) was handed down from my great-grandmother and has been made faithfully by each generation. My siblings and I continue the tradition, making several batches in early September when tomatoes are $5 a peck at local farm markets. Many of our friends have become addicted to the stuff over the years and some make their own. Those who don't, wait anxiously for that special Christmas gift every year! It's the perfect accompaniment to roast meats, especially pork. We also use it as a glaze for meatloaf and to give that *je ne sais quoi* to canned baked beans (along with ketchup and mustard) and stews. My sister is famous for her cheesesteaks (a Philly staple) because of her 'secret' sauce—equal parts ketchup and Tomato Butter!"

MAKES TWELVE 1-CUP JARS

- 14 pounds tomatoes, washed and cored
- 9 cups sugar (4 pounds)
- 2 cups cider vinegar
- 1 tablespoon ground cinnamon
- 1 teaspoon ground cloves

1. Following photos on page 197, peel tomatoes, then remove seeds following photo at right and coarsely chop.

2. Bring tomatoes, sugar, vinegar, cinnamon, and cloves to boil in large Dutch oven, stirring occasionally. Reduce to simmer and cook, stirring often, until tomatoes break down and mixture thickens to jamlike consistency, about 4 hours.

3. Tomato butter can be refrigerated in airtight container for up to 1 month, or canned following Canning 101 steps on page 195. If canning, transfer hot tomato butter to 12 hot, sterilized 1-cup jars and process. Processing times depend on your altitude: 5 minutes for up to 1,000 feet, 10 minutes for 1,001 to 6,000 feet, and 15 minutes for above 6,000 feet.

Notes from the Test Kitchen

Tasters discovered that this sweet, nicely spiced jam was fantastic in countless roles, from being a great match to both hard and soft cheeses (try ricotta or goat cheese) to serving as the "T" in BLTs. Susan's recipe called for 12 to 14 pounds of tomatoes; we found we needed the full amount.

SEEDING TOMATOES

After peeling the tomato, cut it in half and squeeze out the seeds.

Plum Catsup

LEAH HEIDEMAN | COLVILLE, WASHINGTON

When most people think of ketchup, they think of tomatoes, but ketchup (or catsup) was not always synonymous with the tomato. Back in the 17th century, recipes for catsup featured a variety of fruits, vegetables, nuts, and fish. Leah's recipe, made with plums, harks back to those earlier versions. "My grandmother and mother have made this recipe my entire life," she writes, "and my mother has said that her mother made it her entire life. I am happy to say that my children have grown to love plum catsup, and intend on making it for their children as well. The warm, spicy, and sweet flavor on pork chops still reminds me of Grandma Mitchell even after all of these years."

MAKES TWELVE 1-CUP JARS

5	pounds ripe Italian plums, washed, pitted, and chopped coarse
2	tablespoons water
7	cups sugar (3 pounds)
2	cups cider vinegar
1	tablespoon ground cinnamon
1	tablespoon salt
2	teaspoons pepper
1½	teaspoons ground cloves

1. Cook plums and water in large Dutch oven over medium-high heat, stirring occasionally, until plums release their liquid and are softened, about 15 minutes. Bring to simmer and cook until plums are very soft and beginning to disintegrate, about 30 minutes.

2. Mash plums with potato masher until mostly smooth, then stir in sugar, vinegar, cinnamon, salt, pepper, and cloves. Bring to simmer and cook, stirring often, until mixture thickens to jamlike consistency, 1½ to 2 hours.

3. Plum catsup can be refrigerated in airtight container for up to 1 month, or canned following Canning 101 steps on page 195. If canning, transfer hot catsup to 12 hot, sterilized 1-cup jars and process. Processing times depend on your altitude: 5 minutes for up to 1,000 feet, 10 minutes for 1,001 to 6,000 feet, and 15 minutes for above 6,000 feet.

Notes from the Test Kitchen

Leah's unique catsup has an appealing, chunky yet loose texture and slightly sweet flavor that makes it stand out. Her recipe didn't specify to mash the plums but ours didn't cook down enough, even with a longer cooking time and cutting the plums into pieces first, so we found it a necessity. We cut her recipe in half to make a reasonable amount, and scaled down the proportion of clove because tasters felt its flavor came on a little strong. This recipe calls for blue, aka Italian, plums, but if you can't find them regular plums will work fine.

Grandma's Tangy Rhubarb Jam

AUDREY BEAUVAIS | ARLINGTON HEIGHTS, ILLINOIS

"Times were tough when I was a child. Grandma had a kitchen garden, fenced to protect her carefully tended plants from foraging chickens on the small Indiana farm. I hungered for the rhubarb jam she and my mom put up each summer. Memories of toasted homemade bread, buttered, of course, with hand-churned butter and then topped with a generous dollop of jam still make me hungry. Now I use Grandma's tangy spread atop bricks of creamy cheese for an easy appetizer for drop-in guests." Whether you pair it with a cheese platter or sandwiches, or just smear it on buttered toast like Audrey does, this chutneylike jam with raisins and walnuts has a great tangy flavor and appealing texture that is sure to make you a big fan.

MAKES EIGHT 1-CUP JARS

1½   **cups raisins**
1   **orange, washed and cut into 1-inch chunks (do not peel)**
3½   **pounds rhubarb, washed, leaves discarded, stalks cut into ½-inch pieces**
5¾   **cups sugar (2½ pounds)**
1   **cup walnuts, chopped**

1. Pulse raisins and orange chunks in food processor until coarsely ground, about 5 pulses; transfer to large bowl. Stir in rhubarb and sugar and let sit until rhubarb releases some of its liquid, about 30 minutes.

2. Transfer rhubarb mixture to 12-quart pot, bring to simmer, and cook, stirring often, until rhubarb breaks down and mixture thickens to jamlike consistency, about 1½ hours. Off heat, stir in walnuts.

3. Jam can be refrigerated in airtight container for up to 1 month, or canned following Canning 101 steps on page 195. If canning, transfer hot jam to 8 hot, sterilized 1-cup jars and process. Processing times depend on your altitude: 5 minutes for up to 1,000 feet, 10 minutes for 1,001 to 6,000 feet, and 15 minutes for above 6,000 feet.

Notes from the Test Kitchen

Tasters particularly loved the unusual addition of walnuts to Audrey's jam (and since Audrey's recipe called for a range in the amount of nuts, we went on the higher end). We did cut her recipe in half, but we still used the full amount of orange since we liked the bright flavor it lent.

Conversions & Equivalencies

SOME SAY COOKING IS A SCIENCE AND AN ART. We would say that geography has a hand in it, too. Flour milled in the United Kingdom and elsewhere will feel and taste different from flour milled in the United States. So we cannot promise that the loaf of bread you bake in Canada or England will taste the same as a loaf baked in the States, but we can offer guidelines for converting weights and measures. We also recommend that you rely on your instincts when making our recipes. Refer to the visual cues provided. If the bread dough hasn't "come together in a ball," as described, you may need to add more flour—even if the recipe doesn't tell you to. You be the judge.

The recipes in this book were developed using standard U.S. measures following U.S. government guidelines. The charts below offer equivalents for U.S., metric, and Imperial (U.K.) measures. All conversions are approximate and have been rounded up or down to the nearest whole number.

EXAMPLE:

1 teaspoon	=	4.9292 milliliters, rounded up to 5 milliliters
1 ounce	=	28.3495 grams, rounded down to 28 grams

VOLUME CONVERSIONS

U.S.	METRIC
1 teaspoon	5 milliliters
2 teaspoons	10 milliliters
1 tablespoon	15 milliliters
2 tablespoons	30 milliliters
¼ cup	59 milliliters
⅓ cup	79 milliliters
½ cup	118 milliliters
¾ cup	177 milliliters
1 cup	237 milliliters
1¼ cups	296 milliliters
1½ cups	355 milliliters
2 cups (1 pint)	473 milliliters
2½ cups	592 milliliters
3 cups	710 milliliters
4 cups (1 quart)	0.946 liter
1.06 quarts	1 liter
4 quarts (1 gallon)	3.8 liters

WEIGHT CONVERSIONS

OUNCES	GRAMS
½	14
¾	21
1	28
1½	43
2	57
2½	71
3	85
3½	99
4	113
4½	128
5	142
6	170
7	198
8	227
9	255
10	283
12	340
16 (1 pound)	454

CONVERSIONS FOR INGREDIENTS COMMONLY USED IN BAKING

Baking is an exacting science. Because measuring by weight is far more accurate than measuring by volume, and thus more likely to achieve reliable results, in our recipes we provide ounce measures in addition to cup measures for many ingredients. Refer to the chart below to convert these measures into grams.

INGREDIENT	OUNCES	GRAMS
1 cup all-purpose flour*	5	142
1 cup whole wheat flour	5½	156
1 cup granulated (white) sugar	7	198
1 cup packed brown sugar (light or dark)	7	198
1 cup confectioners' sugar	4	113
1 cup cocoa powder	3	85
4 tablespoons butter† (½ stick, or ¼ cup)	2	57
8 tablespoons butter† (1 stick, or ½ cup)	4	113
16 tablespoons butter† (2 sticks, or 1 cup)	8	227

* U.S. all-purpose flour, the most frequently used flour in this book, does not contain leaveners, as some European flours do. These leavened flours are called self-rising or self-raising. If you are using self-rising flour, take this into consideration before adding leavening to a recipe.

† In the United States, butter is sold both salted and unsalted. We generally recommend unsalted butter. If you are using salted butter, take this into consideration before adding salt to a recipe.

OVEN TEMPERATURES

FAHRENHEIT	CELSIUS	GAS MARK (IMPERIAL)
225	105	¼
250	120	½
275	130	1
300	150	2
325	165	3
350	180	4
375	190	5
400	200	6
425	220	7
450	230	8
475	245	9

CONVERTING TEMPERATURES FROM AN INSTANT-READ THERMOMETER

We include doneness temperatures in many of the recipes in this book. We recommend an instant-read thermometer for the job. Refer to the above table to convert Fahrenheit degrees to Celsius. Or, for temperatures not represented in the chart, use this simple formula: Subtract 32 degrees from the Fahrenheit reading, then divide the result by 1.8 to find the Celsius reading.

EXAMPLE:

"Roast until thickest part of chicken thigh registers 175 degrees on instant-read thermometer." To convert:

175°F – 32 = 143°
143° ÷ 1.8 = 79.44°C, rounded down to 79°C

Index

NOTE: *Italicized* page references indicate recipe photographs.

A

Almonds
    Chapel Squares, *154*, 155–56
    Christmas Stollen, **108–9**
    Scripture Cake, 122–24, *123*
Anise Refrigerator Cookies, **144**
Apple(s)
    Biggum's Fried Pies, **186**, *187*
    Bread Pie, Light, **176**, *177*
    Bubbles, **86**, *87*
    Cabbage Rolls, **42–43**
    Cafeteria Lady Cake, **118**
    Chapel Squares, *154*, **155–56**
    Cinnamon Rolls, Double Delicious, **88–89**
    Cake, Mudder's Fresh, **126**
    Pie, Grandma Lena's, **168**
    -Raspberry Pie, Hungarian, **178–79**
    Sunday Supper Strata, *54*, **55**
Apricot(s)
    Coronation Chicken, **52**
    Glaze, Papa Bob's Caramelized Onion Bread
        with, **95**

B

Baba's Bread and Butter Pickles, **191**
Bananas
    Cracker Pie, **173**
Banbury Tarts, *182*, **183–84**
Barley
    Apple Cabbage Rolls, **42–43**
Beans
    Mt. Vernon Short Ribs, **33**
    Sausage Soup, **6**, *7*

Beef
    Apple Cabbage Rolls, **42–43**
    Big Wheel, **66**, *67*
    Bubbe's Passover Brisket, **26**, *27*
    and Dumplings, Nannie's Delicious, **25**
    Edison Street Italian Baptist Church Spaghetti
        and Meatballs, **4–5**
    Grandma Lillian's Oxtail Stew, **24**
    Kapama, **35–37**, *36*
    Mt. Vernon Short Ribs, **33**
    Ox Roast of, **2**
    Polpette alla Nonna, **62**
    Rollettes with Spaghetti, **38–39**
    Sergeant Meatloaf, **58–60**, *59*
    Slumgullion, **3**
    Taglerina, **61**
    Tootie's Tortière Pie, **44**
Biggum's Fried Pies, **186**, *187*
Big Wheel, **66**, *67*
The Bishop's Bars, **157**
Blackberries
    Roly-Boley, **180–81**
Black Currant Tiramisu, *110*, **136–37**
Blarney Stones, **152–53**
Bread pudding. *See* Strata
Bread(s)
    Apple Pie, Light, **176**, *177*
    Bubbles, **86**, *87*
    Caramelized Onion, with Apricot Glaze,
        Papa Bob's, **95**
    Cheese Muffins, **84**
    Christmas Stollen, **108–9**
    Date and Nut, *80*, **100**

Bread(s) *(cont.)*
    Double Delicious Apple Cinnamon Rolls, **88–89**
    German New Year's Pretzel, **105–6**
    Grandma's Sweet Kuchen, **107**
    Grated, and Chocolate Cake, **133–35**, *134*
    Great-Grandma's Potato Rolls, **92**, **93–94**
    Lovie May's Rice Muffins, **82**, *83*
    Minute Muffins, **85**
    Old Time Latvian Rolls, **90–91**
    Pain d'Epices, **101**
    -Pudding Pie, Southern Sweet Potato Pecan,
       170–72, *171*
    Rye, Laura's, **98–99**
    Swedish Coffee, **102–4**, *103*
    Upside-Down Tomato Pan, Grandma Pearl's, **96**, **97**
Brown Sugar Pie, **164**, *165*
Bubbe's Passover Brisket, **26**, **27**
Bubbles, **86**, **87**
Butternut-Pecan Cake with Cranberry–Cream
    Cheese Frosting, *128*, **129–30**

C

Cabbage
    Chow Chow, **188**, *199*
    Grandma's Polish Pierogi, **45–46**
    Rolls, Apple, **42–43**
    Spaetzle and Sauerkraut, **73**
Cafeteria Lady Cake, **118**
Cake pans, preparing, **130**
Cakes
    Ambrosia, Nora Lee's, **127**
    Black Currant Tiramisu, *110*, **136–37**
    Breakfast and Dessert Farina, Nonna's, **115**
    Butternut-Pecan, with Cranberry–Cream Cheese
       Frosting, *128*, **129–30**
    Cafeteria Lady, **118**
    Cookie Top, **125**
    Deutscher Pflaumenkuchen
       (German Plum Cake), **119**
    Fresh Apple, Mudder's, **126**
    Grated Bread and Chocolate, **133–35**, *134*
    layer, cutting in half, **132**
    Marble, Mom's, **120–21**
    Pennsylvania Dutch Shoofly, **112**, *113*

Cakes *(cont.)*
    Prince of Wales, **131–32**
    Raisin, Grandma Lillian's, **114**
    Scripture, **122–24**, *123*
    Tomato Soup, **116**, *117*
Cathedral Windows, **150**, *151*
Chapel Squares, *154*, **155–56**
Cheese
    Beef Kapama, **35–37**, *36*
    Beef Rollettes with Spaghetti, **38–39**
    Big Wheel, **66**, **67**
    Black Currant Tiramisu, *110*, **136–37**
    Chilaquiles, **56**, **76**
    Easy Amazing Noodle Pudding, **74**, **75**
    Eggplant Parmigiana, **12**
    Gnocchi alla Romana, **14**, *15*
    Grandma Pearl's Upside-Down Tomato Pan
       Bread, **96**, **97**
    Greek Shrimp with Feta and Peppers, **78**, **79**
    Italian Love Nests, *40*, **41**
    Lovie May's Rice Muffins, **82**, *83*
    Lynne's Zucchini Parmesan, *10*, **11**
    Mom's Eggplant Deluxe, **13**
    Muffins, **84**
    Nonna's Breakfast and Dessert Farina Cake, **115**
    Polpette alla Nonna, **62**
    Potato Crust Quiche, **71**
    Rum Tum Tiddy, **65**
    Slumgullion, **3**
    Spring Potato Casserole, *1*, **16**
    Squash Casserole with, **9**
    Sunday Supper Strata, *54*, **55**
    see also Cream Cheese
Cherries
    Chapel Squares, *154*, **155–56**
    Christmas Stollen, **108–9**
Chicken
    Biryani, My Grandmother's, **47–49**, *48*
    Coronation, **52**
    Hurry Curry, **77**
    and Mushrooms, Chinese Five-Spice, **50**, *51*
    Tamale Loaf, **8**
Chilaquiles, **56**, **76**
Chinese Five-Spice Chicken and Mushrooms, **50**, *51*

Chocolate
  The Bishop's Bars, **157**
  Cathedral Windows, **150**, *151*
  and Grated Bread Cake, **133–35**, *134*
  grating, **135**
  Mom's Marble Cake, **120–21**
  Pixies, Estelle's Black Walnut, *142*, **143**
Chow Chow, *188*, **199**
Christmas Stollen, **108–9**
Church Cookies, **148**
Collard greens
  Gullah Gratin, **17**
Cookies and bars
  Anise Refrigerator Cookies, **144**
  The Bishop's Bars, **157**
  Blarney Stones, **152–53**
  Cathedral Windows, **150**, *151*
  Chapel Squares, *154*, **155–56**
  Church Cookies, **148**
  Estelle's Black Walnut Chocolate Pixies, *142*, **143**
  Genuine Danish Kleiner (Aegte Danske Klejner),
    138, **158–59**
  Mildred Toogood's Lebkuchen, **149**
  Peppernuts, *146*, **147**
  Rosa Franklin Cookies, **140**
  Scrumptious Orange Bites, **141**
  Svenska Pinners, **145**
Cookie Top Cake, **125**
Corn
  Gullah Gratin, **17**
  Tamale Loaf, **8**
Coronation Chicken, **52**
Crabmeat
  Potato-Mac Salad, **20**
Cracker Pie, **173**
Cranberry–Cream Cheese Frosting, Butternut-Pecan
    Cake with, *128*, **129–30**
Cream Cheese
  Black Currant Tiramisu, *110*, **136–37**
  –Cranberry Frosting, Butternut-Pecan Cake with,
    128, **129–30**
  Prince of Wales Cake, **131–32**
  Southern Sweet Potato Pecan Bread-Pudding Pie,
    170–72, *171*
  Tomato Soup Cake, **116**, *117*

Crème Anglaise, **180–81**
Cucumbers
  Baba's Bread and Butter Pickles, **191**
  Papa Gus's Kosher Dill Pickles, **190**
  Slaked Lime Pickles, **192**, *193*
Curried dishes
  Coronation Chicken, **52**
  Hurry Curry, **77**

D
Date(s)
  Nora Lee's Ambrosia Cake, **127**
  and Nut Bread, *80*, **100**
  Scrumptious Orange Bites, **141**
Desserts. *See* Cakes; Cookies and bars;
    Pies (dessert); Tarts
Deutscher Pflaumenkuchen (German Plum Cake), **119**
Double-Crust Pie Dough, **167**
Double Delicious Apple Cinnamon Rolls, **88–89**

E
Easy Amazing Noodle Pudding, *74*, **75**
Edison Street Italian Baptist Church Spaghetti
    and Meatballs, **4–5**
Eggplant Deluxe, Mom's, **13**
Eggplant Parmigiana, **12**
Eggs
  Eggplant Parmigiana, **12**
  Potato-Mac Salad, **20**
  Sergeant Meatloaf, **58–60**, *59*
Escarole and Potato Soup (Menasha), **68**, *69*
Estelle's Black Walnut Chocolate Pixies, *142*, **143**

F
Farina Cake, Nonna's Breakfast and Dessert, **115**
Fish. *See* Shellfish
Fruits
  Christmas Stollen, **108–9**
  see also specific fruits

G
Genuine Danish Kleiner (Aegte Danske Klejner),
    138, **158–59**
German New Year's Pretzel, **105–6**
German Plum Cake (Deutscher Pflaumenkuchen), **119**

Gnocchi alla Romana, **14**, *15*
Grains
    Apple Cabbage Rolls, **42–43**
    Gnocchi alla Romana, **14**, *15*
    Nonna's Breakfast and Dessert Farina Cake, **115**
    Tamale Loaf, **8**
    see also Rice
Grams's Pickled Peaches, *196, 197*
Grandma Alpha's Barbecue Ribs, **30–32**, *31*
Grandma Lena's Apple Pie, **168**
Grandma Lillian's Oxtail Stew, **24**
Grandma Lillian's Raisin Cake, **114**
Grandma Lucy's Creamed Tomatoes over Biscuits,
    63–64
Grandma Pearl's Upside-Down Tomato Pan Bread,
    96, *97*
Grandma's Gooey Shoofly Pie, **162**
Grandma's Polish Pierogi, **45–46**
Grandma's Sweet and Sour Rabbit, **28–29**
Grandma's Sweet Kuchen, **107**
Grandma's Tangy Rhubarb Jam, **203**
Grandmother Augsburger's Pecan Pie, **163**
Grated Bread and Chocolate Cake, **133–35**, *134*
Great-Aunt Stella's Watermelon Pickles, **198**
Great-Grandma's Potato Rolls, **92**, *93–94*
Greek Shrimp with Feta and Peppers, **78**, *79*
Greens
    Gullah Gratin, **17**
    Menasha (Potato and Escarole Soup), **68**, *69*
    New Orleans Shrimp, French Quarter–Style, *18, 19*
Grits. *See* Gnocchi
Gullah Gratin, **17**

H
Ham
    Lovie May's Rice Muffins, **82**, *83*
    Spaetzle and Sauerkraut, **73**
    Swedish Pea Soup, **70**
Honey
    Pain d'Epices, **101**
Hungarian Apple-Raspberry Pie, **178–79**
Hurry Curry, **77**

I
Ina's Butter Tarts, **185**
Italian Love Nests, **40**, *41*

J
Jam, Tangy Rhubarb, Grandma's, **203**

L
Laura's Rye Bread, **98–99**
Lemons
    Mom's Gone with the Wind Heavenly Pie,
        160, **174–75**
Light Bread Apple Pie, **176**, *177*
Lobster Quiche, Maine, **22**, **53**
Lovie May's Rice Muffins, **82**, *83*
Lulie's Pork Chop Casserole, **72**
Lynne's Zucchini Parmesan, *10*, **11**

M
Main dishes (meat)
    Apple Cabbage Rolls, **42–43**
    Beef Kapama, **35–37**, *36*
    Beef Rollettes with Spaghetti, **38–39**
    Big Wheel, **66**, *67*
    Bubbe's Passover Brisket, **26**, *27*
    Edison Street Italian Baptist Church Spaghetti and
        Meatballs, **4–5**
    Grandma Alpha's Barbecue Ribs, **30–32**, *31*
    Grandma Lillian's Oxtail Stew, **24**
    Grandma Lucy's Creamed Tomatoes over Biscuits,
        63–64
    Grandma's Sweet and Sour Rabbit, **28–29**
    Gullah Gratin, **17**
    Lulie's Pork Chop Casserole, **72**
    Mt. Vernon Short Ribs, **33**
    Nannie's Delicious Beef and Dumplings, **25**
    Ox Roast of Beef, **2**
    Polpette alla Nonna, **62**
    Ribs and Rigatonies, **34**
    Sausage Soup, **6**, *7*
    Sergeant Meatloaf, **58–60**, *59*
    Slumgullion, **3**

Main dishes (meat) *(cont.)*
    Spaetzle and Sauerkraut, **73**
    Swedish Pea Soup, **70**
    Taglerina, **61**
    Tootie's Tortière Pie, **44**
Main dishes (pasta, cheese, and vegetables)
    Easy Amazing Noodle Pudding, **74**, **75**
    Edison Street Italian Baptist Church Spaghetti
        and Meatballs, **4–5**
    Eggplant Parmigiana, **12**
    Grandma's Polish Pierogi, **45–46**
    Italian Love Nests, *40*, **41**
    Lynne's Zucchini Parmesan, *10*, **11**
    Menasha (Potato and Escarole Soup), **68**, **69**
    Potato Crust Quiche, **71**
    Rum Tum Tiddy, **65**
    Slumgullion, **3**
    Squash Casserole with Cheese, **9**
    Sunday Supper Strata, *54*, **55**
Main dishes (poultry)
    Chilaquiles, **56**, **76**
    Chinese Five-Spice Chicken and Mushrooms, **50**, *51*
    Coronation Chicken, **52**
    Hurry Curry, **77**
    My Grandmother's Chicken Biryani, **47–49**, *48*
    Tamale Loaf, **8**
Main dishes (shellfish)
    Greek Shrimp with Feta and Peppers, **78**, **79**
    Gullah Gratin, **17**
    Maine Lobster Quiche, **22**, **53**
    New Orleans Shrimp, French Quarter–Style, *18*, **19**
Maine Lobster Quiche, **22**, **53**
Meat. *See* Beef; Pork; Rabbit
Meatballs
    Polpette alla Nonna, **62**
    Spaghetti and, Edison Street Italian Baptist
        Church, **4–5**
Meatloaf, Sergeant, **58–60**, *59*
Menasha (Potato and Escarole Soup), **68**, **69**
Mildred Toogood's Lebkuchen, **149**
Minute Muffins, **85**
Molasses
    Grandma's Gooey Shoofly Pie, **162**
    Mildred Toogood's Lebkuchen, **149**
    Pennsylvania Dutch Shoofly Cake, **112**, *113*

Mom's Eggplant Deluxe, **13**
Mom's Gone with the Wind Heavenly Pie, *160*, **174–75**
Mom's Marble Cake, **120–21**
Mt. Vernon Short Ribs, **33**
Mudder's Fresh Apple Cake, **126**
Muffins
    Cheese, **84**
    Minute, **85**
    Rice, Lovie May's, **82**, *83*
Mushrooms, Chinese Five-Spice Chicken and, **50**, *51*
My Grandmother's Chicken Biryani, **47–49**, *48*

N

Nannie's Delicious Beef and Dumplings, **25**
New Orleans Shrimp, French Quarter–Style, *18*, **19**
Nonna's Breakfast and Dessert Farina Cake, **115**
Noodle Pudding, Easy Amazing, **74**, **75**
Nora Lee's Ambrosia Cake, **127**
Nuts
    Blarney Stones, **152–53**
    Scripture Cake, **122–24**, *123*
    see also Almonds; Pecan(s); Walnut(s)

O

Old Time Latvian Rolls, **90–91**
Onion(s)
    Caramelized, Bread with Apricot Glaze,
        Papa Bob's, **95**
    Spring Potato Casserole, *1*, **16**
    Taglerina, **61**
Orange(s)
    Bites, Scrumptious, **141**
    Nora Lee's Ambrosia Cake, **127**
Ox Roast of Beef, **2**

P

Pain d'Epices, **101**
Papa Bob's Caramelized Onion Bread with
    Apricot Glaze, **95**
Papa Gus's Kosher Dill Pickles, **190**
Passover Brisket, Bubbe's, **26**, *27*
Pasta and noodles
    Beef Kapama, **35–37**, *36*
    Beef Rollettes with Spaghetti, **38–39**
    Easy Amazing Noodle Pudding, **74**, **75**

Pasta and noodles *(cont.)*
    Edison Street Italian Baptist Church Spaghetti
        and Meatballs, **4–5**
    Italian Love Nests, *40, 41*
    Potato-Mac Salad, **20**
    Ribs and Rigatonies, **34**
    Sausage Soup, **6, 7**
Peaches
    Biggum's Fried Pies, **186,** *187*
    peeling, **197**
    Pickled, Grams's, *196,* **197**
Peanuts
    Blarney Stones, **152–53**
Pea Soup, Swedish, **70**
Pecan(s)
    -Butternut Cake with Cranberry–Cream Cheese
        Frosting, *128,* **129–30**
    Cathedral Windows, **150,** *151*
    Cracker Pie, **173**
    Mudder's Fresh Apple Cake, **126**
    Nora Lee's Ambrosia Cake, **127**
    Pie, Grandmother Augsburger's, **163**
    Rosa Franklin Cookies, **140**
    Scrumptious Orange Bites, **141**
    Sweet Potato Bread-Pudding Pie, Southern,
        170–72, *171*
Pennsylvania Dutch Shoofly Cake, **112,** *113*
Peppernuts, **146,** *147*
Peppers
    Baba's Bread and Butter Pickles, **191**
    Chow Chow, *188,* **199**
    and Feta, Greek Shrimp with, **78, 79**
Pickled Peaches, Grams's, *196,* **197**
Pickles
    Bread and Butter, Baba's, **191**
    Kosher Dill, Papa Gus's, **190**
    Slaked Lime, *192, 193*
    Watermelon, Great-Aunt Stella's, **198**
Pie, Tootie's Tortière, **44**
Pie Dough, Double-Crust, **167**
Pie Dough, Single-Crust, **166**
Pierogi, Grandma's Polish, **45–46**

Pies (dessert)
    Apple, Grandma Lena's, **168**
    Apple-Raspberry, Hungarian, **178–79**
    Bread Apple, Light, **176,** *177*
    Brown Sugar, **164,** *165*
    Cracker, **173**
    double-crust, preparing, **167**
    Fried, Biggum's, **186,** *187*
    Gooey Shoofly, Grandma's, **162**
    Heavenly, Mom's Gone with the Wind, *160,* **174–75**
    1932 Pineapple, **169**
    Pecan, Grandmother Augsburger's, **163**
    Pineapple, 1932, **169**
    rolling out single-crust dough for, **166**
    Sweet Potato Pecan Bread-Pudding, Southern,
        170–72, *171*
Pineapple Pie, 1932, **169**
Plum Cake, German (Deutscher Pflaumenkuchen),
    119
Plum Catsup, **202**
Polish Pierogi, Grandma's, **45–46**
Polpette alla Nonna, **62**
Pork
    Apple Cabbage Rolls, **42–43**
    Chop Casserole, Lulie's, **72**
    chops, preparing for cooking, **72**
    Edison Street Italian Baptist Church Spaghetti
        and Meatballs, **4–5**
    Grandma Alpha's Barbecue Ribs, **30–32,** *31*
    Grandma Lucy's Creamed Tomatoes over Biscuits,
        63–64
    Gullah Gratin, **17**
    Polpette alla Nonna, **62**
    ribs, removing membrane from, **32**
    Ribs and Rigatonies, **34**
    Sausage Soup, **6, 7**
    Sergeant Meatloaf, **58–60,** *59*
    Tamale Loaf, **8**
    Tootie's Tortière Pie, **44**
    see also Ham
Potato(es)
    Bubbe's Passover Brisket, **26, 27**
    Casserole, Spring, *1,* **16**
    Crust Quiche, **71**

Potato(es) *(cont.)*
  Grandma Lillian's Oxtail Stew, **24**
  Gullah Gratin, **17**
  Lulie's Pork Chop Casserole, **72**
  -Mac Salad, **20**
  Menasha (Potato and Escarole Soup), **68, 69**
  My Grandmother's Chicken Biryani, **47–49,** *48*
  Rolls, Great-Grandma's, **92,** *93–94*
  Salad, Sweet and Sour German, **21**
  Sweet, Pecan Bread-Pudding Pie, Southern,
    170–72, *171*
  Tootie's Tortière Pie, **44**
Poultry. *See* Chicken; Turkey
Prince of Wales Cake, **131–32**
Pudding, Noodle, Easy Amazing, **74, 75**

Q

Quiche, Maine Lobster, **22, 53**
Quiche, Potato Crust, **71**

R

Rabbit, Grandma's Sweet and Sour, **28–29**
Rabbit, whole, cutting up, **29**
Raisin(s)
  Banbury Tarts, *182,* **183–84**
  Cafeteria Lady Cake, **118**
  Cake, Grandma Lillian's, **114**
  Christmas Stollen, **108–9**
  Easy Amazing Noodle Pudding, **74, 75**
  Grandma's Tangy Rhubarb Jam, **203**
  Hungarian Apple-Raspberry Pie, **178–79**
  Ina's Butter Tarts, **185**
  Prince of Wales Cake, **131–32**
  Scripture Cake, **122–24,** *123*
Raspberry-Apple Pie, Hungarian, **178–79**
Rhubarb Jam, Tangy, Grandma's, **203**
Ribs and Rigatonies, **34**
Rice
  Hurry Curry, **77**
  Muffins, Lovie May's, *82, 83*
  My Grandmother's Chicken Biryani, **47–49,** *48*
Roly-Boley, **180–81**
Rosa Franklin Cookies, **140**
Rum Tum Tiddy, **65**

S

Salads
  Coronation Chicken, **52**
  German Potato, Sweet and Sour, **21**
  New Orleans Shrimp, French Quarter–Style, *18,* **19**
  Potato-Mac, **20**
Sandwiches
  Big Wheel, **66, 67**
Sauces
  Beef Kapama, **35–37,** *36*
  Crème Anglaise, **180–81**
  Rum Tum Tiddy, **65**
  Taglerina, **61**
Sauerkraut, Spaetzle and, **73**
Sausage(s)
  Edison Street Italian Baptist Church Spaghetti
    and Meatballs, **4–5**
  Grandma Lucy's Creamed Tomatoes over Biscuits,
    63–64
  Gullah Gratin, **17**
  Soup, **6,** *7*
Scripture Cake, **122–24,** *123*
Scrumptious Orange Bites, **141**
Seafood. *See* Shellfish
Sergeant Meatloaf, **58–60,** *59*
Shellfish
  Greek Shrimp with Feta and Peppers, **78, 79**
  Gullah Gratin, **17**
  Maine Lobster Quiche, **22, 53**
  New Orleans Shrimp, French Quarter–Style, *18,* **19**
  Potato-Mac Salad, **20**
Shoofly Cake, Pennsylvania Dutch, **112,** *113*
Shoofly Pie, Grandma's Gooey, **162**
Shrimp
  Greek, with Feta and Peppers, **78, 79**
  Gullah Gratin, **17**
  New Orleans, French Quarter–Style, *18,* **19**
Side dishes
  Gnocchi alla Romana, **14,** *15*
  Italian Love Nests, *40, 41*
  Lynne's Zucchini Parmesan, **10, 11**
  Mom's Eggplant Deluxe, **13**
  Potato-Mac Salad, **20**
  Spring Potato Casserole, *1,* **16**

Side dishes *(cont.)*
    Squash Casserole with Cheese, **9**
    Sweet and Sour German Potato Salad, **21**
Single-Crust Pie Dough, **166**
Slaked Lime Pickles, *192, 193*
Slumgullion, **3**
Soups
    Menasha (Potato and Escarole Soup), **68, 69**
    Sausage, **6, 7**
    Swedish Pea, **70**
    see also Stews
Southern Sweet Potato Pecan Bread-Pudding Pie,
    170–72, *171*
Spaetzle and Sauerkraut, **73**
Spring Potato Casserole, *1,* **16**
Squash
    Butternut-Pecan Cake with Cranberry–Cream
        Cheese Frosting, *128,* **129–30**
    Casserole with Cheese, **9**
    Lynne's Zucchini Parmesan, *10,* **11**
Stews
    Nannie's Delicious Beef and Dumplings, **25**
    Oxtail, Grandma Lillian's, **24**
Stollen, Christmas, **108–9**
Strata, Sunday Supper, *54, 55*
Strawberries
    Cracker Pie, **173**
Svenska Pinners, **145**
Swedish Coffee Bread, **102–4,** *103*
Swedish Pea Soup, **70**
Sweet and Sour German Potato Salad, **21**
Sweet Potato(es)
    Bubbe's Passover Brisket, **26, 27**
    Pecan Bread-Pudding Pie, Southern, **170–72,** *171*

T
Taglerina, **61**
Tamale Loaf, **8**
Tarts
    Banbury, *182,* **183–84**
    Butter, Ina's, **185**
    Roly-Boley, **180–81**
Tiramisu, Black Currant, *110,* **136–37**
Tomato(es)
    Big Wheel, **66, 67**
    Butter, **200,** *201*
    Creamed, over Biscuits, Grandma Lucy's, **63–64**
    Pan Bread, Grandma Pearl's Upside-Down, **96, 97**
    peeling, **197**
    seeding, **200**
    Taglerina, **61**
Tomato Soup Cake, **116,** *117*
Tootie's Tortière Pie, **44**
Tortière Pie, Tootie's, **44**
Turkey
    Chilaquiles, **56, 76**
    Tamale Loaf, **8**

V
Vegetables. *See specific vegetables*

W
Walnut(s)
    Black, Chocolate Pixies, Estelle's, *142,* **143**
    Cafeteria Lady Cake, **118**
    Date and Nut Bread, **80,** *100*
    Grandma Lillian's Raisin Cake, **114**
    Grandma's Tangy Rhubarb Jam, **203**
    Svenska Pinners, **145**
Watermelon Pickles, Great-Aunt Stella's, **198**

Z
Zucchini Parmesan, Lynne's, *10,* **11**